THE NEW
OXFORD BOOK OF
IRISH
VERSE

Edited, with translations, by
THOMAS KINSELLA

Oxford   New York
OXFORD UNIVERSITY PRESS
1989

Oxford University Press, Walton Street, Oxford OX2 6DP
Oxford New York Toronto
Delhi Bombay Calcutta Madras Karachi
Petaling Jaya Singapore Hong Kong Tokyo
Nairobi Dar es Salam Cape Town
Melbourne Auckland
and associated companies in
Berlin Ibadan

Oxford is a trade mark of Oxford University Press

Selection, editorial matter, translations as specified
© Thomas Kinsella 1986

First published 1986 by Oxford University Press
First issued as an Oxford University Press paperback 1989

British Library Cataloguing in Publication Data
The New Oxford book of Irish verse
1. Poetry English. Irish writers. 1985.
Anthologies
I. Kinsella, Thomas, 1928–
821.'.008'09415 891.6'21008
ISBN 0–19–282643–3

Library of Congress Cataloging in Publication Data
The New Oxford book of Irish verse.
Includes indexes.
1. English poetry—Irish authors.
2. Irish poetry—Translations into English.
3. English poetry—Translations from Irish.
4. Irish poetry 5. Ireland—Poetry.
I. Kinsella, Thomas.
PR8851.N48 1986 821'.008'09415 85–21479
ISBN 0–19–282643–3

Set by Wyvern Typesetting Ltd.
Printed in Great Britain by
Richard Clay Ltd.
Bungay, Suffolk

FOR ELEANOR

with love

PREFACE

THE previous *Oxford Book of Irish Verse*, edited by Donagh MacDonagh and Lennox Robinson, contained a selection from 'XVIIth Century to XXth Century'. It opened with a carol by Luke Wadding, the Catholic Bishop of Ferns in Cromwellian times, and ended with a number of poems by myself.

Between these the editors ranged the glories of Anglo-Irish liter- ature: Swift, Goldsmith, Wilde, Yeats, Synge, Joyce. Also Davis, Mangan, and Ferguson—the three significant poets of the nineteenth century, as Yeats has named them—with many others, and many oddities and old favourites. It included, without specific comment, a tiny handful of translations from the Irish.

It was clearly no part of the book's purpose, as interpreted by its editors, to deal seriously with poetry in the Irish language—a poetry which had served its people, in whatever ways a poetry does, for a thousand years before the curse of Cromwell fell upon them, and it, and which for some hundreds of years afterwards flourished in decline. With that interpretation it appears to me that an opportunity, even an obligation, was missed.

Irish poetry is important in both languages. At certain times it functioned in one language, in certain ways; at other times in both. It is a main aim of the *New Oxford Book* to present an idea of these two bodies of poetry and of the relationships between them.

The translations from the Irish, with the exception of the 'versions' by Mangan and the translation by Patrick Pearse of his 'Renunciation', are my own. As to the possible use of other translations, where they exist, there is a great unevenness in the range covered by these, and no agreement on verbal accuracy or, what is often more important, on accuracy of tone or rhythm. The dual tradition in Irish poetry is still in need of adequate translations. It seemed better to use all new versions: these transmit the essential contents of the originals in their major basic rhythms. Some have been published previously, as part of a more comprehensive specialized collection, in *An Duanaire: Poems of the Dispossessed 1600–1900* (Dolmen Press, 1981).

CONTENTS

CONTENTS

CONTENTS

English

SIXTEENTH CENTURY

MAGHNAS Ó DOMHNAILL (d. 1563)

LOCHLANN ÓG Ó DÁLAIGH (*fl.* mid 16th cent.)

TADHG DALL Ó HUIGÍNN (1550–1591)

LAOISEACH MAC AN BHÁIRD (*fl.* late 16th cent.)

ANONYMOUS

English

ANONYMOUS

SEVENTEENTH CENTURY

CONTENTS

CONTENTS

SEVENTEENTH TO NINETEENTH CENTURIES: FOLK POETRY

Folk Poems and Songs, Prayers and Charms from the Irish

Ballads in English

xvii

BOOK III: THE NINETEENTH AND TWENTIETH CENTURIES

CONTENTS

CONTENTS

INTRODUCTION

THE earliest datable Irish poem is *Amra Choluim Chille*, a poem in praise of Saint Colum Cille, whose death is recorded in AD 597. The poem is attributed to the poet Dallán Forgaill and was greatly treasured: it was copied again and again through the centuries as an act of devotion, even when the scribes had clearly ceased to understand parts of it. The version included here, though it is complete, is highly conjectural.

That the *Amra* is the first major item in the anthology is appropriate for a number of reasons. Firstly for its very survival across the catastrophes of the years. Then for its Christian origin; Christianity, from its beginnings in Ireland, worked intimately with poetry, and it was due largely to Christian literacy that so much of early Ireland's non-Christian oral literature survived. Finally, for the poem's incantatory character: it is a poetry facing both ways, giving a hold on the actuality of pre-Christian art.

Something of the same pre-Christian quality, though far weaker, can be sensed in the eighth-century 'Saint Patrick's Breastplate'. It is stronger in the *Cétamain* ('First of summer . . .'), a ninth-century text but an ancient gesture welcoming the season; and in the songs of Amergin, which occur in a late ninth-century prose narrative; and in all the early epic literature, mainly prose narratives but with important verse passages of various kinds, which it has been possible to represent only slightly in the anthology. And it is possibly a 'pagan' purity of view which gives the lyrics of the early Christian hermits their extraordinary directness and force.

But it is Christianity that is the dominant element in early Irish poetry. And it is mainly through the Christian element that we see the others. Even the image of the Hag of Béara—the *cailleach*, an embodiment of pagan sovereignty—survives from the ninth century in a figure interpreted as that of a Christian nun (with the word *cailleach* itself probably a derivative of *pallium*). It might seem appropriate, therefore, to open the anthology, before the *Amra* itself, with a few short poems offering a gesture of farewell to an older world. There is, in fact, some doubt about the antiquity of the first poem: even here, in the rhyming of the original, there is evidence that Christian monastic influence may have been at work. But there is no doubt about the sense of a past heavy with loss—as there is no doubt, in the second poem, of the sharpness of that loss in an individual case; and none, in the third poem, of the threat associated with the new Christians at their altars, the tonsure reminding the poet of the cutting edge of an adze.

By the seventh century, with 'The Boyhood of Christ', Christian theme and native tongue were as one, and the circumstances were right for the early monastic poems and glosses. The immediacy of these early poems, the freshness as of a beginning, was maintained over unlikely stretches of time: into the eleventh century and later, as in the lyric 'Praise of God' or the nature poetry of the mad Suibne or the Fenian poetry of the twelfth century.

In the twelfth century the next 'stranger' came. The Normans, unlike the Christians, did not mix easily. And unlike the Vikings they did not absorb or disappear. They settled early in strength in County Wexford. There are still traces there, as elsewhere, of their order on the landscape. They understood the function of the town as a device in permanent settlement and the maintenance of rule. Within a hundred years of their arrival great walls were being built around New Ross, a town that in its time seemed a rival to Dublin in status, and a long and lively poem in Norman French survives to celebrate the event. Within another hundred years the transitional French-speaking period had passed, and there are the first traces of Irish poetry in the English language: pious, comic, delicate, powerful . . . And the counter-tradition has begun.

Poetry in the Irish language, meanwhile, had grown and strengthened through the same centuries, absorbing some external influences but mainly self-sufficient. It is full of the life of the people, and a series of notable individual poetic careers can be distinguished: Muireadhach Albanach Ó Dálaigh in the thirteenth century, Gofraidh Fionn Ó Dálaigh in the fourteenth, and a whole caste of professional bardic poets.

*   *   *

At the opening of Book II, entering the fifteenth century, the scene is still one of stability in the Irish-speaking world. There is a lament by Tadhg Óg Ó hUigínn, for his teacher and elder brother, which dwells on the procedures of the formal schools of poetry almost as if they were laws of nature. There is a body of love poetry, anonymous yet with a kind of skill that distinguishes it from folk poetry or folk song as usually understood, and suggesting we may owe these poems to the professional poets in their unprofessional moments. There is also the first surviving translation into English of an Irish song, a sign of how the two languages were to come to terms, of the element of translation in a future 'Anglo-Irish' literature.

By the close of the eighteenth century there had been a series of profound political and social changes, and the literatures in both languages had followed them. The new Anglo-Irish literature was dominant, being particularly rich in drama and with its main audience in England and a new Georgian Dublin. Bardic poetry in Irish had disappeared, with the extermination of the Irish aristocracy who were its patrons. The Irish language itself was in retreat, into isolated areas, apparently on the way to extinction, and taking an entire literature with it. The loss was not regretted in English-speaking Ireland, in so far as it was felt at all: Goldsmith knew the early sagas, for example, but found them merely barbaric.

A reading of bardic poetry gives a view of these violent events. Originally the bardic order of poets had developed in close relationship with a conservative ruling class. They fulfilled a largely social function in a stable society; their poetry became, and remained, a standardized medium, with a high respect for precedent, with rigorous requirements as to syllabic count, alliteration, and the like, and with a fixed array of formal phrases and references. As Osborn Bergin put it: 'Practically all bardic poetry is written in one standard literary dialect, which remained almost unchanged for five hundred years.'[1] The conservatism should be felt even through the translations. But the dialect was a toughly elegant one, and a fit vehicle for real feeling in the proper hands. And bardic poetry offers one of the great achievements of the Irish tradition when, at the close of the seventeenth century, with the final defeat and expulsion of the Catholic nobles, it rose above its fixed modes and employed its old-established resources in an extraordinary act of commentary on its own extinction. A reading of even the few poems it has been possible to include—by Ó hEoghusa, Ó Gnímh, Ó Hifearnáin—illustrates the swift transition from the old world into a painful new one, in which the old poetry knows that it has no place.

But a 'new' poetry had already appeared in Irish, different in character, accentual and open. For the 'new' poets the world was just as painful a place, but the pain was directly in the nature of things, not in a fall from a privileged past. In the seventeenth century the new poets accompany the old: Céitinn, a priest and historian; Haicéad, a priest also, who studied on the Continent during the Penal times; Ó Bruadair, one of the last to attempt the career of professional poet, and who died in misery.

By the eighteenth century the distinctive role of the poet in Irish was that of outcast, and the tradition found one of its strongest voices in Aogán Ó Rathaille, a major poet whose search for a patron ended in a bitter turning toward the grave. After Ó Rathaille the main creative power in the language was in the voices of the people, in their remarkable songs and prayers and charms—poetry as a useful and

[1] Osborn Bergin, *Irish Bardic Poetry* (Dublin Institute for Advanced Studies, 1970), p. 13.

necessary art. There are also, however, two prolonged utterances of fierce individual energy, 'The Lament for Art Ó Laoghaire' and 'The Midnight Court', matching masterpieces standing at the close of this phase of the tradition. The first is a love poem and lamentation of absolute directness, the second a nightmare comedy in which courtly love, Irish society, and the poets of the past, not excluding Ó Rathaille, are parodied.

Against these is set the anthology's solitary choice in Irish in the nineteenth century: Blind Raftery's own image of himself, a beggar singing to beggars. The Great Famine is soon to come, after which (in Douglas Hyde's phrase) the Irish language 'withered off the face of Ireland'. And the foundation is laid for the opening scene of *Ulysses*, where the *cailleach*, inured to conquest and not even recognizing the Irish language on the lips of the 'stranger', attends to the loudest, domineering mouth.

*   *   *

It is in Book III, with the nineteenth century and the total preponderance of the English language, that the familiar 'Anglo-Irish' elements dominate, in a long preparation (as it can seem) for the career of Yeats. Yeats himself has suggested where we might look in the nineteenth century if we choose to view it in that way:

> Nor may I less be counted one
> With Davis, Mangan, Ferguson,
> Because, to him who ponders well,
> My rhymes more than their rhyming tell
> Of things discovered in the deep,
> Where only body's laid asleep . . .

> ('To Ireland in the Coming Times')

Here Yeats is as much claiming (or confessing) his mystical concerns as he is establishing some recent forebears. And he is certainly not mentioning Thomas Moore.

It is not necessary to make heavy weather of Moore. There is critical agreement that he was not an important poet, and Moore would join in that assessment, being a modest man. But in many minds, even still, he was Ireland's national poet. Moore's *Melodies* is possibly the most popular book ever produced in Ireland. The songs, snugly fitted to their facile and graceful airs, and full of deathless phrases, are still widely sung. Moore is probably the most *successful* Irish poet, in either language, who has ever lived, reaching a wide audience and satisfying it, and continuing to do so. None of this popular poetry bears close scrutiny. Its grasp on actuality is slight. Its designs are on the emotions more or less to the exclusion of the intelligence. But in certain satirical political poetry of Moore's, a poetry which plays no part in the standard image of him—in a poem like 'The Petition of the Orangemen of Ireland'—his considerable intelligence is re-engaged. And in 'Oh! blame not the bard' his admissions partly forestall criticism: in the time of testing he has proved inadequate, withholding his talents from the service of the oppressed and choosing to entertain the oppressor.

Davis and Mangan, on the other hand, spent themselves in the direct effort, Davis in active nationalist journalism, Mangan in contriving to produce, during a brief and luckless life—and though he knew no Irish—one of the first important bodies of 'translation' from Irish poetry. Earlier acts of retrieval had included Charlotte Brooke's *Reliques of Irish Poetry*, published toward the end of the eighteenth century, and Hardiman's *Irish Minstrelsy*, a generation later. One of the early reviewers of Hardiman's book was the poet and antiquarian Samuel Ferguson, who himself produced many versions and verse re-tellings from the Irish during a long and respectable career.

Out of the ill-starred enthusiasms and the miscellaneous activities of his chosen predecessors, Yeats, in his early career, put together a kind of literary nationalism and strengthened it with his great gifts of particularity and drama. He became, on this basis, the first major poet in the new language.

The Irish tradition has always presented an intimate fusion of literature and history. At certain times the literature and the history are functions of one another, as with the first settlement and expansion of Christianity, or with the circumstances leading to the destruction of the bardic order and the emergence of the 'new' poetry. So again in the early twentieth century, with revolution, the symbolic martyrdoms of 1916, and civil war. In Yeats's maturing poetry the tradition found a voice for significant events and made its first move, with complex past intact (though at an enormous remove), into modern poetry.

The complexity of that past and the nature of that remove are suggested in the selection of poetry that follows. It should be clear at least that the Irish tradition is a matter of two linguistic entities in dynamic interaction, of two major bodies of poetry asking to be understood together as functions of a shared and painful history. To limit a response to one aspect only, as is often done—to the literature in Irish, through specialized academic concerns or out of nationalist emotion, or to the literature in English as an annexe to British literature, an 'aspect of the Anglo-Saxon experience' (as I have heard it put), or out of mere convenience—is to miss a rare opportunity: that of responding to a notable and venerable literary tradition, the oldest vernacular literature in Western Europe, as it survives a change of vernacular.

For the modern Irish writer this tradition now provides, after more than a century of retrieval and self-analysis, as living a link with the significant past as any stable, monolingual tradition could do, and with the possibility of great richness and scope of reference. But this is merely an opportunity, and not a requirement, and the response among recent writers, faced with the usual other demands, has been varied, ranging from blind commitment to an impatient indifference.

*   *   *

In the final phase of the anthology (and even though, beginning with the nineteenth century, it was felt that the coverage could be a little more generous) the element of risk increases, in general diagnosis as well as in individual choice. But some things seem certain.

In the generation immediately after Yeats there are two poetic careers that demand special attention: those of Austin Clarke and Patrick Kavanagh. These poets disagree in their attitude to the tradition: Clarke's early poetry made much of the literature and legend of Ireland's past; Kavanagh dismissed it virtually complete. But they agree in a radical unevenness: they were capable of writing poorly at any stage in their working lives, yet both were capable also of poetry of the highest force, and on a wide front—in social comment, lyric observation, and occasional psychic penetration.

In Irish (the language refusing to expire) there was one poet, Seán Ó Ríordáin, born in 1916, who had responded, before his death in 1977, to the demands and opportunities of modern poetry.

Poets currently writing have tended to make use of the opportunity offered them by Ireland's dual tradition. If there is a shared characteristic among them it is in an area of dual responsibility, as they struggle to meet, as best they can, the growing demands of the poetic medium, as it invades and illumines the area of the self, and the demands of a peculiarly insistent and rewarding past. That past is no longer something which can be exploited simply for its drama; for the entertainment, however charming (as with Moore), or the manipulation, however electrifying (as with Yeats), of an inert audience. Although there are, of course, writers who continue to attempt things of the kind. Ireland's tradition continues in a phase of self-exploration, and insists, in its complexities and coherences, on a careful, active, and comprehensive response. A number of poets who began to write in the 1950s have shown an awareness of this in their different ways and in different degrees. A selection of their poetry that might have been made in other ways has been made partly so as to illustrate this. Richard Murphy, for example, conscious of his place in an Anglo-Irish ascendancy family, and that the ascendancy has had its day, has turned back in his poetry to expose some relevant raw points in history. It is in the early Gaelic tradition that John Montague found his hero-feast, as brutal as he can make it. Certain domestic images out of my own childhood insisted on sharpening until they found the image of the *cailleach*. I believe that these are processes at a level beyond the use of local colour, the ethnic as entertainment. And they are accompanied, not only in my own case, by an amount of personal repossession in the form of commentary and translation.

Most of Ireland's contemporary writers in English do, in fact, know modern Irish reasonably well. 'The language' was established as a compulsory school subject in de Valera's nationalist Ireland during the 1930s. It was taught unimaginatively on the whole, in an exclusivist and authoritarian atmosphere, so that it was usually dropped as soon as the school years were over. But there appears lately to be a change in the general feeling, associated possibly with the renaissance in Irish traditional music brought about by Seán Ó Riada; certainly the authoritarian element has disappeared.

One outcome has been the recent strong popular response to what might seem a specialist book: a collection of one hundred poems, with original texts and English translations, chosen from the period of the 'new' poetry covered (though very thinly) in Book II of this anthology.[2] It is not only the writers who are active in repossession.

*　　*　　*

Here, perhaps, is the place to say that it has been impossible, within the scope of this book, to represent the tradition really adequately. The choices have tried, therefore (as with the period of Irish bardic poetry), to pick a 'thematic' path through the many possibilities, taking advantage of a poem's documentary value. Also, it could be no suggestion of their relative calibres, for instance, that Ó Bruadair should have so few poems while Thomas Moore (not to mention others) should have more. And one does not come to such an anthology for a full view of the careers of Ó Rathaille or Yeats.

It would have been possible to produce a very different book with a lesser emphasis on the poetry in Irish; another with a slightly greater; another still with less of the early poetry and a greater emphasis on twentieth-century poetry in English—this differing, in its turn, as the emphasis was laid on an 'Age of Yeats' or on the years since the Second World War, or with the scope adjusted so as to absorb certain problems

*　　*　　*

[2] *An Duanaire: Poems of the Dispossessed 1600–1900*, edited by Seán Ó Tuama with translations by Thomas Kinsella (Dolmen Press, 1981).

of definition by including, say, Robert Graves. A former editor has found a place for Emily Brontë . . .

As to the anthology's closing choices, these (exclusions as well as inclusions) can amount to no more than a personal gesture at the end of such a book: the selection of a few poems that may confirm one of the themes or that have been personally important. The last ten pages are selected from the work of a number of poets born around the time of Yeats's death. The adequate presentation of contemporary careers would require another book. Similarly with any current 'movements'. Though it is clear already, with the most insistent of these, that it is in the context of a dual responsibility, toward the medium and toward the past, that Seamus Heaney's and Derek Mahon's poetry registers so firmly, rather than in any 'Northern Ireland Renaissance'.

The idea of such a renaissance has been strongly urged for some time (with the search for special antecedents usually settling on Louis MacNeice), and this idea by now has acquired an aspect of official acceptance and support. But it is largely a journalistic entity. The past, in Northern Ireland, is not. It has, in fact, two aspects there: the one adjusting normally in the psyche, the other kept irritated at the political surface. Heaney, at his best, can handle both of these aspects clearly and dispassionately, with a dominating instinct for mimesis. For Mahon, the past is significantly present particularly through poetry: his 'early crone' and her vision in 'Derry Morning', his scribe in 'The Woods', have clear, remote echoes.

The anthology closes with a gesture by the Limerick poet Michael Hartnett. He wrote his first poetry in English but has since begun writing in Irish. It is too soon to tell if this will continue, but his 'Farewell to English' has a stern ring to it, very like a convert.

BOOK I

—

FROM THE BEGINNING TO THE FOURTEENTH CENTURY

TO THE SIXTH CENTURY

ANONYMOUS

1   The *rath* in front of the oak wood
     belonged to Bruidge, and Cathal,
     belonged to Aedh, and Ailill,
     belonged to Conaing, and Cuilíne
     and to Mael Dúin before them
     —all kings in their turn.
     The *rath* survives; the kings
     are covered in clay.

2   Three rounded flanks I loved
     and never will see again:
     the flank of Tara, the flank of Tailtiu
     and the flank of Aed Mac Ainmirech.

3   He is coming, Adzed-Head,
     on the wild-headed sea
     with cloak hollow-headed
     and curve-headed staff.

     He will chant false religion
     at a bench facing East
     and his people will answer
     'Amen, amen.'

attributed to DALLÁN FORGAILL

4   *A Poem in Praise of Colum Cille*

     God, O God, whom I have begged
        (ere I stand before His face)
     for chariots for the battle;
        the God of Heaven, that He might not

3

abandon me with the crowds wailing
  before the enormous smoke;
the Great God, to save me from the fiery walls,
  my eyes stretched with tears;
the God of Truth near me, that He might hear
  my pitiful cry to cloudy Heaven:

Here is no slight news out of Niall's people
  nor sighing from a single plain
with great sorrow and a great burden unbearable.
  This verse tells of a Dove
lifeless and without sanctuary.

How can a simple one speak of Him?
  Even Nera could not, the sage of God
who sat himself in Sion and lived not long.
  There is no increase amongst us.
Our seer lives no longer.
  Our souls' light is hidden.
Our keeper of life is dead.
  He has died, our lawful leader,
he is gone, our witness of the Word:
  the wise one who took away our terrors,
the strict one who taught us truth in words,
  the teacher who could chant for us
the tribes of the whole world.
  We are a harp without a peg,
a church without an abbot.

*

In God's time he rose on high,
  Colum of the companies,
servant of the shining shrine.
  All his life he kept vigil.
His span was short, his fill frugal.
  He led in learning on every hill,
to doctors of the law a citadel.
  Countries and kingdoms he set alight
and their firm-hearted peoples.
  He made a good death.
He rose on high with the angels of God.

*

He has reached the arms of the ranked archangels;
   reached a place where there is no night;
reached Moses' land (for we have faith);
   reached that plain where music is self-born,
where the wise do not die,
   where the King of Priests has abolished all toil.

*

His pangs were brief before his triumph.
   He was a torment to the Devil.
To him pleasure was temptation
   from his powerful calling.
Stoutly he supported the law.
   He knew wisdom and the tomb.
Theology was fixed for him.
   His death was good indeed.
He knew the embrace of angels.
   He lived by the judgements of Basil.
He would not have anything done
   by throngs enormous, enormous choirs.

*

He saw his course and seized it.
   Returning good for evil
the wise one wove the Word,
   made clear the commentaries.
He established the Psalms,
   laid down the books of the Law
(by Caseon held so dear).
   He won the battle of the belly.
He followed the books of Solomon,
   foretold fair weather and foul.
He singled out the sections
   of all the books of the Law.
He read the holy secrets
   revealed in the schools of Scripture
and harmonized together
   the moon and the path it makes
and its course with the sun's stations,
   and the ocean's actions also.

He numbered the stars of Heaven,
 this teacher of all things,
this Dove, this Colum Cille.

     *

Who has lived, or ever shall,
 more notable in our lands
than this learned one from the North-East?
 There spoke with us, and lately,
a man who knew no meanness,
 who did only deeds of virtue,
who rose to the upper world
 by a vessel of the vast city,
who was lifted up and made king
 before the Maker had made men.
Desire of the eyes he put aside,
 a perfect sage with faith in Christ.
No ale he wanted, no excess;
 he gave up meat.
He was learned and clean-lived.
 He was loving; a rock for victory.
His was a great goodness.
 He abounded in goodness to his guests.
He was eager. He was noble;
 noble his death.
He was gentle.
 Sages held him close to their hearts.
He was our jewel.
 He talked with Axal!
He died of abstinence.
 He was sweet to listen to.
Being a priest was but one of his callings.
 To people he was inscrutable.
He was a roof to the naked,
 a tit to the poor.
All heaviness harassed him
 and caused him new suffering.
From this Colum who guards our lands
 let us hope for high honour and manna.
Long he abased himself
 but Christ set him among the righteous.

     *

6

The wise sage found the Fourfold Path
    that would bring him, after his cross,
into Heaven, with music.
    He held one hundred churches
under waves of ample offerings.

A high hero, with no idols,
    he gathered no crooked companies
but gathered all in the milk of penance.
    He neither taught nor took heed of heresy.
He delighted in nothing outside the King's Law
    lest he might have everlasting death.
His name lives, and his soul.
    He prepared many in the law of the Saints.
Sickness attacked his side.
    He destroyed the desires of the body.
He destroyed meanness.
    Is that not a true son of Conn?

He caused no offence through envy.
    He caused no offence through jealousy.
Wise men know his grave is good
    against hardships of the stormy season.
In a country of idols he took to violence
    in his holy chariot
and sought the Truth in strife everlasting
    warring against the flesh
lest the King-Son come, a Second God
    with second voice and second verse.
Before he reached old age,
    or failing strength, he was buried.
Through terror of Hell
    he went to Alba.

*

Aed commissioned a solid song
    out of our mighty music:
how the hero came to Heaven
    no unloved, no slight soul,
nor worldly-wise; a hero
    not by alliance with Conall

but quietening with a blessing
   the bitter lips of those
in Alba through the king's will.

Far from the ways of men
   he sat down with God.
Though fasting and abstemious, yet
   he offered in Conall's city
hospitality great and clean.
   A just elder in judgement,
true head of a household.
   He conversed with angels;
he could speak Greek grammar.
   A noble one I tell of
who sought out the North
   —Fedlimid's son, who found a limit
up in the Northern land.

None left this world with thoughts
   more totally fixed on the Cross;
all his formulations
   were fulfilled in the fact,
so that there sprang therefrom
   an honourable outcome
not from Niall only
   but from the Holy Spirit.
No deed deserving death he did.
   When he went to his death
all the professions of Conn
   broke in grief by dint of his goodness.

Son-Name of the Cross:

The life until now
   plain as the sky
      I have told it all.

He cried aloud
   a sweet lion
      encountering the snow.

*

How can I show before I die
  a way for the body into Heaven?

He found tranquil joy in his choice.
  This good man solved the obscure.
Not wailed by one house
  nor wailed on one string,
a weight on the world
  is the heavy word.
He lit the King's lamp
  that had been put out.

This is in praise of the King who kinged me.
  May it turn us toward Sion.
May it take us past torments
  and drive off my dark mood.
May Coirpre's child in his noble city
  behold me without a stain.

A great circuit is finished.
  But a great heaven poem
without its sun
  —that is not my wish.

No slight news out of Niall's people.

From the Latin

COLUMBANUS

5
A Boat Song

The driving keel, cut from the forest—look—travels the current
of the twin-horned Rhine, and slides over the water like oil.
Together, men! Let the sounding echo return our cry.

The winds raise their breath, the harsh rain hurts us,
but men's proper strength prevails and drives off the storm.
Together, men! Let the sounding echo return our cry.

The clouds fade in time, and so the storm will yield.
Our efforts will tame it. Steady toil conquers all.
Together, men! Let the sounding echo return our cry.

Stand fast, and hold yourselves ready for better things.
You have suffered harder, and God will end even this.
Together, men! Let the sounding echo return our cry.

So the foul fiend works: he tires our hearts with fury,
and with evil temptation shakes our innermost hearts.
Keep Christ in your minds, my men, and let your cry re-echo.

Stay stern in your resolve, spurn the lures of the enemy
and seek your safety in the weapons of virtue.
Keep Christ in your minds, my men, and let your cry re-echo.

Firm faith and a blessed zeal will conquer all.
The ancient enemy will fail and shatter his arrows.
Keep Christ in your minds, my men, and let your cry re-echo.

The King of every good, the source, the height of power,
gives promise as we strive, gives the prize when we succeed.
Keep Christ in your minds, my men, and let your cry re-echo.

SEVENTH CENTURY

ANONYMOUS

6   *The Boyhood of Christ*

When He was barely five
Jesus, the Son of God,
blessed twelve water puddles
He moulded out of clay.

He made a dozen birds
—the kind we call the sparrow—
He made them on the Sabbath,
perfect, out of clay.

A Jew there criticized Him
—Jesus, the Son of God!—
and to His father Joseph
took Him by the hand.

'Joseph, correct your son,
he has committed wrong.
He made clay shapes of birds
upon the Sabbath day.'

Jesus clapped His palms,
His little voice was heard.
Before their eyes—a miracle—
the little birds flew off.

The sweet, beloved voice was heard
from the mouth of Jesus pure:
'So they will know who made you
off with you to your homes.'

A man who was there told everyone
the wonderful affair
and overhead they all could hear
the singing of the birds.

EIGHTH CENTURY

ANONYMOUS

7   *Saint Patrick's Breastplate*

Today I put on
a terrible strength
invoking the Trinity,
confessing the Three
with faith in the One
as I face my Maker.

Today I put on the power
of Christ's birth and baptism,
of His hanging and burial,
His resurrection, ascension
and descent at the Judgement.

Today I put on the power
of the order of Cherubim,
angels' obedience,
archangels' attendance,
in hope of ascending
to my reward;
patriarchs' prayers,
prophets' predictions,
apostles' precepts,
confessors' testimony,
holy virgins' innocence
and the deeds of true men.

Today I put on
the power of Heaven,
the light of the Sun,
the radiance of the Moon,
the splendour of fire,
the fierceness of lightning,
the swiftness of wind,

the depth of the sea,
the firmness of earth
and the hardness of rock.

Today I put on
God's strength to steer me,
God's power to uphold me,
God's wisdom to guide me,
God's eye for my vision,
God's ear for my hearing,
God's word for my speech,
God's hand to protect me,
God's pathway before me,
God's shield for my shelter,
God's angels to guard me
from ambush of devils,
from vice's allurements,
from traps of the flesh,
from all who wish ill,
whether distant or close,
alone or in hosts.

I summon these powers today
to take my part against every implacable power
that attacks my body and soul,
the chants of false prophets,
dark laws of the pagans,
false heretics' laws,
entrapments of idols,
enchantments of women
or smiths or druids,
and all knowledge that poisons
man's body or soul.

Christ guard me today
from poison, from burning,
from drowning, from hurt,
that I have my reward,

Christ beside me,
    Christ before me,
        Christ behind me,

Christ within me,
  Christ beneath me,
    Christ above me,

Christ on my right hand,
  Christ on my left,

Christ where I lie,
  Christ where I sit,
    Christ where I rise,

Christ in the hearts of all who think of me,
Christ in the mouths of all who speak to me,
Christ in every eye that sees me,
Christ in every ear that hears me.

Today I put on
a terrible strength,
invoking the Trinity,
confessing the Three,
with faith in the One
as I face my Maker.

Domini est salus.
Domini est salus.
Domini est salus.
Salus tua, Domine, sit semper vobiscum.

8　　　*Epitaph for Cú Chuimne*

Cú Chuimne in his youth
  studied half the truth,
then turned from the second half
  and studied women.

With the fullness of years
  he developed wisdom,
and turned away from women
  to complete his studies.

BLÁTHMAC MAC CON BRETTAN

from *A Poem to Mary*

I call you with honest words,
Mary, my lovely queen,
that I may talk with you
and pity your poor heart,

lamenting Christ the bright
from my whole heart with you,
luminous, precious jewel,
mother of the mighty Lord.

If I ruled with every honour
earth's peoples to the far sea
they would come with me, and with you,
to lament your Son the King,

men, women, children
beating their hands without cease
in lament on the hills
for the King Who created the stars.

But I cannot: so I will mourn
your Son profoundly with you
if, at some time,
you will come to visit me.

That we may talk together
in the pity of an unstained heart,
o head of purest faith,
come to me, loving Mary.

EIGHTH/NINTH CENTURY

From *The Ulster Cycle* (10–13)

from *Exile of the Sons of Uisliu*

10   *Two Poems of Derdriu*

. . . She was kept a year by Conchobor. In that time she never gave one
smile, nor took enough food or sleep, nor lifted up her head from her
knees. If they sent musicians to her, she would say this following poem:

> 'Sweet in your sight the fiery stride
> of raiding men returned to Emain.
> More nobly strode the three proud
> sons of Uisliu toward their home:
>
> 'Noisiu bearing the best mead
> —I would wash him by the fire—
> Ardán, with a stag or a boar,
> Anle, shouldering his load.
>
> 'The son of Nes, battle-proud,
> drinks, you say, the choicest mead.
> Choicer still—a brimming sea—
> I have taken frequently.
>
> 'Modest Noisiu would prepare
> a cooking-pit in the forest floor.
> Sweeter then than any meat
> the son of Uisliu's, honey-sweet.
>
> 'Though for you the times are sweet
> with pipers and with trumpeters,
> I swear today I can't forget
> that I have known far sweeter airs.
>
> 'Conchobor your king may take delight
> in pipers and in trumpeters
> —I have known a sweeter thing,
> the three sons' triumphant song.

16

'Noisiu's voice a wave roar,
a sweet sound to hear for ever:
Ardán's bright baritone;
Anle, the hunter's, high tenor.

'Noisiu: his grave-mound is made
and mournfully accompanied.
The highest hero—and I poured
the deadly drink when he died.

'His cropped gold fleece I loved,
and fine form—a tall tree.
Alas, I needn't watch today,
nor wait for the son of Uisliu.

'I loved the modest, mighty warrior,
loved his fitting, firm desire,
loved him at daybreak as he dressed
by the margin of the forest.

'Those blue eyes that melted women,
and menaced enemies, I loved;
then, with our forest journey done,
his chanting through the dark woods.

'I don't sleep now,
nor redden my fingernails.
What have I to do with welcomes?
The son of Indel will not come.

'I can't sleep,
lying there half the night.
These crowds—I am driven out of my mind.
I can neither eat nor smile.

'What use for welcome have I now
with all these nobles crowding Emain?
Comfortless, no peace nor joy,
nor mansion nor pleasant ornament.'

If Conchobor tried to soothe her, she would chant this following poem:

'Conchobor, what are you thinking, you
that piled up sorrow over woe?
Truly, however long I live,
I cannot spare you much love.

'The thing most dear to me in the world,
the very thing I most loved,
your harsh crime took from me.
I won't see him till I die.

'I feel his lack, wearily,
the son of Uisliu. All I see—
black boulders on fair flesh
so bright once among the rest.

'Red-cheeked, sweet as the river-brink;
red-lipped; brows beetle-black;
pearly teeth gleaming bright
with a noble snowy light.

'His figure easiest to find,
bright among Alba's fighting-men
—a border made of red gold
matched his handsome crimson cloak.

'A soft multitude of jewels
in the satin tunic, itself a jewel:
for decoration, all told,
fifty ounces of light gold.

'He carried a gold-hilted sword
and two javelins sharply tipped,
a shield rimmed with yellow gold
with a knob of silver at the middle.

'Fergus did an injury
bringing us over the great sea.
How his deeds of valour shrank
when he sold honour for a drink!

'If all Ulster's warriors
were gathered on this plain, Conchobor,
I would gladly give them all
for Noisiu, son of Uisliu.

'Break my heart no more today.
In a short while I'll be no more.
Grief is heavier than the sea,
if you were but wise, Conchobor.'

'What do you see that you hate most?' Conchobor said.

'You,' she said, 'and Eogan mac Durthacht!'

'Go and live for a year with Eogan, then', Conchobor said.

Then he sent her over to Eogan.

They set out the next day for the fair of Macha. She was behind Eogan in the chariot. She had sworn that two men alive in the world together would never have her.

'This is good, Derdriu', Conchobor said. 'Between me and Eogan you are a sheep eyeing two rams.'

A big block of stone was in front of her. She let her head be driven against the stone, and made a mass of fragments of it, and she was dead.

from *How the Bulls were Begotten*

11   *The Two Bulls*

This was the Brown Bull of Cuailnge—
dark brown dire haughty with young health
horrific overwhelming ferocious
full of craft
furious fiery flanks narrow
brave brutal thick breasted
curly browed head cocked high
growling and eyes glaring
tough maned neck thick and strong
snorting mighty in muzzle and eye
with a true bull's brow
and a wave's charge
and a royal wrath
and the rush of a bear
and a beast's rage
and a bandit's stab
and a lion's fury.
Thirty grown boys could take
their place from rump to nape
—a hero to his herd at morning
foolhardy at the herd's head
to his cows the beloved
to husbandmen a prop
the father of great beasts
overlooks the ox of the earth.

A white head and white feet
  had the Bull Finnbennach
  and a red body the colour of blood
  as if bathed in blood
  or dyed in the red bog
  or pounded in purple
  with his blank paps
  under breast and back
  and his heavy mane and great hoofs
  the beloved of the cows of Ai
  with ponderous tail
  and a stallion's breast
  and a cow's eye apple
  and a salmon's snout
  and hinder haunch
  he romps in rut
  born to bear victory
  bellowing in greatness
  idol of the ox herd
  the prime demon Finnbennach.

from *The Táin*

12   *The Armies Enter Cuailnge*

. . . Now it was that the Morrígan settled in bird shape on a standing
stone in Temair Chuailnge, and said to the Brown Bull:

'Dark one are you restless
    do you guess they gather
to certain slaughter
    the wise raven
groans aloud
    that enemies infest
the fair fields
    ravaging in packs
learn I discern
    rich plains
softly wavelike
    baring their necks
greenness of grass
    beauty of blossoms

        on the plains war
                grinding heroic
    hosts to dust
                cattle groans the Badb
    the raven ravenous
                among corpses of men
    affliction and outcry
                and war everlasting
    raging over Cuailnge
                death of sons
    death of kinsmen
                death   death!'

13   *Before the Last Battle*

... The men of Ulster were settled before sunset. The ground between
the armies lay bare.

  In the half light between the two camps, the Morrígan spoke:

            'Ravens gnawing
                    men's necks
            blood spurting
                    in the fierce fray
            hacked flesh
                    battle madness
            blades in bodies
                    acts of war
            after the cloaked one's
                    hero heat
            in man's shape
                    he shakes to pieces
            the men of Cruachan
                    with hacking blows
            war is waged
                    each trampling each.
            Hail Ulster!
                    Woe men of Ireland!
            Woe to Ulster!
                    Hail men of Ireland!'

This last ('Woe to Ulster') she said in Connachtmen's ears only, to hide
the truth from them ...

Toward Winter

Four Fragments

Sliab Cua, dark and broken, is full of wolf packs.
The wind sweeps down its glens,
wolves howl about its dykes,
the fierce dark deer bellows
across it in the Autumn,
and the crane cries out across its rocks.

* * *

The night is cold on the Great Bog.
The storm is lashing—no small matter.
The sharp wind is laughing at the groans
echoing through the cowering wood.

* * *

We are shattered and battered, engulfed,
O King of clear-starred Heaven!
The wind has swallowed us like twigs
swallowed in a red flame out of Heaven.

* * *

Want and Winter are upon us.
The lake-side is flooded.
Frost has shrivelled the leaves.
The pleasant wave has started muttering.

NINTH CENTURY

ANONYMOUS

15   *An Ivied Tree-Top*

No great house is finer
than my cell in Tuaim Inbir
with its stars all in order
and its sun, and its moon.

It was Gobbán who built it
(you have all heard the story)
and beloved God in Heaven
the Thatcher made its roof.

Rain does not reach it.
There is no fear of spears.
It is bright as a garden,
and with no fence around it!

16   *The Hag of Béara*

I am ebbing—but not like the sea.
It is age drains my colour
bringing me only grief,
while the sea's glad tide will return.

I am Buí, the hag of Béara.
I had new shifts once to wear
but am so cast down today
I haven't one cast-off shift.

Possessions,
not people, is all you value.
As for me, when I was young
it was people only I loved.

Tuaim Inbir] lit. 'the ridge, or tumulus, by the estuary'; a monastery in Meath
Gobbán] a mythical craftsman

16 Béara] peninsula of Beare, south-west Cork

And the people I loved the most,
I travelled across their land
and they looked after me well
and boasted little about it.

Now people ask politely
but won't give much away,
and little though they give
they boast about it greatly.

Chariots at high speed
and horses seizing the prize,
there was a flood of them once.
And I bless the King who gave them.

Now my body gropes out sourly
sensing its destined home,
and whenever it suits God's Son
let Him come and recover His loan.

Nothing but narrow bones
you will see when you look at my arms.
But they did sweet business once
round the bodies of mighty kings.

Look at my arms: you will see
nothing but narrow bones.
They are not worth lifting up
to circle a sweet young man.

Young girls fill with pleasure
when Beltaine comes round,
but misery suits me better,
an ancient thing, past pity.

There's no honey in my talk,
no sheep are killed for my wedding.
My hair is scarce and grey.
If my veil is thin, what matter?

And no matter
if the veil on my head is white
—who had veils of every colour
and drank the best of beer.

Beltaine] the festival of May-time

So I'll envy no ancient thing
except the hill of Femen:
I have worn out age's garment
but Femen's hair holds its yellow.

The royal stone at Femen
and Rónán's *cahir* at Bregon
—it is long since the storm first touched them
yet their cheeks are not old or worn.

Winter begins to waken
the sea's great roaring wave
and I cannot look forward now
to company high or low.

It is many a day
since I sailed the seas of youth.
The years of my beauty are over
and all my lust is spent.

Many a day
since I have felt the heat.
I go full dressed in the sun.
I feel old age upon me.

The summer of my youth
and the autumn, too, are spent.
And winter that ends it all
—its first days have touched me.

I wasted my youth from the start
and I'm glad I chose to do it.
If I'd 'leaped the wall' only a little
would this cloak be any the newer?

Lovely the cloak of green
that my King has thrown on the hill
and great is the One who dyed it
and Who makes soft wool from coarse.

Femen] a plain in Co. Tipperary   *cahir*] a dwelling place   Bregon] on Femen plain
leaped the wall] gone wandering; in modern usage, to leave a convent   thrown on
the hill] lit. 'on Drumain', an unidentified place

Pity me: only a wretch.
Every acorn rots away.
The feast of bright candles is over
and I'm left in this darkened cell.

I had business once with kings
and drank their mead and wine.
But I drink whey-water now
with other withered ancients.

For beer, a cup of whey . . .
But my trials be all God's will.
I pray Thee, living God,
avert my blood from rage!

With age's stained cloak around me
my senses start to deceive.
Grey hair grows out of my skin
like rot on an ancient tree.

My right eye taken from me,
down-paid on the Promised Land.
And the left eye taken too
to make the title sure.

There is a wave at the flood
and another at the swift ebb
and what the flood wave gives
the ebb takes from your hands.

The flood wave
and that other wave at the ebb,
both have come upon me
and I know them well.

The flood wave
couldn't reach my cellar now.
I had great following once
but a hand fell on them all.

If the Son of Mary knew
He'd lie under my cellar-pole!
There's nothing much for Him there
but I never said no to a man.

Everything is wretched
and the wretchedest thing is Man.
He sees the flood-tide ebb
but his ebb without an end.

Happy the isle in the ocean wide
where the flood follows the ebb.
As for me, after my ebb
I can look forward to nothing.

There is scarcely a single house
I still can recognize.
What once was full in flood
has ebbed to the full at last.

17   *Créide's Lament for Dínertech*

Créide, the daughter of King Guaire, sang these verses for Dínertech,
son of Guaire mac Nechtain, after the battle of Aidne, when she saw him
with seventeen wounds in the breast of his tunic. She loved him, and
said:

'These are the arrows that kill sleep
in the cold night at all hours:
love-lament for my nights spent
with the man from Roigne border.

'My love for that man from another land
beyond all living men
has drained my colour till I've little left
and will not let me sleep.

'His speech was sweeter than any song
(save worship of the King of Heaven)
—a glorious flame, and shyly spoken,
a slim spouse with soft thighs.

'I was modest as a child
and unused to sins of desire.
Now I have reached unsettled age
I am confused by lust.

17 Roigne] unidentified; see note to poem 24

'I have all I need with Guaire,
the king of chilly Aidne,
but my thoughts stray from my people
out to the land of West Luachar.

'Round the walls of Colmán's churchyard
they are chanting, in the land of Aidne,
of a glorious flame called Dínertech
from South Limerick of the grave mounds.

'O chaste Christ, his hard death
torments my harassed heart.
These are the arrows that kill sleep
in the cold night at all hours.'

A Selection of Monastic Poems (18–25)

18

All alone in my little cell
with no one for company,
I love this place of pilgrimage
now while I still have life.

A hut remote and hidden
for repenting of all sin,
with upright conscience, unafraid
in the face of holy Heaven.

With a body that good habits
made holy, treading it down,
and eyes worn out and tearful
with penance for my desires,

with weak, subdued desires
and denial of the wretched world,
with innocent, eager thoughts,
so let us sue to God.

17 West Luachar] a district comprising north-east Kerry and the adjoining parts of
Cork and Limerick   Colman's churchyard] attached to a monastery in Aidne

With sincere lamentations
up to cloudy Heaven,
earnest devout confession,
intense tears in torrents;

on a cold, nervous bed
—as a doomed man might lie down—
with short, anxious sleep
and prayer early and often.

As to property and food
our one wish—to abstain.
For certain what I eat
will be no cause of sin:

dry bread measured out
with virtuous head bowed low,
and water from the bright hill
our proper draught to drink.

A salt and meagre diet
with mind bent on a book;
no disputation, visitation;
conscience serene and calm.

How wonderful it would be
—some pure and holy blemish,
cheeks dried and sunken in,
skin leathery and lean!

Christ, God's Son, to visit me,
my Maker and my King,
my spirit turning toward Him
and the Kingdom where He dwells.

And let the place that shelters me
behind monastic walls
be a lovely cell, with pillars pure,
and I there all alone.

19   *Four 'Glosses'*

A wall of woodland overlooks me.
A blackbird sings me a song (no lie!).
Above my book, with its lines laid out,
the birds in their music sing to me.

The cuckoo sings clear in lovely voice
in his grey cloak from a bushy fort.
I swear it now, but God is good!
It is lovely writing out in the wood.

*   *   *

How lovely it is today!
The sunlight breaks and flickers
on the margin of my book.

*   *   *

A bird is calling from the willow
with lovely beak, a clean call.
Sweet yellow tip; he is black and strong.
It is doing a dance, the blackbird's song.

*   *   *

The little bird
let out a whistle
from his beak tip
    bright yellow.
He sends the note
across Loch Laíg
—a blackbird, a branch
    a mass of yellow.

Loch Laíg] Belfast Lough

30

Pangur Bán

I myself and Pangur Bán,
we each have our particular skill.
   His mind is fixed upon the hunt,
   mine upon my chosen craft.

Peace I love beyond all fame
in diligence above my book.
   Pangur Bán is never jealous,
   holding dear his childish art.

It is never tiresome while we two
are here together in our home,
   our interest endless while we have
   something to try our skills upon.

Often, after the hard hunt,
a mouse will tangle in his net,
   while into mine there falls a rule
   of dark meaning and difficult.

He directs his pure bright eye
along the wall surrounding us.
   I direct my clear eye,
   weak though it is, at hard knowledge.

He takes delight in rapid action;
a mouse sticks in his sharp claw.
   Solving a dark and valued crux
   I, for my part, take delight.

However long we work together
neither one disturbs the other.
   Each enjoys his own skill
   finding pleasure for himself.

He, for his part, is the master
of his daily job of work.
   Bringing darkness into light
   is the work that I do best.

   Pangur Bán] lit. 'the white fuller'

21 A busy yellow bee, after his mighty quest
    from cell to cell in the sunlight,
    flies contented across the great plain
    home to his welcome in the honeycomb.

22 A sweet little bell
    struck on a windy night:
        I would rather answer that
    than meet with a wicked woman!

23 Adore we the Lord
        and His wonderful works:
    great Heaven bright with angels,
        Earth's sea white with waves.

24   *The Hermit Marbán*

King Guaire Hermit Marbán,
    why can't you sleep in your bed?
    You spend your nights so often
    with your tonsured head on the fir-grove ground.

Marbán I have a hut here in the wood
    that nobody knows but my Lord.
    An ash tree one side is its wall,
    the other a hazel, a great *rath* tree.

    Two posts of heather prop it up,
    its lintel a honeysuckle.
    The forest sheds a crop of nuts
    on the plump pigs by its open door.

    My hut is small, and yet
    encircled by well-known paths.
    And look who is singing sweet on my gable
    in a blackbird-coloured shift!

    24 *rath*] a fortification and dwelling-place

The stags of Druim Rolach spring
up out of the glittering stream.
Roigne you can see, all red,
and noble Mucruime, and Moen Plain.

It is a humble, hidden house
—but the path-filled forest is mine.
Will you come to see it with me?
Though if not I am content . . .

The slender mane
of a yew-green tree
    will show you where,
and the beauty around it
—great green oaks—
    will make you certain.

Fruits of the apple,
abundant blessing,
    abound in the *bruiden*
and fine clumped crops
on the small-nut hazels,
    branching and green.

Fresh spring wells
and falls of water
    delicious to drink
break forth in plenty,
with yew-tree berries,
    and cherry and privet.

Tame pigs and goats
and baby pigs
    at home all round it,
and wild pigs also,
tall deer and their does,
    badgers and their brood.

In peaceful parties
crowds from the country
    visit my home:
foxes gather
in the woods before it
    and that is lovely.

        bruiden] a dwelling-house

Lovely feasts
come into my kitchen
   quickly prepared:
the purest water,
the choicest fruits
   and trout and salmon,

the fruit of the rowan,
black sloe-berries
   from the brown thorn-tree,
acorns to eat
and smooth-skinned berries
   from the bare hill-face,

clutches of eggs,
nuts, onion and honey
   —the gift of God—
sugary apples,
red bog-berries
   and berries of the heather,

beer and herbs,
strawberry patches,
   a lovely plenty,
haws from the hawthorn,
fruits of the yew
   and nutty kernels.

A cup of mead
from the noble hazel
   swiftly served;
brown fruit of the oak
and manes of the briar
   with fine blackberries.

Summer brings
gay garments of plenty
   and tasty flavours:
ground-nuts, mint,
tresses from the stream
   all green and pure.

The music of pigeons
in their glossy throats
   makes lovely stir,
and the murmur of thrushes
sweet and homely
   over my house;

beetles, bees,
with their tiny buzzing
   and delicate hum;
wild barnacle geese
(it will soon be Samain!)
   with their wild dark music;

the busy linnet,
brown restless spirit
   on the hazel bough,
and then woodpeckers,
speckle-hooded,
   in enormous flights;

they come, the white ones,
gulls and herons,
   till the harbour echoes
and (no sad music)
the brown hen fowl
   in the russet heather.

The heifer is rowdy
in time of summer,
   the shining season.
Work is no burden
on the pleasant plain,
   smooth and delightful.

The voice of the wind
through the branchy wood
   under clouds of grey,
and the river rapids
babbling on rocks,
   are lovely music.

Samain] feast at the end of summer

The pleasant pine
makes music for me,
   and not for payment.
There is never a time
by grace of Christ
   when I'm poorer than you!

Though you delight
in your private pleasures,
   all wealth exceeding,
I render thanks
for what is given
   by Christ in His goodness.

Not one hour's quarrel
or noise or clamour
   the like of yours.
I thank the Prince
Who grants all good
   to me in my hut.

King Guaire   I would give my ample kingdom
and my share of Colmán's birthright,
all claims to the hour of death,
to be with you, Marbán!

25   *The Calendar of Oengus*

from the *Prologue*

This sad world we inhabit,
brief are its kingdoms.
The King who rules the angels
is Lord of all lands.

Even in this our land
where all run after riches
we have a great example
of God's power to instruct us:

24 Colmán] Colmán Mac Duach, another 'saint' with a hermitage (now Kilmacduagh, 'Mac Duach's Sanctuary') in Co. Galway

Tara's great palace perished
with the fall of its princes
while great Armagh remains
with all its worthy choirs.

Quenched—and great the fall—
brave Loegaire's fame
while, proud and honoured, Patrick's name
is spreading still.

The Faith has spread
and will last till the Day of Doom
while evil pagans are borne off
and their *raths* deserted.

Cruachan's *rath* is vanished
with Ailill, sired in triumph;
a quiet pride, past reach of princes,
lives in the *cahir* of Cluain.

The proud palace of Aillin
perished with its braggart hordes;
great, triumphant is Brigit
and lovely her thronged convent.

The *dún* of Emain is vanished,
only its stones remain,
while thronged Gleann Dá Loch
is the monastery of the western world.

Fine and splendid shines
strong Ferna of the yew trees
while gone are the proud throngs
of Bécc Mac Eogain's *rath*.

Let us then take note
of the judgement of our King:
Bécc Mac Eogain gone
while Aed Mac Sétna lives!

The pagans' ancient *cahirs*
not permitted to last long
—they are wastes without worship now
like the place of Lugaid—

while the little places taken
by two people, or three,
now are crowded shrines,
with hundreds and with thousands!

Paganism is ruined
though it once spread far and bright
while the Father's realm is ample
—ocean and earth and sky!

And closer at hand we have
a sign of the power of God
like a holy psalm, a judgement
from now till the end of the world:

proud Donnchadh, red and wrathful,
or valorous Bran from the Berb,
stir not a trace of grief
when I visit their monuments

while Mael Ruain, whose life was short,
the great sun of South Mide's plain,
heals all hearts of their hurt
beside his pure tombstone.

The great kings are brought low
—all the Domhnalls—as by disease
while the Ciaráns are crowned
and the Crónáns set on high.

The great evil mountains
are cut down as with blades
while from former valleys
mountains now are made.

ANONYMOUS

26

First of summer, lovely sight,
season of perfection!
At the slightest ray the sun sends
blackbirds sing their full song.

The hardy vigorous cuckoo calls
all hail to high summer.
The bitter weather is abated
when the branched woods were torn.

Summer dries the stream down small,
the swift herd searches for a pool.
Heather spreads its hair afar.
The pale bog-cotton, faint, flourishes.

Buds break out on the hawthorn bush.
The sea runs its calm course
—the salt sea the season soothes.
Blossom blankets the world.

Bees' feet, with tiny strength,
carry their bundles, sucked from blossom.
The hill-fields call to the cattle.
Ants are active in swarming plenty.

The woods' harp works its music;
the harmony brings total peace.
Dust blows out of all our houses,
haze blows from the brimming lake.

The sturdy corncrake-poet speaks.
The cold cataract calls its greeting
down to the warm pool from on high.
Rushes begin to rustle.

Slim swallows flash on high:
living music rings the hill.
Moist fruits grow fat and heavy.
. . . the marsh . . .

. . . the lovely marsh:
grass in a fine, packed path.
The speckled fish makes a leap
at the swift fly—worthy warriors.

Man thrives: all things flourish.
The great slopes are full of gifts.
Each forest glade is shining bright
and bright each broad and lovely plain.

The whole season full of wonder:
Winter's harsh wind is gone.
The fruitful woods are fair.
Summer is a great ease.

A flock of birds settles to earth:
they have seen a woman there.*
The green field echoes
where a stream runs brisk and bright.

Horse riding; wild ardour;
ranked hosts ranged around.
Tree-white freed across the land,
giving up an iris-gold!

A delicate and timorous thing
is singing ceaseless in the air,
and rightly, from a full throat:
'First of summer, lovely sight!'

27   *Epitaph for Mael Mhuru*

Rich earth has not pressed down,
to towers of Tara will not come,
Eriu's fields have not embraced
pure and mild Mael Mhuru's like.

Ne'er cheerfully drank death,
nor found fellowship with the dead,
nor has ploughed earth enwrapped
historian more fine.

28   *An Insult*

I hear
he won't give horses for poems.
He gives what his style allows:
cows.

* conjectural

29 *The Lovely Étan*

I don't know who it is
that Étan is going to sleep with.
But I know the lovely Étan
will not be sleeping alone.

From the Latin (30–34)

DONATUS
*c.*829–876

30 *The Land Called Scotia*

It is said that that western land is of Earth the best,
that land called by name 'Scotia' in the ancient books:
an island rich in goods, jewels, cloth, and gold,
benign to the body, mellow in soil and air.
The plains of lovely Ireland flow with honey and milk.
There are clothes and fruit and arms and art in plenty;
no bears in ferocity there, nor any lions,
for the land of Ireland never bore their seed.
No poisons pain, no snakes slide in the grass,
nor does the chattering frog groan on the lake.

And a people dwell in that land who deserve their home,
a people renowned in war and peace and faith.

SEDULIUS SCOTTUS
d. 858

31 *Request for Meat and Drink*

Now the crops grow green and the fields flourish with life,
now the vines fatten, and now is the year most lovely,
now the colourful birds soften the heavens with song,
now the ocean smiles, and the earth, and the stars of the sky.

But I am dejected for lack of a drink of sweet juice;
mead is missing, and the gifts of Ceres and Bacchus;
and flesh in its various forms has failed, alas;
though mild earth and the dewy air produce them still.

A writer I am, I declare, a musician—an Orpheus!—
an ox at your threshing: I wish you may have increase.
I am your champion, equipped with the weapons of wisdom.
So off to the Bishop, my Muse, and make my request.

32   *Death of a Ram*

What pangs did he merit—so simple, without misdeed?
   Not Bacchus's gift—no alcohol—did he touch;
not drunkenness drove him from the narrow path,
   nor feasts with kings, nor banquets with lofty captains.
The grass of the field to him was his solemn meal
   and his pleasant drink the gift of the limpid Maas.
He lusted not after ruby raiment nor pearl
   but contented himself with a simple tunic of skin.
He followed his proper course on his own four feet,
   not haughty on horseback over the lovely grass,
nor did he lie, nor speak in empty words,
   but uttered the mystic syllables 'Báá' and 'Béé'.

Great king of the snow-white herd, all hail, farewell!
   You might have used my garden, alas, and lived.
I might have prepared a heated bath, my friend,
   in accord with the laws of hospitality,
and scrubbed the water, with a diligent breast,
   onto your hoofs and onto the horns of your head.
Say only I loved you, your widow and mother also.
   And your brothers too, I shall ever love. Farewell.

33   from *The Defeat of the Norsemen*

Heavens, ocean, and all earth, rejoice!
And rejoice, O people who blossom in Christ.
Admire the acts of the Lord of thunder
   and potent Father.

.   .   .   .   .   .

The vigorous arm of a powerful Father
has levelled with sudden anger—behold it!—
the rebel Northman, foe of the faithful,
   glory to God!

Battle is joined on the open plain,
brightness of weapons glints in the air,
warriors' manifold voices shake
   the frame of the sky.

Opposing armies shower their spears,
the unhappy Dane counts his wounds,
a mighty army aims and strikes
   with showers of iron.

Those who have thirsted through the years
drink the blood of a raving tyrant
and find a sweetness in sating their breast
   with slaughter of men.

Diggers of pitfalls tumble in;
an overweening tower tumbles;
a swelling enemy host—behold—
   is crushed by Christ.

A people great and powerful humbled,
a cursed mass ground utterly down
—death's mouth has swallowed an evil stock:
   praise, Christ, to Thee.

Reckon that overthrow of people:
not counting the humble and lesser kinds
more on that hideous field in blood
   than thrice three thousand.

The judge is just, the world's ruler,
Christ the glory of Christian people,
prince of glory, subduer of evil,
   in rule supreme.

A strong tower, salvation's shield,
he worsts the mighty giants in battle,
He whose name exceeds all others
   and is blessed.

Avenger of a faithful people,
Who drove the sea in swollen tempest
in Egypt once, on chariots and riders
    and whelmed all.

    .   .   .   .   .   .

34   I read, or write. I teach or study wisdom.
        I call on the Heavenly Throne by night and day.
    I eat and drink as I can. I rhyme at the Muse.
        Sleeping, I snore. Waking, I pray to God,
    my woken mind bewailing the sins of my life.
        O Christ and Mary, pity your wretched one.

ANONYMOUS

35   Getting to Rome
    is great labour, little use.
    The King you look for here
    you won't find unless you bring Him.

36   The wind is wild tonight.
    It tosses the sea's white hair.
    What harm . . . It is calm seas
    bring the sharp warriors from the North.

37   Cold! Cold!
    Wide Lurg Plain is cold tonight.
    Snow covers the hill.
    The deer cannot reach their feed.

    Cold without end,
    foul weather has spread over all:
    every downhill ditch a river,
    every ford a full pool,

37 Lurg Plain] the plain near Boyle, Co. Roscommon

every pool a full lake,
every full lake a great sea.
There is no crossing Ros Ford
on horseback any more than on foot.

The fish of Inis Fáil are swarming.
The waves have no end or beginning.
There are no badgers seen in the land.
The hills are hidden, the crane silent.

The wolves of Cuan Wood in their lairs
get no peace or sleep.
The little wren can find nothing
to cover its nest on Leitir Lon.

A terror to the little bird morsels
are the sharp wind and the cold ice
and the beetle-black blackbird finds
no shelter for his flank in Cuan Wood.

Our pot is snug on its hook
but the byres on Leitir Lon are uneasy.
The woods are flattened under snow.
It is hard climbing, with your cow-horn stick.

The bird in his old age in Glen Ridh
finds misery in the bitter wind.
He is in great suffering and pain.
The ice blows into his mouth.

Believe me, it makes no sense
to leave your bed of flock or down.
There is ice over all the fords.
Is it any wonder I say: 'Cold!'

38   I bring you news:
                 the stag roaring,
                 winter flooding,
             summer gone.

37 Inis Fáil] Ireland   Glen Ridh] the Vale of Newry, Co. Armagh

45

Wind high and cold,
   the sun low,
    its path short,
the ocean swift.

The bracken red,
   its outline lost,
    and every day
the cry of geese.

Cold caught
   in birds' wings.
    An icy season.
That's my news.

39

Look out there
to the north-east
at the noble ocean
   teeming,
the home of agile
shining seals:
it is swollen
   to full flood!

40   *Líadan and Cuirithir*

It is miserable
what I have done.
I have tortured the thing I loved.

It was foolish
not to let him have his way,
but for fear of the King of Heaven.

He thought it
no harm, the love he longed for
—reaching Paradise with no pain.

It was a little thing
turned Cuirithir against me,
I who showed him such tenderness.

I am Líadan.
I loved Cuirithir.
It is true what they say.

A little while
I was with Cuirithir.
He thought well of my company.

Forest music
sang to me, with Cuirithir,
and the sound of the blazing sea.

I thought
I could never have angered Cuirithir,
however I managed our love.

I cannot hide it:
he was my heart's love,
no matter how I might love others.

A roar of flame
has torn my heart:
I know it will not last without him.

41   *Amergin's Songs*

I

The winds rose against them so that the gravel of the sea-bottom rose to
the surface and the storm drove them westward until they were lost and
exhausted. Then Amergin said:

'I call the land of Ireland
much travelled fertile ocean
fertile fruitful mountains
fruitful showery woods
falls showering in rivers
falls of deep-pooled lakes
deep-pooled source on the hilltop
source of people gathering
gathering of kings on Tara
Tara hill of tribes

tribes of the sons of Míl
Míl of boats and vessels
and the greatest vessel Ireland
great Ireland darkly sung
in song of darkest wisdom
great wisdom of Bres's women
wives of Bres of Buaigne
and the greatest woman Eriu
by Eremon overborne
by Ír and Eber called.
I call the land of Ireland.'

And immediately a tranquil calm came over the sea.

II

Setting his right foot on land at Inber Scéne, Amergin made this chant:

'I am wind on sea
I am wave in storm
I am sea sound
and seven-horned stag
I am hawk on cliff
a drop of dew in the sun
a fair flower
a boar for valour
I am salmon in pool
lake on plain
a hill with ditches
a word of art
a piercing point
   that pours out rage
the god who fashions
   fire in the head.

'Who makes smooth the stony mountain?
Who announces the phases of the moon?

Míl] one of the ancestors of the Celtic race   Bres] one of the rulers of Ireland before the arrival of the Celts; he was renowned for his meanness and was deposed by the first satire ever made in Ireland   Eriu, Eremon, Ír, Eber] names from the first invasion of Ireland. The invaders, the sons of Míl, meet three queens in turn—Eriu, Banba, and Fódla—and promise that the country will be named after them   Inber Scéne] the estuary at Kenmare

And who the place of the sun's descent?
Who calls the cows from the house of Tethra?
On whom do the cows of Tethra smile?
Who is the force, who is the god
   who shapes blades on a hill of sickness?
Spear wailing,
   wailing in the wind?'

III

Afterward he sang this, to increase the fish in the rivers:

'Fish-teeming sea
abounding land
a flood of fish
fish under wave
like flights of birds
in the hard ocean.

'A bright torrent
salmon in hundreds
plump creatures
harbour song:
"A flood of fish
fish-teeming sea!" '

Tethra] chief of the Fomorians; overcome by the sons of Míl, he becomes King of the Dead

49

ANONYMOUS

42

I'm ashamed of my thoughts
   and how they escape me.
I fear dreadful danger
   on Doom's endless day.

They stray, in the Psalms,
   down paths not proper,
run riot, make mischief
   in great God's eyes,

through bustling throngs
   and flocks of wild women,
through forests and towns,
   more swift than the wind.

One time they will travel
   by paths that are pleasant;
by paths not so pleasant,
   I confess, at another.

So crooked, they cross
   the sea without ships,
or spring in one leap
   from Earth up to Heaven.

They run their mad races
   near and afar,
then return to their home,
   their wild wandering done.

Though you try to restrain them
   or fetter their feet
they're too fickle and thoughtless
   to try to stand still.

No blade and no whiplash
   can keep them in place.
They slip like an eel-tail
   out of my grasp.

No lock, no arched dungeon,
   no fetters on earth
—fort, ocean, bleak stronghold—
   can hamper their course.

Beloved, chaste Christ,
   Who beholdest all eyes,
gracious seven-formed spirit,
   control them and check.

Govern my heart,
   elemental dread God.
Be Thou my Beloved
   that I bend to Thy will.

May I join with Thee close
   in union, O Christ,
Thou not thoughtless nor fickle,
   unlike to myself.

43   Alone up here on the mountain
may my track, Sun-King, be straight
—though I would not die of its crookedness,
or the lack of three thousand men . . .

For though I had three thousand
tough-skinned and fiery youths
let swift death come a-hunting
and no defence will stand.

There is no safe place on earth
when a mortal man is doomed.
And who has ever heard
of a path where the saved will die?

A man may seek my ruin,
greedy for my goods,
yet has no power, for all his plots,
unless the Lord so wills.

And no one has the power
to cut my lifetime short
but the King who shapes the summer,
the Lord of Heaven and Earth.

—So it won't delay my journey
if someone sneezes near me!
The sod for my grave appointed:
I get there when I must.

—Nor stop my setting out alone:
life shaped and will not break me.
The end comes only when it will.
It is the ripe nut falls.

The hero risking his fair skin
with sharp bravery in the ford
is he nearer death, by his wildness,
than the shrewd one lagging after?

Why then should the traveller
search out the surest way?
Where is the assurance
will keep him safe from death?

Amen, and so be it.
Let a man avoid his end,
the deadly day approaches
all at the end of life.

So, watched by noble, glorious God,
nine ranks of angels, the Holy Ghost,
let me not dread pale death,
though the horror come when I am alone.

44   *Manchán's Prayer*

This is the prayer of Manchán of Liath:

O Son of the living God,
ancient eternal King,
grant me a hidden hut
to be my home in the wild,

with green shallow water
running by its side
and a clear pool to wash off sin
by grace of the Holy Ghost;

a lovely wood close by
around it on every hand
to feed the birds of many voices,
to shelter them and hide;

southward facing for warmth,
with a stream in its grounds,
and choice land of thick growth
good for every crop;

some sensible disciples
(their number I will fix)
modest and obedient
praying to the King:

four times three—or three fours—
correct for every need;
two sixes within the church
on the north side and the south,

six pairs besides myself
gathered all about me
praying for all Eternity
to the King who lights the Sun;

a lovely church, with linen,
a home for Heaven's King,
with bright lamps shining down
on the clean bright scriptures;

and a special house to go to
for minding of the body,
with no lust or luxury
or any harmful thought.

And the things that I will have there
and tend there, for certain,
are hens, fresh and fragrant leeks,
bees and speckled salmon . . .

Ample food and raiment
for the King of fairest fame
and I seated somewhere
praying to God a while.

OENGUS CÉILE DÉ

fl. late 10th century

45

The time is ripe and I repent
every trespass, O my Lord.
Pardon me my every crime,
Christ, as Thou art merciful.

By Thy incarnation sweet,
by Thy birth, my sacred King,
by Thy lasting baptism here,
pardon me my every wrong.

By Thy hanging, filled with love,
by Thy rising from the dead,
all my passions pardon me,
Lord who art truly merciful.

By Thy ascension—glorious hour—
to holy Heaven, to the Father
(promised ere Thou didst depart)
pardon me my evil-doing.

By Thy coming—holy word—
to judge the hosts of Adam's seed,
by Heaven's orders nine revealed,
be my offence forgiven me.

By the ranks of prophets true,
by the martyrs' worthy throng,
by the train of noble Fathers,
pardon the crimes that mastered me.

By the band of pure apostles,
by the chaste disciples' host,
by each saint of royal favour,
pardon me my evil deeds.

By the great world's pious virgins,
by the prime lay-womanhood,
by Mary, Maiden wonderful,
pardon me my earthly crimes.

By Earth's peoples (sweet the word)
and those of bright and blessed Heaven
grant Thy pardon excellent
for all my crimes, since I repent!

ANONYMOUS

46 Ah blackbird, giving thanks,
from your nest in the thorn . . . Hermit
that use no bell: soft, sweet,
from the otherworld, your whistle!

ELEVENTH CENTURY

ANONYMOUS

47

Eve am I, great Adam's wife.
I wronged Jesus long ago.
I stole Heaven from my kin.
It is I should hang upon the Tree.

I had a royal house to rule
but evil choice has brought me shame.
An evil crime has withered me.
My hand, alas, it is unclean.

I it was that plucked the apple.
It overcame my greedy will.
As long as womankind shall live
they will not lose their foolishness.

No ice anywhere would there be
nor winter bright with all its blasts.
There'd be no Hell, there'd be no grief,
there'd be no terror, but for me.

MAEL ÍSU Ó BROLCHÁIN

d. 1086

48

To an Elderly Virgin

Old virgin, your airs are proper,
modest, no longer young.
Once, north in the land of Niall,
we passed our nights together.

My age, when you settled with me
(a bold maiden of pointed wit
and an easy, kind, pure-hearted
upright boy) was seven sweet years.

On Banba's steadfast earth we lived,
no stain on body or soul.
My face shone full of your love,
an innocent, free of temptation.

Your correct counsel on hand:
I chose it at every point.
I loved your sharp wisdom better
than converse calm with a king.

Then you stayed with another four
after me, and reaped no ill,
for I know—it is living knowledge—
you are free of sin with a man.

You have found me again at last
after many travels, a test of skill.
A cloud has covered your face,
though it is not evil aged you.

You are my blameless love,
here's my welcome unrestrained.
We will not drown in pains:
I find pure virtue with you.

Endless earth is full of your fame,
your travels wondrous on every track.
Only follow your verse each day
and we'll reach the dread God safe.

You offer your silent precepts
to all on this earth below.
Pour it daily for us all.
Not vain is earnest prayer to God.

Restore our aspect, O God,
who do Thy will with gentle mind,
and the King's clear countenance shine upon us
when we have leaped from our bodies old.

Banba] Ireland

49

My sins in their completeness,
spoken or hid in the heart,
the hideous haste of my career,
forgive me, God in Heaven.

When I was a tender youth
I was ignorant of the right.
Foolish kissing was my joy
with dear white-teethed women.

Now that I am an old man
and have known each wretched fall
I would not take a day of drink
for these tears upon my cheek.

50

I give Thee thanks, my King,
who workest our weal on earth:
since I found the bed of sickness
it is six months yesterday.

I am a victim in the stocks
—all evils visit me.
Tonight my soul yearns upward
yet my body seeks the ground.

I have been thrown in chains
(at all times good for the soul!)
Weakened from head to foot,
I am feeble indeed, I find.

It is plain what troubles drain me,
stern God's good Son . . . Yet rather them
than a feast of drink in my own north land
or gold in hand, dross-free and pure.

And worst of woes should I be a fool
through crime and treachery.
No cruel stroke, no deadly blow,
Thy lofty lash has dealt me.

A pitch-blind man am I,
my side weak to the wall
—alas, beloved God—
a wretch in my own home.

My strength is gone. I cry aloud:
Father of Hosts, come near!
Thou has shackled me to a cross
in this fine land of Munster.

Because of the weight of gloom
my two eyes are chained tight,
but I hope, O King of the stars,
to be happy on high thereby.

I am only a little thing
like a mouse caught in a trap
or rattled in a cat's claw.
No pleasure—but my thanks!

I rise up—agh!—with a groan.
I cannot answer the bell's call.
But my ills are nothing to my evil.
My thanks to Thee, God, tonight.

ANONYMOUS

51 *Praise of God*

It is senseless for any man
to cease in the praise of God.
The birds, they never cease
and their souls are only air.

52 A great tempest on the Plain of Ler,
fierce, beyond all bounds:
the wind risen, harsh winter attacks
across the great sea, rough and bright.
Cruel winter's weapon has found us.

52 Ler] sea god

The sea-surface, Ler's broad plain, in motion
terrifies our long-suffering troops
—it is monstrous, defeating all.
What more overwhelming
than its great outcry, unanswerable?

When the wind blows from the east
the wave's spirit is roused
and it urges past us westward
toward the place where the sun sets
into the rough green wide sea.

When the wind blows from the north
the wave presses cruel and dark
into the southern world,
waging war on the expanse of heaven.
Listen then to the cry of the swans!

When the wind blows from the west
over the brine's swift currents
it urges past us eastward
toward the sun-tree to seize it
in the wide far-distant ocean.

When the wind blows from the south
from the land of Saxons, of the sturdy shields,
the wave strikes against Inis Scít
and reaches to the top of Calad Nit
and its grass-edged grey-green cloak.

Then the sea is full—the ocean a flood—
the home of ships, and beautiful!
A sandy wind sets up currents
around the harbour of Dá Ainmech.
The rudder trembles in the wide water.

Then sleep is troubled (a bad omen)
with fevered victory or raging battle.
The thronged sea surface and its creatures
are covered in swan white.
The mane of Manannán's wife is tossed!

Inis Scít] Skiddy Island, Cork   Calad Nit] unidentified   harbour of Dá
Ainmech] unidentified   Manannán] son of Ler

The wave falls in powerful fury
across wide, dark river-mouths.
The wind rushes. Rough winter attacks.
A full, fierce mountainous torrent pours
about Ceann Tíre and the land of Alba.

Son of the Father, of mighty armies,
save me from terror of hard tempests.
Righteous Lord of the Holy Feast,
save me from the awful blast
and this high tempest out of Hell!

From the Latin

BISHOP PATRICK

d. 1084

53   *An Invocation*

Almighty God, who fillest the recesses of the heavens,
press back with Thine oar the grey-locked waves of the deep ocean.

Here begins the prologue of the book
of the blessed bishop Patrick:

Hurry, my ship,
on the wide sea.
Christ on the waves,
let Him be thy steersman
with sure oar
in a cloudless sky.

Fly, my ship,
on the deep-channelled sea,
slicing asunder
the pallid waves
dewy with foam,
driven by the ocean's
favouring blasts.

52   Ceann Tíre] 'land's end', the Mull of Kintyre   Alba] Scotland

Hurry, my booklet.
An angel go with thee
on the broad sea,
to visit the home
of our pleasant patron
to see is he well
—most worthy of honour
and sweet in love.
O drive out care
and sing out gladness
by night and by day
with your singing voice
up to the sun
and the highest stars.

Hurry, my page,
by the holy power
of the high cross.
Let swell your sails
on the pure sea waves.
Learn, my ship,
to race in safety
on the plains of ocean,
alike in that
to the dire sea beasts
and monsters swimming
in open water.

Hurry, my booklet,
travel in joy
through the waves and the winds.
The scaly hosts
shall travel beside you,
and the rhythmic cry
sweet in tone
of the steersman also
shall strongly sound.

Fly, my ship,
in joy through the waves.
Let the peaks of your sails
be swollen full
by breaths from the east.

May the breezes come
without a cloud . . .
May no error strike
as you are borne
on safe passage
to the fields of England.

Hurry, my page,
with the following thoughts
to keep you company:
I am led by love
to visit the cherished
children of peace,
the faithful in Christ,
our pleasant patron
—though all equally,
with fitting salutes
three times ten
in fair order.

Hurry my book,
with faltering song
and ask, as is right,
with faithful mind:
in the name of Patrick
be my comrade crowned
with a thousand blessings.

Thus the prologue.

A Selection of Poems attributed to
Colum Cille (54–58)

54
O Son of God, it would be sweet,
    a lovely journey,
to cross the wave, the fount in flood,
    and visit Ireland:

to Eolarg Plain, by Foibne Hill,
    across Loch Febail,
and listen there to the matching music
    of the swans.

Flocks of gulls would fill with pleasure
    as we sailed swiftly
into the welcome of Port na Ferg
    in our 'Red-with-Dew'.

I am full of sorrow that I left Ireland
    when I had my strength
and then grew tearful and full of sadness
    in a foreign land.

Grave the journey imposed upon me,
    O King of Mysteries:
I wish I never had started out
    for Cúl and the conflict.

For he was happy, the son of Dimma,
    in his pious cell,
where I have heard, west there in Durrow,
    what delights the mind:

the sound of wind against the elm
    making music,
the lovely song of the grey blackbird
    as she claps her wing,

Eolarg Plain] near Derry   Foibne Hill] overlooking Lough Foyle   Loch Febail] Lough Foyle   Port na Ferg] 'Harbour of Angers'; unidentified   Red-with-Dew] Colum Cille's boat   son of Dimma] Colum Cille's friend Cormac Ó Liathain, abbot of Durrow, Co. Offaly

listening early in Ros Grencha
   to the herds of stags
or the cuckoo chorus out of the forest
   on the verge of summer.

The fields of Ireland I have loved
   and that's no lie.
To stay with Comgall, to visit Caindech,
   it would be sweet.

55   Mary mild, good maiden,
            grant us thine aid,
        shrine of the Lord's body,
            casket of mysteries.

        Queen of all rulers,
            holy maid and chaste,
        pray we be forgiven
            our wretched sin through thee.

        Forgiving one, O merciful,
            graced with spirit pure,
        pray with us to the just King
            for His fair, fragrant kin.

        Branch out of Jesse's tree
            from the mild hazel wood,
        entreat I have forgiveness
            for my crooked sin.

        Great lovely jewel, Mary,
            who have saved our seed,
        ample and lovely light,
            garden of kings,

        O splendid, O shining,
            who practise purest deeds,
        golden coffer, sweet-candled,
            holy born from Heaven.

54 Ros Grencha] the district around Durrow   Comgall, Caindech] other friends
of Colum Cille who visited him in exile

Mother of all truth,
   excelling over all,
pray to your Firstborn
   at the Judgement to save me.

Secure, O triumphant,
   with retinues, with power,
pray to potent Christ with me,
   thy Father and Son.

Glorious and chosen star,
   tree under bloom,
torch choice and powerful,
   sun warming all,

ladder of mighty rungs
   that the virtuous ascend,
be thou our protection
   till we reach holy Heaven.

Fair, fragrant city
   that the King chose out,
great the guest within thy womb
   three measures of time.

Chosen royal door
   through whom was made flesh
the Sun choice and shining,
   Jesus, of the living God;

for the Sweetly-conceived
   set in thy womb,
for the Only-conceived,
   High King of the World;

for the sake of His cross,
   most noble cross of all;
for the sake of his burial,
   interred in a rock;

for the sake of His ascension,
   uprisen before all,
and of His holy family
   gathering to the Judgement,

66

be thou our guardian
to God's sweet realm,
that we join baby Jesus—
So I'll pray while I live.

56   If I owned all of Alba
entire, from shore to shore,
   I would rather my chosen place
   on the plain of gentle Doire.

The reasons I love Doire:
its calmness, its purity
   and the number of white angels
   from one end to the other!

There is not a single leaf
in Doire, so full and fine,
   but has two virgin angels
   going with every leaf.

I could find no place on earth
so full of pure fine angels!
   No more than nine waves' distance
   would I choose to go from Doire.

I am sad for the tearful cries
from the two shores of Loch Febail:
   the cries of Conall and Eogan
   lamenting as I left.

Since I bound me to those brothers
   (now I will tell my secret)
I swear not a night will pass
   but this eye will shed a tear.

Cut away from the men of Ireland
in whom my regard is fixed
—I care not, after that,
   if my life last but one night.

56 Doire] modern Derry. Literally, an oak-wood; hence the reference later to acorns, and the relevance of the saint's own religious name, the 'dove' of the sanctuary   Conall, Eogan] the two northern peoples, on either side of Lough Foyle. The names form part of the county names Tyrone and the now obsolete Tyrconnell (Donegal)

I am Irish, and I owe
  my honour to Irishmen,
my learning to Irishmen
  and to Irishmen my beauty.

O the outcry that I hear
  —how is it I am still alive?
The great cry of Doire's people
  has broken my heart in four.

Our Doire, with all its acorns,
sad, spiritless, sunk in tears:
  it hurts my heart to leave it
  and turn toward alien people.

That beloved woodland
  —and I driven, loveless, away.
  Great woe to Niall's women
  my banishment, and to his men.

Dire is my currach's speed
  and its stern turned toward Doire,
a drear journey on the high sea
  sailing for the shores of Alba.

The seagulls of Loch Febail
before me and behind me
  do not fly near my currach.
  We are parting in misery.

My foot on the humming currach,
my heart in woe, and weeping,
  a man of no skill, exhausted,
  ignorant and blind.

I stare back across the sea
at the plain of plentiful oaks,
  my clear grey eye in tears
  seeing Ireland fall behind me.

There is a grey eye
fixed on Ireland in goodbye.
  Never shall it see again
  women of Ireland, or her men.

Morning and noon I lament
  the journey I make, alas.
My name—let me make a riddle:
  'A Back Turned on Ireland'.

Iona I behold:
God bless every eye that sees it.
  That man who minds his friend
  minds himself thereby.

Take my blessing with you westward.
My heart breaks in my side.
  Death will come, if it comes,
  through my love for the men of Ireland.

57   Three places most loved I have left
  on this peopled earth:
Durnmag, Doire—high place of angels—
  and the land of Lugaid.

Had I leave from the King of Angels
  and the Sun
I would choose to be buried in Gartán
  out of all three.

58   My claw is tired of scribing!
Not thick, this great sharp thing,
my thin-beaked pen, emitting
its beetle-dark drink of bright-blue ink

but a steady stream of wisdom pours
from my fine brown handsome hand
and spills along the leaf a drink
of ink from the green-skinned holly.

I send my little dripping point
through a set of great bright books
without rest for our men of skill to treasure.
Hence my claw is tired of scribing.

57 Durnmag] present-day Durrow; this, with Derry, was one of Colum Cille's
monasteries   Gartán] the saint's birthplace, in Tír Luigdech, 'the land of Lugaid'

ANONYMOUS

The Fort of Árd Ruide

There are three plenties
always in the fort of Árd Ruide:
a plenty of young men, plenty of horses
and a plenty of Mac Lugaid's hunting hounds.

With three sorts of music
sweet for its king to hear:
the harp, the drum echoing,
and the bass of Fer Tuinne Mac Trogain.

There are three calls
heard there always in plenty:
the call of the lamb on the green,
the calls of racing, the call of cattle.

And three other calls:
of black, fat-backed pigs,
of crowds on the palace green,
high company and drink.

There are three harvests
always there on the branches:
a first harvest falling,
a harvest in bloom, and a harvest ripening.

Lugaid left three sons
—where are their riches now?
Ruide, Eochaid, the manly Fiachu,
three sons of Lugaid the Broad.

This I will say for Ruide,
on whom the three plenties fell:
no one ever begged him in vain,
and he never begged from anyone.

This I will say for Eochaid:
he never stepped back in battle
and never told a lie;
none has a finer fame.

And this I will say for Fiachu
—where are his riches now?
He was never long without music
or without a drink of beer . . .

Thirty princes, thirty champions,
thirty chiefs—a king's following:
and the size of his people assembled
three times thirty hundred.

TWELFTH CENTURY

A Selection of Verses attributed to Suibne Geilt

60   I am in great misery tonight:
           the clear wind has pierced my body,
      my feet are transfixed, my cheek grey
           —I have good reason, great God!

Last night I spent on Benn Boirche.
    Raindrops beat me on cold Echtga.
Tonight my members fall asunder
    in a tree-fork in bright Gáille.

Many merciless blows have I suffered
    since the feathers grew on my body.
And every night and day
    I suffer a greater hurt.

Frost racks me, wicked weather.
    Snow beats me on Sliab Mac Sin.
The wind wounds me tonight
    far from sweet Glen Bolcáin's heather.

I have lost my sense and my wits.
    I shift restless everywhere
from Line Plain over Lí Plain
    and from Lí Plain over wild Liffe.

Over Segas I make for Sliab Fuait.
    I reach Rath Mór in my flight
then across Ai Plain and Lurg Plain swiftly
    to the handsome hill of Cruachan.

Benn Boirche] the Mourne Mountains, Co. Down   Echtga] Aughty Mountain, between Clare and Galway   Gáille] a river in east Connaught   Sliab Mac Sin] a mountain probably in Kerry   Glen Bolcáin] Suibne's 'home'; possibly in north Antrim   Line Plain] 'Moylinny'; near Lough Neagh   Lí Plain] west of the river Bann   Liffe] the Liffey valley   Segas, Sliab Fuait] Fews Mountains, Armagh   Rath Mór] a 'great *rath*' on Line Plain   Ai Plain, Lurg Plain] near Boyle, Roscommon   Cruachan] Rathcroghan, Co. Roscommon: ancient royal residence of Connaught

From Sliab Cua (no simple matter)
   I reach fair Gáille river.
I land a long step from the Gáille
   at sweet Sliab mBreg in the east.

A wretched life without a house
   —a piteous life, sweet Christ!
The green-topped evergreen cress is enough
   and cold water from the clean stream.

Dropping from decayed bough-tops,
   travelling through gorse—I have done it:
shunning people, companion to wolves,
   racing the red stag over the moor.

A night spent in the woods with no blanket
   in a tree-top thick and bushy,
hearing no voice or sound,
   it is great misery, Son of God.

I fly to the hills in madness
   with a speed few have surpassed.
I have lost my unequalled looks.
   Great misery, Son of God!

*   *   *

My fixed abode is Glen Bolcáin.
   I have taken it for my own.
Many a night I have spent
   running hard across its hills.

If I wandered by myself
   the hills of the wide world
I would pick a place for my shed
   in glorious Glen Bolcáin.

Its pure green water is good
   and good its rough clean wind.
Its cress is good, the green cress,
   and its tall brooklime is better!

Sliab Cua] Knockmealdown Mountains, Waterford   Sliab mBreg] mountain in
Co. Louth

Its ivy trees pure and good
   and good its clean fine willow;
good its yews among all yew-trees,
   and its sweet birches better!

*   *   *

A rich tuft of ivy
   climbs through a twisted tree.
If I were at the very top
   I would be frightened to come out.

I fly before the larks,
   running hard and lively.
I leap across the reeds
   up on the mountain tops.

The proud wood-pigeon
   when it rises up before me
I overtake it suddenly
   now that my feathers have grown.

When the stupid clumsy woodcock
   rises up before me,
I see a raging enemy
   in the blackbird raising alarm.

And every time I leap
   down onto the ground
I see the little fox
   down there chewing bones.

Fiercest of dogs, he would catch me
   quickly in the ivy
except I leap so swiftly
   up to the mountain peak.

Little foxes creeping
   up toward me and away,
and wolves moving about
   —I fly from the very sound!

They tried to overtake me
    coming running hard,
but I fled away before them
    along the mountain peaks.

My sin comes against me
    everywhere I turn
and I learn, as I weep,
    I'm a sheep without a fold.

*   *   *

The starry frost descends
    and settles on every pool:
I am wretched and astray
    and abandoned on the peaks.

There are herons, with their crying,
    in cold Glen Aigle;
a quick flight of birds
    toward me and away.

I do not like the love-talk
    men and women make.
I would rather have the blackbird
    singing where he sits.

I do not like the trumpetings
    I hear in the early mornings.
I would rather badgers badgering
    out on the badger slopes!

I do not like the horn calls
    I hear, all tense.
I would rather the bellowings
    of a stag with forty prongs!

*   *   *

Bellower with the antlers
    and your roar so sweet,
sweet is the rumbling
    you make in the glen.

Glen Aigle] Glenelly, near Strabane, Co. Tyrone

A longing for my home
    comes over my mind:
for the plants on the plain
    and the fawns on the hill.

For the tufted, leafy oak,
    loftiest of trees,
and the branchy little hazel,
    hoard of hazel nuts!

Alder—no enemy!—
    lovely your gleam,
not grievous or prickly
    where you grow in the gap.

Blackthorn, all thorny,
    all dark with berries.
Green cress from the brink
    of the blackbird's well.

Little thing of the pathway,
    sweetest of herbs,
green thing—so green!—
    strawberry plant.

The apple—all the apples
    that we shake so hard.
Rowan-berry bearer,
    lovely your bloom.

Ridge-backed bramble
    that grant no quarter
nor cease from your scraping
    till you're covered with blood.

Yew, of the yew kind,
    in graveyards seen,
and ivy, all the ivy
    in the dark wood found!

Holly giving shelter,
    a door against the wind.
Ash, a woeful weapon
    in the warrior's hand.

Blessed, blossomed birch,
　swelling and sweet,
each tangled branch lovely
　in your head so high.

The poplar, all trembling,
　is what I hear next,
the leaves quickly stirred
　—like an enemy coming!

What I fear in the woods
　(I will tell no lie)
is the leafy oak sapling
　moving and restless!

      *　　*　　*

Sweet voice of the Garb
　as it meets the first wave:
lovely great fish-swarms
　swimming in its heart.

How fast the time passes:
　I watch the flood fill,
great Garb's mighty current
　forced back by the brine.

Pleasantly they struggle,
　the flood, the cold ebb,
one upon the other
　down and up, for ever.

Such music in the winter light
　I hear in the Garb.
I sleep to its uproar
　in the ice-cold night.

The shore birds and their voices,
　always that music:
I hear it with longing
　as they cry out the hours.

      *　　*　　*

Garb] tidal waters of the Barrow, south Carlow

I am Suibne the wanderer.
  I run swift across the valley.
It is no proper name.
  'Horn Head' would be better.

*   *   *

Though my wanderings are many
  my clothes are few.
I keep my own watch
  on the mountain peak.

Bracken red and deep,
  your cloak is dyed red:
no bed for an outlaw
  among your spiky tips!

My last resting place
  will be south by the fierce Taidiu.
At Mo Ling's house, of endless angels,
  by a horn point I shall die.

A Selection of Fenian Poems (61–66)

61   Caílte said this poem:

'Cold is the winter. The wind is risen.
The wild, red-raging stag is aroused.
  No warmth tonight on the bare mountain,
  hence the fierce stag is grumbling.

'The stag on Sliab Carn, our gathering place,
will not lay his flank to the ground.
  And the stag on bitter cold Echtga Head
  is listening to the wolves' music.

Taidiu] a 'mill-race' on the Dubglass (Glynn) river, near St Mullins, Carlow

61 Sliab Carn] Slievecarran in the Burren, Co. Clare   Echtga] the Aughty Mountains

'I, Caílte, and brown-haired Diarmait
and Oscar, eager and slight,
    used to hear that wolf music
    at the close of a freezing night!

'The brown stag sleeps sound.
His hide is pressed against Corann
    as though under the Wave of Tuag
    at the close of a bitter night.

'I am old now, an ancient man,
I know only a few people
    —though I shook a brutal spear-point
    on bitter icy mornings!

'I thank the King of Heaven,
the Son of the maiden Mary,
    I could bring great silence on armies
    —though tonight I am freezing cold.'

62   *Créide's Lament for Cael*

And Caílte told how Créide came and stretched herself beside Cael and made a lamentation and great wailing. 'How can it be', she said, 'that I am not dead of grief for my mate when the roving wild beasts are dying of grief for him?' Then the girl said:

'The harbour roars out
over the fierce flow of Rinn Dá Bharc.
The hero from Loch Dá Chonn drowned:
the wave mourns it against the shore.

'The heron is crying
in the marsh of Druim Dá Thrén.
She cannot guard her young:
the two-coloured fox is stalking them.

'Mournful is the whistle
of the thrush on Druim Caín.
And no less mournful is the call
of the blackbird on Leitir Laíg.

61 Diarmait, Oscar] other members of the Fianna   Corann] in Co. Sligo
the Wave of Tuag] in the mouth of the river Bann

'Mournful the music
of the stag on Druim Dá Léis:
the doe of Druim Silenn is dead
and the great stag roars at her loss.

'My grief
that hero dead, who lay with me,
that woman's son from Doire Dá Dos
with a cross set at his head.

'My grief that Cael
is fixed by my side in death,
that a wave has drowned his pale flank.
His great beauty drove me wild.

'Mournful is the roar
the ebbing wave makes on the strand.
It has drowned a fine and noble man.
My grief Cael ever went near it.

'Mournful the sound
the wave makes on the northern shore,
rough about the lovely rock,
lamenting Cael who is gone.

'And mournful the fall
of the wave on the southern shore.
As for myself, my time is over,
my face the worse, for all to see.

'There is unnatural music
in the heavy wave of Tulach Léis:
it is telling its boastful tale
and all my wealth is as nothing.

'Since Crimthann's son was drowned
I will have no other love.
Many leaders fell at his hand
but his shield on the day of need was silent.'

And the girl stretched out beside Cael and died of grief. The two of
them were buried together in one grave. 'I myself', said Caílte, 'had the
stone set up over them where they lie . . .'

63 *Goll Mac Morna Parts from his Wife*

Goll   Take my tunic, woman.
        Rise up, and leave me here.
        Leave me—red-cheeked and pure—
        now before I am killed.

Wife   Goll, where can I go?
        I have few friends, alas.
        What luck has any lady
        without her head and lord?

Goll   Find Finn's camp, and the Fian,
        here in the westward quarter.
        Lie there—red-lipped and sweet—
        with some fine fitting man.

Wife   What man should I lie with there,
        great Goll who have guarded me?
        West or east where will I find
        one for my bed like you?

Goll   Take Finn's son Oisín,
        or Aonghus, Aodh Rinn's son,
        or handsome blood-stained Cairell,
        or fleet-foot Corr the hundred-killer.

Wife   And my father Conall of Cruachan!
        I, fostered with Conn of the Hundred Battles!
        With Céidghein, Conall Red-Hand's son,
        in the north land for my brother!

        It is harder now to leave
        my chosen cheerful man
        now that seven brave years have passed
        since you took me to bed, my husband.

        From that night until this
        you were not hard-hearted ever.
        And from this night I will take
        ease with no man on earth.

Thirty days without food, alive
—was there ever your like before?
A hundred heroes, Goll, by your hand
fell on the narrow rock.

Goll Wide is the ocean round us
and I on a narrow rock.
By hunger I am beaten,
by thirst I am undone.

And though it is hunger beats me,
though fierce this war of five battalions,
my cheeks are faded more
through drinking the bitter brine.

If one of the Fian slew
my nine and twenty brothers
I would make my peace with him
if it eased my thirst one night!

Wife Goll Mac Morna from Maon Plain
eat one of those corpses near you.
After that meat I will ease your thirst:
you can drink the milk from my breasts.

Goll Conall's daughter, I will tell no lie,
it is wretched the tale turned out.
But I never followed, north or south,
woman's counsel, and never will.

Wife Goll, it was a cruel case:
five battalions or six against you
and you in an angle of hard rock
high and bare and cold.

Goll My only fear on land or wave
(red mouth that were once so sweet)
was Finn and his Fian in pursuit
and I starved in a narrow crack.

I reddened my spears rightly
in the bodies of Tréanmór's tribe!
Trouble and strife I gave them.
I killed Cumhall of the mighty shaft!

Munster's men I brought to grief
that Tuesday on Léan Plain.
I waged a lovely war
that morning on Eanach Plain!

Eochaidh Red-Limb, son of Mál,
proud-faced High King of Ulster
—I mixed my spear in that hero!
I brought him to grief, woman!

64   Oisín said:

'There once was a time
   I had curled, yellow hair.
Now there's nothing on top
   but short grizzled fuzz.

'I would prefer
   hair black as the raven
to cover my head,
   not a short grey fuzz.

'The wooing should stop
   when the women won't come.
Now my hair has turned grey
   and I'm not what I was.'

65   Oisín, Finn's son, sang this:

'My hands are withered,
my doings at an end.
   The flood is gone, the ebb has come
that has destroyed my strength.

'I thank the Creator
I found good, and great joy.
   Long my days in this wretched life
and I had beauty once.

'Handsomest once among all,
I had loose and lavish women.
    Not timidly do I leave this world
though my spring torrent is past.

'The breadcrumbs you break small
for this starving woeful wretch
    —there's a bit on stone, a bit on bone
and a bit on this withered hand.'

66   Caílte said:

'The Place of the Fian is bare tonight
where Finn came once with naked blade.
    That prince without grief is dead
    and noble Alma is bare.

'His good people live no more
and Finn lives not, the true prince.
    The shining troops and captains
    attend no more the Fian's king.

'All Finn's Fian are dead
who travelled valley after valley.
    I am ruined after those great kings,
    after Diarmait and Conán;

'after Goll Mac Morna from the plain
and Ailill with his hundreds,
    Eogan, and his grey spear, lost
    and Conall first in the fray.

'Now I say to you,
and true is what I tell:
    it is our great loss we lack
    Dub Drumann and his straight spear.

66 The Place of the Fian] lit. 'The Look-Out', in the Mourne Mountains, Co.
Down   Alma] the Hill of Allen, Co. Kildare

84

'A pity I did not perish
when the hosts and hundreds fell!
   They have vanished, far and wide,
      though once the Place was thronged.'

And Caílte wept bitterly.

ANONYMOUS

67
   The blackbird calls in grief.
   I know what harm has happened.
   Someone has broken his home
   and killed his little birds.

   The harm now happened him
   not long since happened me.
   Blackbird, I know your story,
   you with your home destroyed.

   The act of an ignorant man,
   blackbird, scalded your heart.
   Your nest without eggs or young
   —to that cowherd it is nothing.

   Once, at your clear call,
   your family used to come.
   No birds come now from your home.
   There are nettles at the lip of your nest.

   That cowherd has killed them all,
   your whole family in one day.
   And a similar fate had I.
   My family live no more.

   She was feeding there at your side,
   your bird-mate from over the sea,
   when she fell into the snare
   and died at the cowherd's hands.

O You who made the world,
Your bias is hard to bear:
friends all around me are spared,
their women and young survive,

but a host from the *síd*, in a blast,
came and killed my family.
And though I escaped unharmed
that is worse than wounding with weapons.

Grief for wife and children
is anguish heavy upon me.
They bustle about me no more.
Hence the grief that is in my heart.

síd] the 'other' world

MUIREADHACH ALBANACH Ó DÁLAIGH

fl. early 13th century

68   Mighty Mary, hear me.
      To you I would wish to pray.
Turn not your back on your brother,
      mother of the high elemental King.

I recall your mother's story.
      For long it has been told:
a gentle girl with dark brows
      and tresses heavy about her head.

Anna she was, grandmother of God,
      whose bright brother begot a king.
She yielded in cheer to no woman
      and to three men she was wed.

To each good man she bore a daughter.
      Fair, bright, noble, she conceived
three daughters, her children dear,
      with slim bright sides and waving hair.

Blue their eyes, their manners pleasing,
      never a scandal touching them,
three ladies sought by the whole world
      and Mary the name of each.

Three husbands they took, the three of them,
      three Maries from saintly Heaven.
Pregnant, slow-paced, the three became,
      with thick and rich tress-heavy hair.

The women bore three sons
      who grew from strength to strength.
Where find a mightier, modest six?
      And the youngest of these was God.

One girl the mother of James,
   shielded from every care.
One Mary the mother of John
   (no usual theme in verse).

And you, Mary, the mother of God,
   no usual beauty yours,
triple-branched royal stem:
   in your womb true Heaven's King.

Summon me, both of you,
   to your fine house and your fort,
mighty Mary, my soul,
   yellow gold, rich apple tree!

Food and clothes, by your clemency,
   O branched locks like a garden;
Mother, Sister, Beloved,
   guide this wretched brother well.

Your great Son is my brother,
   noble mother, stately branch.
Guard this good brother, it is right;
   one fair grandmother had we both.

Till I put myself in your Husband's hands,
   fair Mary, O tresses thick,
black coals a-plenty were in my heart.
   It is right I should cleanse them now.

Let us make peace, mother of God
   —bright brown in hue your hair.
Mighty Mary, calm your wrath,
   red gold in vessel of clay.

From Heaven He came, that fair body,
   that waist like the noble stream.
No little kinship I have with Him,
   O fair, pure, curling locks.

O Trinity, O Mary mild,
   all glory ebbs but yours.
Four Persons, hear my poem.
   I will take no gold in payment:

Virgin Mary, dark of brow,
   mighty vine, O garden bright,
grant, of women most beloved,
   Heaven for my humility!

Sedate and great, of David's line,
   there is no tree but you.
From Abraham your waving locks,
   sweet branching tresses about your head.

Husband and Son within your womb
   —bright His fist and bright His wrist!
Your Husbandfather in your side:
   so your Husband's art is shown.

A wondrous child at your white breast,
   your fresh and fair pure hair;
a Son and Husband both in one
   on your knee, bright noble branch.

A pleasant pair indeed you were
   as you fled from vale to vale:
a black-browed, white-gripped noble Son,
   a gravid, fair, unhurried girl.

And while you curled His locks
   and minded Him on the ass
your palm, pure Virgin Mary,
   curled yellow paths in a King's hair!

Always you were His peace,
   your white breast in His palm.
When you washed that graceful Branch
   you kissed His dear palm and foot.

A yellow-gold heath your noble head,
   my sister Mary of the slow eyes.
A smooth, bright, heavy breast on your side
   and a high-born Baby suckling it.

Accursed who rebukes your pure locks
   —no easy thing, for you never sinned.
If your womb, lady, is not pure
   there's no nut on a lovely branch in the wood.

Robbers' children we will not mention,
soft-tipped, ringleted, curling hair:
who with any wit could doubt you,
beloved locks, all ridged with light?

Your womb below filled full
like the mid-belly of a trout:
the Lord, though He never lay with you,
made with you the Son of Mary.

Mighty Mary, but for you
wretched man would never know
his greater peace—O curling hair—
is never to go with wicked women.

Your only Son has your waving hair,
noble sapling with rounded eyes.
He has your hands, that slender Boy,
and your fair nails shaded brown.

Blue-eyed, gleaming, is your face,
with dark-ridged eyebrow over it;
fair-branching, slender, is your hand:
I owe a poem that does not lie.

Pure, wholesome, yellow hair,
a vine of curls about your head;
round, thin-fingered, pure palm,
O firm, slim, well-shaped foot.

No like-born woman ever was;
your like (no lie) will never be.
Woman like you ne'er tasted life,
bright womb where God has gone.

Give me beer and bed,
O head untouched by soil.
The false feast that has no end
be it not mine, O strong white teeth.

May your dark brow nobly plead,
pure love, for the love of your soul.
(If I pray to your white bright teeth,
Mary, that Man will not be jealous.)

O curled, ridged, yellow hair,
   Mary of slender brows,
give me no other judge
   but the welcome of your heart.

Let us feast to your shapely figure
   —swift, mighty—side by side.
Accept my best poems and songs,
   bright-languid, noble, decorous one.

No woman but you in my home;
   its mistress may you be.
False women and all the wealth I see,
   none of mine will pay them heed.

May I never care for wealth
   or horses or hounds, pure swan,
or others' hounds or drinking horns
   or women, or choice pastures.

Turn your dark brow toward me,
   your face calves' blood in colour.
Turn it so I may see
   your noble fair locks' branching paths.

Turn toward me your sole and palm
   and your brown hair in beauty,
your keen green young round eye
   —may I fall in feast on your moist locks!

69   Young man of alien beauty,
        of an alien-Gaelic people,
        youthful, high-born, slim
        —who are your foreign guests?

        These people in your house
        visiting from abroad
        are used to receiving wine
        from a king's hand or a knight's.

They have taken their share often
from an abbot's hand or a bishop's.
They disturb no foreign houses
with noise and drunken chatter.

Yet I could be their teacher.
I was often at foreign courts.
I make small ceremony
of sitting in a High King's presence.

My power derives from kings.
It pleases me to travel.
In the East my rank is lofty,
with always a knight on hand.

But I needn't dwell on that,
FitzWilliam, my hero-hound!
Prince of Leinster, no need of talk:
praise follows the virtuous man.

Better someone else than himself
should praise him, if good he be.
A man much praising himself
is only seeking blame.

But I come to you now in flight
since I dare delay no longer
under the feet of Clann Chuinn
on account of Domhnall's anger.

FitzWilliam, surrender me not
to Domhnall of Doire and Druim Cliabh.
That northern prince would not surrender
one who offended you.

And my quarrel with him so slight:
that an ignoramus abused me
and that I slaughtered the slave.
Is that cause for bad blood, dear God?

Clann Chuinn] descendants of Conn Céadcathach, of the Hundred Battles
Doire] Derry   Druim Cliabh] Drumcliff

But the king of Ess Rua in anger
commenced to threaten me
so I look to the Saxon hawks
because they have sworn me safety.

For your honour, and that of the stranger,
and of all who carry steel,
slim champion, fierce and pure,
take my quarrel upon your head.

For so your home might gather
the poets of all five provinces.
Ask in the foremost schools,
the finest in Western Ireland.

Not every poet is wise,
nor every scholar a fount.
Wisdom's surface is smooth,
yet two-thirds is hidden study.

The fingers are not one length
nor all men equally strong.
No chessboard lacks its king.
No litter lacks a leader.

And you are head of your kin,
FitzWilliam, aglow like gold,
the choicest of every stock
being head of that family.

But little you know, I think,
who am I, of the men of Ireland.
From my poems be assured:
Ó Dálaigh of Meath am I!

Young Richard, of fairest land,
now your father William is dead
all Clan William yields
to your round, curled, flaxen head.

Ess Rua] Assaroe

Meadhbh's mighty Cruachan is yours,
of Tara you are lord,
and Tara being your home
I hail her local kings:

The fort of Mac an Duinn is yours,
Ó Conaing Castle by name.
Yours also the stone rampart
where Mac Coise first prevailed.

The walls of that house were lovely
when last we looked upon them.
Eye never looked on household
more thronged, that ever I heard,

of such pale, tapering hands
or slenderer white-soled feet,
hair clustered high and gleaming
or linen lustrous more,

shoulders or bosoms brighter,
ladies more purple-lipped,
of waving locks, pure yellow,
green eyes with bluer lashes.

A house richer in golden treasures,
more full of serving men,
more full of fine cup-bearers,
was ne'er built, nor shall be.

Richard of Beann Bladhma,
fail not the men of art.
No matter a man's achievements,
there's no fame without good name.

Judge fairly, alien prince,
nor leave the weak to the strong.
Credit not the lying tale
nor utter the lying word;

The fort of Mac an Duinn . . . Ó Conaing Castle] Castleconnell, Co. Lim-
erick   Mac Coise] a poet who was allegedly entitled to all the revenues of Ireland for
one year   Beann Bladhma] Slieve Bloom

94

be not soft toward the enemy,
nor proud toward the High King,
nor quarrelsome with the Church,
nor with abbots nor with bishops;

nor craven toward the warrior,
nor warlike against women
—nor hard against a poet,
O King of Connacht's clans!

It was no cause, once, for wonder,
Sir Richard, when I handled
a swift steed—gift of the stranger—
or the lipped and lidded goblet!

70   Last night my soul departed,
  a pure body, most dear, in the grave,
her stately smooth bosom taken
  from me in a linen sheet,

a lovely pale blossom plucked
  from a limp downcurving stem,
my heart's darling bowed low,
  heavy branch of yonder house.

I am alone tonight, O God.
  It is a crooked, bad world you see.
Lovely the weight of the young flank
  I had here last night, my King.

That bed there, my grief,
  the lively covers where we swam
—I have seen a fine lively body
  and waved hair in your midst, my bed!

One of a gentle countenance
  lay and shared my pillow.
Only the hazel bloom is like
  her womanly dark sweet shade.

Maol Mheadha of the dark brows,
    my vessel of mead, by my side,
my heart, the shade who has left me,
    a precious flower, planted and bowed.

My body is mine no longer.
    It has fallen to her share:
a body in two pieces
    since she left, fair, lovely and gentle

—one foot of mine, one flank
    (her visage like the whitethorn;
nothing hers but it was mine):
    one eye of mine, one hand;

half my body, a youthful blaze
    (I am handled harshly, O King,
and I feel faint as I speak it)
    and half of my very soul.

My first love her great slow gaze;
    curved, ivory white her breast;
nor did her body, her dear side,
    belong to another before me.

Twenty years we were as one
    and sweeter our speech each year.
Eleven babies she bore me
    —great slender-fingered fresh branch.

I am, but I do not live,
    since my round hazel-nut has fallen.
Since my dear love has left me
    the dark world is empty and bare.

From the day the smooth shaft was sunk
    for my house I have not heard
that a guest has laid a spell
    on her youthful brown dark hair.

Do not hinder me, you people.
    What crime to hear my grief.
Bare ruin has entered my home
    and the bright brown blaze is out.

The King of Hosts and Highways
  took her away in His wrath.
Little those branched locks sinned,
  to die on her husband, young and fresh.

That soft hand I cherished,
  King of the graves and bells,
that hand never forsworn
  —my pain it is not beneath my head!

71   *On the Gift of a Knife*

My friend's knife by my side
  —not slight my love for that lady!
Nor will it fade as the days pass
  till her giver gets safely home.

No mean, poor-seeming thing,
  nor coarse, but shining fair.
The one who gave me this blue blade
  is free with horse and horn and weapon.

Gold she wears in plenty
  and a dainty band at her lip.
A dark brown branch has given me
  a sharp new jewel, blue-sheathed.

Her point keen and slender,
  dainty and sleek her flank.
That soft-haired ringleted one
  gave grey hard iron for my belt!

A braided scabbard guards it,
  brand new, showing in pride
on its side a thick gold ridge,
  with a bare branch, red-gold, under.

A lady from the south country
  with a finish of fairy ivory
—a fine Munsterwoman at my belt,
  fine-flanked, grey-backed, clean.

Donnchadh Cairbreach, of the fine hounds,
    no plunderer of poets,
soft-tressed and fair, like gold:
    enough that his knife is beneath my cloak.

*

Maol Ruanaidh, now, the king's carver,
    with the yellow plaited curls
and honoured face like blood or wine,
    works hard, my knife, till all are served.

GIOLLA BRIGHDE MAC CON MIDHE

fl. mid 13th century

72   *A Defence of Poetry*

*(addressed to a priest claiming to bring from Rome
a condemnation of the Irish bards)*

Messenger from Rome,
laying down instructions,
show where it is written
—the script, not just the seal.

This cross from Peter's Heir
give out just as you brought it.
This dark and rigid page,
if sent, present it so.

As it in Rome was spoken
so speak it—spare your preaching.
There is no further message
could make us suffer more.

But you were not told in Rome
to banish bards, my priest!
In some non-Rome or other
you got that foul instruction!

Where is the script prescribes
our art must be abolished?
Do as I have commanded:
take the seal from off your script.

It was never found in book
fine verse should earn us nothing.
An ugly alien teaching
would banish Ireland's poets.

A sweet poem is *Donum Dei*
deep in the body of our learning.
Take it; dissect the meaning.
'God-Gift' it plainly means.

If decent men are told
to give no pay for poems
it is to say, No satire,
but praise all round, my priest!

If it's to spare expense
that poets must be deprived
have people not enough, my priest,
without resort to that?

Why did devoutest Patrick
not banish all the poets
when he came from the land of Rome
to the soft-grassed isle of Ireland?

Or what caused Colum Cille,
who uttered only truth,
each Thursday, rapt toward Heaven,
to leave out pay for a poem?

The poets of grassy Fódla
were driven out once before.
It was Colum, and at once,
who brought their restóration.

Blessed Mobhi, the level-visaged,
most honourable and noble,
gave his life, a generous act
—monstrous—at a poet's asking.

Did that statue not take off
her shoe for a noble poem,
though arrogant the demand?
She is barefoot now, for certain.

Mary's great Son will grant me
a prize no man can give
for a poem of my lovely craft:
I'll have Heaven, like Ó hIfearnáin!

To praise man is to praise
the One who created him,
and man's earthly possessions
add to God's mighty praise.

All metre and mystery
touch on the Lord at last.
The tide thunders ashore
in praise of the High King.

And a poem, though a fantasy,
gives a lasting one for one that fades:
great wealth is a fantasy
—and the man that a poem praises.

A man, though great his meanness,
gains no more gold or steeds.
Scorning all poets on earth,
will that enhance his herds?

If poetry went, my people,
with its lore and ancient lays
man's knowledge would reach back
no further than his father.

If the well of wisdom dried,
the nobles, unless we lived,
would be ignorant of their rights
and the complex kin of the Gael,

and the great fiery warriors
would have their stories hidden
for ages long (no little loss)
nor know the roots that reared them.

The fights and frays of Ireland's men
obscured—there is a loss!
Forgotten, for all their spirit,
true princes and their blood.

Guaire now is dead—but lives;
Cú Chulainn of the Red Branch;
and (his name known east and west)
Brian is living still.

Conall and Conchobar live
because their praises live
and Fergus is with us still
his name being known abroad.

Lugh was killed by the son of Coll,
not a bone of his body left,
but his name travels the world,
and so is Lugh renewed.

If poems did not give life
to their deeds, however great,
a pall would settle far and wide
on Niall and Cormac and Conn.

The kingdoms of Cruachan and Corc's Caiseal
—poets are their blossoms' root.
And they are the props of the three *brughs*:
Da Thi of Tara, and Tuathal.

But for poems there would not be
(and the sweet-stringed harp and drum)
news of the good man gone,
nor his glory, nor his skill.

Noble people would not have
access to their past, or rights.
Let them have these put in a poem
or farewell to the ancient things!

brughs] the great houses of hospitality

Lose the lore of Conn's people,
Domhnall, with your poems,
and your nobles and your dog-boys
are equal: slavish-free!

If the men of Ireland suffer
their poetry to be banished
the Gael will lose respect
and freemen turn to clowns.

From the Norman French

ANONYMOUS

73   from *The Fortification of New Ross*

I have a whim to speak in verse,
If you will list what I rehearse
(For an unheeded tale, I wisse,
Not worth a clove of garlic is).
Please you then to understand
'Tis of a town in Ireland
For its size the one most fair
That I know of anywhere.

But the town had cause of dread
In the feud two barons spread:
Sir Maurice and Sir Walter—see,
Here their names shall written be.
Also that fair city's name:
'Ross' they then did call the same.
'Tis the new bridge-town of Ross
Which no walls did then inclose . . .

Commons both, and leading men,
Gathered in the council then,
What for safety to devise
In shortest time and lowest price.
'Twas that round the town be thrown
Walls of mortar and of stone . . .

Candlemas it was the day
They began to delve in clay
Marking out a fosse, to show
Where the future wall should go.
Soon 'twas traced, and then were hired
Workmen, all the task desired.
More than a hundred workmen ply
Daily 'neath the townsmen's eye,
Yet small advance these fellows made
Though to labour they were paid.

So the council sat again.
Such a law as they passed then!
Such a law might not be found
Nor on French nor English ground.
Next day a summons read aloud
Gathered speedily a crowd;
When the law proclaimed they hear
'Twas received with many a cheer:
Vintners, drapers, merchants, all
Were to labour at the wall! . .

Monday, they began their labours,
Gay with banners, flutes and tabors.
Soon as the noon hour was come
These good people hastened home
With their banners proudly borne.
Then the youth advanced in turn
And the town they made it ring
With their merry carolling;
Singing loud and full of mirth
Away they go to shovel earth.
And the priests, when Mass was chanted,
In the fosse they dug and panted.
Quicker, harder, worked each brother,
Harder far than any other,
For both old and young did feel
Great and strong with holy zeal.
Mariners came next, and they
Pass'd along in fair array
With their banners borne before
Which a painted vessel bore . . .

Tuesday came coat-makers, tailors,
Fullers, cloth-dyers and 'sellers',
Right good hands, these jolly blades,
Were they counted at their trades . . .

Wednesday, following, down there came
Other bands who worked the same:
Butchers, cordwainers, and tanners
Bearing each their separate banners . . .

Thursday came the fishermen
And the hucksters followed then,
Who sell corn and fish: they bear
Divers banners, for they were
Full four hundred: and the crowd
Carolled and sung aloud;
And the wainwrights, they came too—
They were only thirty-two;
A single banner went before,
Which a fish and platter bore.

On Friday came the porters then,
Three hundred fifty solid men;
Their banners out before them toss
Along the margin of the fosse.

Then on Saturday the stir
Of blacksmith, mason, carpenter
. . . And they toiled with main and might;
Needful knew they 'twas, and right.

Until on Sunday there came down
All the dames of that brave town
. . . On the ramparts there were thrown
By their fair hands many a stone
. . . In no lands where I have been
Such fair dames digging have I seen
. . . Many a banner was displayed
While the work the ladies aid.
When their gentle hands had done
Piling up rude heaps of stone
Then they walked the fosse along
Singing sweet a cheerful song;

And returning to the town
All these rich dames there sat down
Where, with mirth and wine and song
Pass'd the pleasant hours along.

Then they said a gate they'd make,
Called the Ladies', for their sake,
And their prison there should be.
Whoso entered, straightway he
Should forgo his liberty.
Lucky doom I ween is his,
Who a lady's prisoner is;
Light the fetters are to wear
Of a lady kind and fair.
But of them enough is said,
Turn we to the fosse instead.

Twenty feet that fosse is deep,
And a league in length doth creep.
When the noble work is done,
Watchmen then there needeth none:
All may sleep in peace and quiet
Without a fear of evil riot.
Fifty thousand might attack
And yet might turn them bootless back.
. . . I warrant you the town's prepared
'Gainst all enemies to guard.

Here I deem it meet to say
No desire for war have they
But to keep their city free.
Blamed of no man can they be.
When that wall is carried round
None in Ireland will be found
Bold enough to dare to fight.
Let a foeman come in sight,
If the city horn twice sound
Every burgess will be found
Eager in the warlike labour
Striving to outdo his neighbour.

So God give them victory!
And say amen for charity.

In no other isle is known
Such a hospitable town;
Joyously the people greet
Every stranger in the street.
Free is he to sell and buy
And sustain no tax thereby.
Town and people once again
I commend to God. Amen!

FOURTEENTH CENTURY

GOFRAIDH FIONN Ó DÁLAIGH
d. 1387

74   *A Child in Prison*

Woe to him by this world enticed.
Short a success in its mighty lists.
Woe who bethinks him not of this
during a hard and evil life.

A mighty realm for a puny pleasure.
Eternal life for a tiny span.
Turning from God is a luckless thing
for the fleeting time of this little world.

The bliss of the hosts in Heaven
as they circle about the Lord,
all bliss under Heaven save that
is the life of a man in a cave.

You who have found good fortune
and pleasure that seems not slight
your happiness seems sufficient
because you have known no greater.

In proof of which, here is a tale
bears witness to that truth
—not in itself a claim on Heaven
though the Scripture is the source.

*

A pregnant woman (sorrow's sign)
once there was, in painful prison.
The God of Elements let her bear
in prison there a little child.

The little boy, when he was born,
grew up like any other child
(plain as we could see him there)
for a space of years, in prison.

That the woman was a prisoner
did not lower the baby's spirits.
She minded him, though in prison,
like one without punishment or pain.

Nothing of the light of day
(O misery!) could they see
but the bright ridge of a field
through a hole someone had made.

Yet the loss was not the same
for the son as for the mother:
her fair face failed in form
while the baby gained in health.

The child, raised where he was,
grew better by his bondage,
not knowing in his fresh frail limbs
but prison was ground of Paradise.

He made little playful runs
while her spirits only deepened.
(Mark well, lest you regret,
these deeds of son and mother.)

He said one day, beholding
a tear on her lovely face:
'I see the signs of sadness;
now let me hear the cause.'

'No wonder that I mourn,
my foolish child', said she.
'This cramped place is not our lot,
and suffering pain in prison.'

'Is there another place', he said,
'lovelier than ours?
Is there a brighter light than this
that your grief grows so heavy?'

'For I believe,' the young child said,
'mother, although you mourn,
we have our share of light.
Don't waste your thoughts in sorrow.'

'I do not wonder at what you say,
young son', the girl replied.
'You think this is a hopeful place
because you have seen no other.

'If you knew what I have seen
before this dismal place
you would be downcast also
in your nursery here, my soul.'

'Since it is you know best, lady,'
the little child replied,
'hide from me no longer
what more it was you had.'

'A great outer world in glory
formerly was mine.
After that, beloved boy,
my fate is a darkened house.'

At home in all his hardships,
not knowing a happier state,
fresh-cheeked and bright, he did not grudge
the cold and desolate prison.

And so is the moral given:
the couple there in prison
are the people of this world,
imprisoned life their span.

Compared with joy in the Son of God
in His everlasting realm
an earthly mansion is only grief,
prisoners all the living.

GEARÓID IARLA MAC GEARAILT

d. 1398

75   Woe to him who slanders women.
       Scorning them is no right thing.
     All the blame they've ever had
       is undeserved, of that I'm sure.

     Sweet their speech and neat their voices.
       They are a sort I dearly love.
     Woe to the reckless who revile them.
       Woe to him who slanders women.

     Treason, killing, they won't commit
       nor any loathsome, hateful thing.
     Church or bell they won't profane.
       Woe to him who slanders women.

     But for women we would have,
       for certain, neither kings nor prelates,
     prophets mighty, free from fault.
       Woe to him who slanders women.

     They are the victims of their hearts.
       They love a sound and slender man
     —not soon do they dislike the same.
       Woe to him who slanders women.

     Ancient persons, stout and grey,
       they will not choose for company,
     but choose a juicy branch, though poor.
       Woe to him who slanders women!

ANONYMOUS

Two Fragments

76
Icham of Irlaunde
Ant of the holy londe of irlonde
Gode sir pray ich ye
for of saynte charite,
come ant daunce wyt me,
in irlaunde.

*   *   *

77
Alas! How should I sing?
Yloren is my playing.
How should I with that old man
To leven, and leave my leman,
    Sweetest of all thing?

78   *The Land of Cokaygne*

Fur in see bi west Spayngne
Is a lond ihote Cokaygne.
Ther nis lond vnder heven riche
Of wel, of godnis hit iliche.
Thogh paradis be miri and bright,
Cokaygn is of fairer sight.
What is ther in paradis
Bot grasse and flure and grene ris?
Thogh ther be ioi and grete dute
Ther nis mete bote frute;

77 Yloren] lost   leven] live

78 Cokaygne] Cooking   ihote] called   heven riche] heaven's kingdom
Of wel, of godnis hit iliche] like it for wealth, for goodness   ris] twigs   dute]
delight   nis mete bote frute] is no meat but fruit

Ther nis halle, bure no benche
Bot watir man is thursto quenche.
Beth ther no men bot two,
Elijah and Enok also;
Elinglich mai hi go,
Whar ther wonith men no mo.

In Cokaigne is met and drink
Withvte care, how and swink;
The met is trie, the drink is clere
To none, russin and sopper.
I sigge for soth, boute were,
Ther nis lond on erthe is pere,
Vnder heuen nis lond iwisse
Of so mochil ioi and blisse.
Ther is mani swete sighte,
Al is dai, nis ther no nighte.
Ther nis baret nother strif,
Nis ther no, ac euer lif,
Ther nis lac of met no cloth,
Ther nis man no womman wroth,
Ther nis serpent, wolf no fox,
Hors no capil, kowe no ox,
Ther nis schepe no swine no gote
No non horwgh la, god it wote,
Nother harace, nother stode,
The lond is ful of other gode.
Nis ther flei, fle no lowse
In cloth, in toune, bed no house;
Ther nis dunnir, slete no hawle
No none vile worme no snawile
No non storme, rein no winde;
Ther nis man no womman blinde,
Ok al is game, ioi and gle,
Wel is him that ther mai be.
Ther beth rivers gret and fine
Of oile, melk, honi and wine,

nis] is not (in)	Elinglich] sadly	Whar ther wonith men no mo] where dwell
no more men	how] anxiety	swink] toil	trie] choice	none] noon
russin] lunch	sopper] supper	I sigge for soth, boute were] I say for sooth,
without a doubt	baret nother] quarrel or	lac] lack	capil] nag
horwgh] dirt	harace] stable	stode] stud	toune] farm	dunnir]
thunder	hawle] hail	game, ioi and gle] sport, joy, and glee

Watir servith ther to no thing
Bot to sight and to waiissing,
Ther is al maner frute,
Al is solas and dedute.

Ther is a wel fair abbei
Of white monkes and of gre.
Ther beth bowris and halles
Al of pasteiis beth the walles,
Of fleis, of fisse and rich met,
The likfullist that man mai et.
Fluren cakes beth the schingles alle
Of cherche, cloister, boure and halle,
The pinnes beth fat podinges,
Rich met to princes and kinges.
Man mai tereof et inogh,
Al with right and noght with wogh,
Al is commune to yung and old,
To stoute and sterne, mek and bold.
Ther is a cloister fair and light,
Brod and lang, of sembli sight.
The pilers of that cloister alle
Beth iturned of cristale,
With har bas and capitale
Of grene Iaspe and rede corale.
In the praer is a tre
Swithe likful for to se,
The rote is gingeuir and galingale,
The siouns beth al sedwale,
Trie maces beth the flure,
The rind canel of swet odur,
The frute gilofre of gode smakke,
Of cucubes ther nis no lakke;
Ther beth rosis of rede ble
And lilie likful for to se.

sight] seethe	waiissing] washing	solas] ease	dedute] delight
fleis] flesh	fisse] fish	likfullist] pleasantest	Fluren] flour
schingles] shingles	pinnes] pins (of the shingles)	Man] one	et inogh]
eat enough	wogh] wrongdoing	sembli] seemly	praer] lawn Swithe
likful] very pleasant	rote] root	siouns] shoots	sedwale] zedoary
Trie] choice	canel] cinnamon	gilofre] gillyflower	smakke] scent
cucubes] cubebs	lakke] lack	ble] complexion	

Thai faloweth neuer dai no night—
This aght be a swet sight.
Ther beth IIII willis in the abbei
Of triacle and halwei,
Of baum and ek piement,
Euer ernend to right rent
Of thai stremis al the molde:
Stonis preciuse and golde.
Ther is saphir and vniune,
Carbuncle and astiune,
Smaragde, lugre and prassiune,
Beril, onix, topasiune,
Ametist and crisolite,
Calcedun and epetite.

Ther beth briddes mani and fale:
Throstil, thruisse and nightingale,
Chalandre and wedwale,
And other briddes without tale,
That stinteth neuer bi har might
Miri to sing dai and night.

Yite I do thow mo to witte:
The Gees irostid on the spitte
Fleeth to that abbai, god hit wot,
And gredith: 'gees, al hote, al hote!'
Hi bringeth garlek gret plente,
The best idight that man mai se.
The leuerokes that beth cuth
Lightith adun to man is muth,
Idight in stu ful swithe wel,
Pudrid with gilofre and canel.
Nis no spech of no drink,
Ak tak inogh withute swinke.

faloweth] fadeth   willis] wells   triacle] treacle   halwei] balsam
baum] balm   piement] spiced wine   ernend] running   rent] purpose
molde] beds/courses   briddes] birds   fale] numerous   Chalandre]
goldfinch?   wedwale] oriole?   without tale] beyond count   stinteth]
cease   might] strength   Yite I do thow mo to witte] yet I tell you more
irostid] roasted   gredith] crieth   leuerokes] larks   adun to man is
muth] down into men's mouths   Idight in stu ful swithe wel] prepared in stewpan
very well   Pudrid] stuffed   no spech of no drink] no question of a lack of
drink   swinke] trouble

Whan the monkes geeth to masse,
Al the fenestres that beth of glasse
Turneth into cristal bright
To give the monkes more light.
Whan the masses beth iseiid
And the bokes up ileiid,
The cristal turnith into glasse,
In state that hit rather wasse.

The yung monkes euch dai
Aftir met goth to plai.
Nis ther hauk no fule so swifte
Bettir fleing bi the lifte
Than the monkes heigh of mode
With har slevis and har hode.
When the abbot seeth ham flee,
That he holt for moch gle;
Ak natheless al ther amang
He biddith ham light to evesang.
The monkes lightith noght adun,
Ac furre fleeth in o randun.
Whan the abbot him iseeth
That is monkes fram him fleeth,
He takith a maidin of the route
And turnith up hir white toute
And betith the taburs with is hond
To make is monkes light to lond.
Whan is monkes that iseeth,
To the maid dun hi fleeth
And geth the wench al abute
And thacketh al hir white toute
And sith aftir hir swinke
Wendith meklich hom to drinke
And geth to har collacione,
A wel faire processione.

fenestres] windows   iseiid] said   rather] formerly   hauk] hawk
fule] fowl   fleing bi the lifte] flying in the air   heigh of mode] in high
spirits   slevis] sleeves   hode] hood   holt] considers   Ak natheless]
but none the less   light to evesang] descend to evensong   furre fleeth in o
randun] fly far in furious course   toute] buttocks   dun hi] down they
And geth . . . abute] and go about   thacketh] thwacketh   sith aftir hir
swinke] then after their labours

115

An other abbei is ther bi,
For soth a gret fair nunnerie,
Up a river of swet milke,
Whar is plente gret of silk.
Whan the somer is dai is hote,
The yung nunnes takith a bote
And doth ham forth in that river
Both with oris and with stere.
Whan hi beth fur fram the abbei
Hi makith ham nakid forto plei
And lepith dune in to the brimme
And doth ham sleilich for to swimme.
The yung monkes, that hi seeth,
Hi doth ham up, and forth hi fleeth
And commith to the nonnes anon,
And euch monke him taketh on,
And snellich berrith forth har prei
To the mochil grei abbei,
And techith the nunnes an oreisun
With iambleue up and down.
The monke that wolde be stalun gode
And kan set aright is hode,
He schal habe withoute danger
XII wives euch yere,
Al throgh right and noght throgh grace
For to do him self solace.
And thilk monke that slepith best
And doth is likam al to rest,
Of him is hoppe, god hit wote,
To be sone uadir abbot.

Whoso wl com that lond to,
Ful grete penance he mot do:
Seve yere in swine is dritte
He mote wade, wol ye iwitte,
Al anon up to the chynne,
So he schal the lond winne.

---

bote] boat   oris] oars   stere] rudder   sleilich] timidly   snellich] swiftly   mochil] great   techith] teach   oreisun] prayer   iambleue] ambling   Of him is hoppe] there is hope for him   Whoso wl com] who wishes to come   in swine is dritte] in swine's dirt   chynne] chin

Lordinges gode and hend,
Mot ye never of world wend,
Fort ye stond to yure cheance
And fulfille that penance,
That ye mote that lond ise
And never more turne aye.
Pray we god, so mote hit be,
Amen, pur seint charite.

BROTHER MICHAEL OF KILDARE

fl. early 14th century

79   *Swet Jesus*

Swet Jesus, hend and fre
That was istrawght on rode tree
Now and ever with us be
And us schild from sin.
Let Thou noght to Helle te
Thet that beth herein!
So bright of ble, Thou hear me,
Hope of all mankynne,
Do us i-se the Trinite
And Hevenriche to winne!

This worldeis love is gon awai,
So dew on grasse in someris dai,
Few ther beth, weilawai,
That lovith goddis lore.
Al we bith iclung so clai,
We schold rew that sore;
Prince and King, what menith thai,
To libbe evir more?
Leveth yur plai and crieth ai:
Jesu Crist, thin ore.

Mot ye never . . . wend] may you never leave   Fort] unless   cheance]
opportunity   ise] see   turne aye] relapse in sin

79 hend] gracious   fre] noble   istrawght] stretched   schild] shield   te]
draw   ble] countenance   Do us i-se] make us to see   Hevenriche] the
Heavenly Kingdom   iclung so] shrunken as   menith] thinketh   ore]
compassion

Alas, alas, ye riche men,
Of muck whi wol ye fille yur denne?
Wende ye to ber hit henne?
Nai, so mote I thrive!
Ye sulle see that al is fenne,
The catel of this live.
To criste ye ren and falleth o knen,
That wondis tholiid five;
For ye beth trenne worthi to brenne
In bittir helle kive.

Godde you havith to erthe isent,
Litil dwel you havith ilent,
He schal wit, how hit is spent,
I rede you, tak hede.
If hit be hidde, ye beth ischent,
For helle worth yur mede.
The bow is bend, the fire itend
To you, if ye beth gnede.
Bot ye amend, ye sul be wend
In ever glowind glede.

Pouir was thin incomming,
So ssal be thin outegoing,
Thou ne ssalt of al thi thing
A peni ber to molde.
That is a rewful tithing,
Whoso hit hire wold.
Louerd king, to hori ding
What maketh man so hold?
In pining give a farthing
He ne sal, though he wold.

Riche man, bethenche ye,
Tak gode hede, wat thou be!

Wende ye] think ye   fenne] dung   catel] chattels   ren] run   knen]
knees   wondis] wounds   tholid] suffered   trenne] trees   brenne] burn
kive] pit   dwel] space   ilent] on loan   schal wit] want to know   rede]
counsel   ischent] destroyed   worth yur mede] is your desert   itend]
kindled   gnede] mean-spirited   glede] coals   Pouir] poor   thing]
property   A peni ber to molde] take a penny into the earth   hire] hear
Louerd] lord   hori ding] filthy dung   pining] suffering (in Hell)

Thou ne art bot a brotil tre
Of schorte seven fote,
Ischrid withoute with gold and fee
—The ax is at the rote.
The fent unfre halt al to gle
This tre adun to rote.
So mote ich se, Ich rede the: fle
And do thi sowlis bote.

Now thou art in ro and rest
Of al the lond thou art the mest
Thou doist no streinth of godis hest;
Of deth whi neltou thenche?
Whan thou wenist libbe best
Thi bodi deth sal quench;
The pouer chest ssal be thi nest
That sittist bold a bench;
East and West schal be thi qwest,
Ne might thou nothing blench.

Be thou baron other knighte
Thou salt be a sorful wighte,
Whan thou liest in bere itight
In fulle pouer wede.
Nastou nother main no mighte
Whil thou no man drede;
With sorwghful sight—and that is right—
To erthe man sul the lede;
Then ssal thi light turn into nighte.
Bethench, man, this i red.

The pouer man bit uche dai
Gode of the, and thou seiist ai:
'Begger, wend a devil wai!
Thou denist al min ere.'

---

brotil tre] unstable tree   Ischrid] clothed   fent unfre halt al to gle] ignoble
fiend takes delight   So mote ich se] as I may thrive   sowlis bote] soul's cure
Now thou art] now that you are   ro] peace   mest] most important   doist
no streinth of] give no importance to   neltou thenche] wilt thou not think   wenist
libbe] expect to live   pouer chest] poor box (coffin)   a] on   blench] shrink
from   other] or   bere itight] bier arrayed   wede] garment   Nastou
nother] thou hast neither   the lede] thee carry   red] counsel   bit uche
dai] begs each day   denist] deafenest

Hunger-bitte he goth awai
With mani sorwful tere.
A wailowai! thou clotte of clai!
Whan thou list on bere,
Of fow no grai no rede no rai
Nastou bot a here.

Crist tellith in holi writte
That a man of withir witte
Ibiriid was in helle pitte,
That in this lif was riche;
Ssal he never than flitte
Fram the sorful diche.
He sal sitte in helle flitte
Withoute wyn and miche,
The fent sal sitte is knot to knitte
Sore mai he skriche.

The pouer man goth bifor the
Al idriid als a tre,
And gredith: 'Louerd, help me,
Hunger me havith ibund.
Let me dei pur charite,
Ibroght ich am to grund.'
So mot I the and crist ise:
If he dei that stund
His lif sal be icrauid of the
That thou gif him no wonde.

I the rede: rise and wake
Of the hori sinne lake.
If thou be ther in itake,
Iwisse thou schalt to helle,
To woni with the fendis blake
In that sorful wille.

---

withir witte] wicked disposition   Ibiriid was] was buried   flitte] escape   helle
flitte] Hell's strife   wyn and miche] wine and bread   fent] fiend   is knot
to knitte] to tie his fate   bifor the] up to thee   idriid als] as dry as   gredith]
shall cry   ibund] bound   Ibroght ich am] I am brought   the and crist ise]
prosper and see Christ   that stund] at that time   icrauid of the] your respon-
sibility   hori] filthy   itake] taken   Iwisse] truly   woni with the
fendis blake] dwell with the black fiends   wille] well

Thi wei thou make, thou dri the stake,
To prest thi sinnes telle;
So wo and wrake sal from the rake
With fendis grimme and felle.

If in sinne thi live is ladde,
To do penance ne be noght sadde;
Who so doth, he nis noght madde,
As holi churche vs techithe;
Thereof be thou noght adradde
Crist sal be thi lech,
Thus Crist us radde, that rode spradde
With a blisful spech.
Whan he so bad, thou might be gladde
Ne lovith he no wreche.

Iesu, king of heven fre,
Ever iblessid mot thou be!
Louerd, i besech the,
To me thou tak hede;
From dedlich sinne thou ghem me,
While i libbe on lede!
The maid fre that bere the
So swetlich vnder wede,
Do vs to se the Trinite—
Al we habbeth nede!

This sang wroght a frere menour,
Iesus Crist be is socure,
Louerd, bring him to the toure.
Frere Michel Kyldare;
Schild him fram helle boure,
Whan he sal hen fare!
Leuedi, flur of al honur,
Cast awai is care;
Fram the schoure of pinis sure
Thou sild him her and thare! *Amen.*

dri the stake] endure the hardship   wrake] punishment   rake] depart
clotte] clod   list on bere] liest on bier   fow no grai no rede no rai] fur: grey, red, or striped   ladde] led   adradde] in dread   thi lech] thy physician
radde] spoke   rode spradde] stretched on cross   bad] ordered   fre] noble
ghem] keep   on lede] among men   wede] garments   frere menour] friar minor   hen fare] fare hence   Leuedi] Lady   schoure] onslaught   pinis] pains

BOOK II

——

FROM THE FOURTEENTH TO THE EIGHTEENTH CENTURY

FOURTEENTH/FIFTEENTH CENTURY

TADHG ÓG Ó HUIGÍNN
d. 1448

80   *Lament for Fearghal Ruadh*

The schools break up tonight,
their beds left abandoned,
and we who used those beds
lament as we depart.

Many slept peaceful there
where I have passed the nights.
This night we are more likely
to lie awake than to sleep.

I have lived in a lovely place,
and will see the like no more.
Dear God, how unworthy now!
There's a text for who can read it.

Toward Samhain it was a place
where the men of art would meet.
If a certain man still lived
we would not be parting now.

All who lived with him there
finding art and shelter
had reason to detest
hearing the cuckoo's call!

For then the school broke up,
each student left for home
—who will not leave his father's house
in quest of art again.

The school that Fearghal gathered:
its summer break seemed endless.
Longer now than any break
is our gentle teacher's loss.

But better shut down than search
for one to take his place.
It would be a prison sentence, God,
to take another teacher.

As Ireland's schools have ended
on Fearghal's sole account
so Banba's schools of old
broke up for one man of art:

Dallán's school, at his loss,
knew that they must disperse
whatever grief it caused them,
having faith in no other teacher.

Dallán Forgaill's poet-school,
confused in their heavy sorrow,
could neither leave nor stay.
It is so with this company.

As Inis Fáil's noble schools'
prime grief was for Dallán
today our schools disperse
with a great new grief for Fearghal.

The misery I have hidden
breaks forth when I meet my friends.
The schools have broken up
and all comfort turns to longing.

Brother and foster-son,
soon I must follow him,
troubled not just for a teacher
but the long loss of a brother.

Dallán Forgaill] poet of the sixth century, reputed poet of the *Amra Choluim Chille*
(no. 4)

If I were granted two lives
or this one life prolonged
it still would not suffice:
I am lonely, now he is gone.

Thirty years or longer
I was (to speak it plain)
full of prideful breath
when anguish came and chilled me.

Now my feats in his banquet hall
are paid in draughts of sorrow.
If ever I sought for pleasure
I have sorely paid, my God.

He did not cease in my training,
not for a single night,
till he turned me loose at the birds . . .
I shared one hut with Ó hUigínn.

A word whispered to him
against me, to do me harm,
availed him naught who said it:
he brooked no breath against me.

From childhood he shared with me
all his eager plans
(and God requite him for it)
until it was time to part.

Such teaching as I can give
to his students now he is dead
I had from Fearghal Ruadh.
Lord, may I do as well.

Utmost honour and kindness
and favour toward myself
were mine—by a sore heart's charter—
over all Ó hUigínn's pupils.

I swear I could not repay him,
Fearghal, for all his labours
with soul-sickness enough
though I should mourn for ever.

It is wrong to cut grief short
before its attack is spent:
ease taken, forgetting sorrow,
that would torment my heart.

Though care for my teacher's loss
might leave me for a while
soon the grief returns.
Easy kindle a live coal!

But I will not weep aloud
after Fearghal Ó hUigínn.
Let my wretched share of grief
be known by my sighing only.

I shall not go while I live
to the place where I knew Fearghal.
The huts where we lived are gone.
I would hear no friendly voice.

If I saw, with Ó hUigínn gone,
that couch we shared together,
any sorrow I have been spared
believe me I would pay.

I love the strange hut of poetry.
I know that, now he is lost.
You empty hut there before me
had once no neighbour near.

The son of Áine dead
has robbed poetry of her pleasure.
A stave gone in the side of a barrel
—the wall of learning is broken.

FIFTEENTH CENTURY

ANONYMOUS

81   Gormlaith said:

'You are desolate, fort of kings.
    And no wonder: Niall is gone.
Though decay has seldom touched you
    you are lonely for him tonight.

'But though tonight you are lonely
    you once were a hill of poets.
You were not often empty
    in Niall's time, of the Nine Hostages.

'All realms but the realm of God
    shall pass, and that is truth.
This world holds nothing to wish for.
    You are desolate, fort of kings.'

82   Gormlaith said:

'Monk, step further off.
Move away from Niall's side.
You settle the clay too heavy
on him with whom I have lain.

'You linger here so long
settling the clay on noble Niall:
he seems a long while in the coffin
where his soles don't reach the boards.

'Aed Finnliath's son, of the drinking feasts,
under a cross—it is not my will.
Stretch the slab upon his bed.
Monk, step further off.

'Over Uisnech's famous family
Deirdre stood as I do now,
till her heart swelled in her side.
Monk, step further off.

'I am Gormlaith, maker of verses,
Flann's noble daughter from Dún Rois.
My grief that slab is not above me!
Monk, step further off.'

English

ANONYMOUS

83 from *A Letter sent by the Mayor and Inhabitants of the
Citie of Waterford unto Walter, archbishop of the Citie
of Dublin, the Mayor and Citizens of the same, in the
time of their Rebellion*

. . . O thow archbishop and metropolitan,
The chief lampe of pastorall dignitie
Of all this land, for thow is vertue began,
If thow be cause of this perversitie
That late is fallen against all equitie
We know it not; but certain we can saie
Thou keepest silence, and saidst not once nay.

. . . Ye may see, by common experience,
What vengeance God have shewd in your country
By murther, slaughter and great pestilence;
The fruits dearer than they were wont to be,
And manie of your men drowned in the sea.
Theis are not without cause, after our intent.
But we be not privie to Gode's judgement.

What is he that have read in cronicle,
In old stories, or in anie writing,
Or in the volume of the Holie Bible

So rude a matter and so strange a thinge
As a boy in Dublin to be made a kinge;
And to receave therein his unction,
The soleymne act of his coronation?

. . . It is tyme for you to be reconciled.
Of this matter now we will end.
Ye have been to long from trouth exiled.
The tyme is now come for you to amend.
A convenable tyme is to you sent:
The tyme of Lent, the mirrour of mercy,
For all them that will reverse their folie.

. . . O Ireland, Ireland! by what conclusion
Is thy mirrour of beautie eclipsed all?
By murder, slaughter and great rebellion
Thy fertill bondes have had great fall,
Thy stynge of venyme, as bitter as gall.
Fortune have cast on thee so her chaunce
That alwaies thow must stand in variaunce . . .

FIFTEENTH/SIXTEENTH CENTURY

ANONYMOUS LOVE POETRY

84

Keep your kiss to yourself,
   young miss with the white teeth.
I can get no taste from it.
   Keep your mouth away from me.

I got a kiss more sweet than honey
   from a man's wife, for love,
and I'll get no taste from any kiss
   till doomsday, after that.

Until I see that same woman
   (grant it, gracious Son of God)
I'll love no woman young or old
   because her kiss is—what it is!

85

Take my song of love to heart,
   lady of the lying love:
you and I from this time on
   must endure each other's loss.

If you hear them talk of me
   in the cottages or the big house
don't discuss me like the rest.
   Don't blame me or defend me.

In the chapel, in the abbey,
   the churchyard or the open air,
if we two should chance to meet
   don't look, and I won't look at you.

You and I, we mustn't tell
   my family or Christian name.
Don't pretend, and I won't,
   I ever looked at you before.

86   I will not die for you,
    lady with swanlike body.
Meagre men you have killed so far,
    and not the likes of me.

For what would make me die?
    Lips of red, or teeth like blooms?
A gentle hand, a lime-white breast?
    Should I die for these?

Your cheerful mood, your noble mind?
    O slender palm and flank like foam,
eye of blue and throat of white,
    I will not die for you.

Your rounded breasts, O skin refined,
    your flushed cheeks, your waving hair
—certainly I will not die
    on their account, unless God will.

Your narrow brows, your hair like gold,
    your chaste intent, your languid voice,
your smooth calf, your curved heel
    —only meagre men they kill.

Lady with swanlike body,
    I was reared by a cunning hand!
I know well how women are.
    I will not die for you.

87   You that are jealous and have a wife
    go face the rain like other men.
If you want a hope of peace
    question not your woman's moods.

She's woman born, and must so stay
    whatever pain she has of it.
She is the servingmaid of love
    and not herself responsible.

Don't trust the sight of your own eyes.
    Half of what you know, know not.
Take proven news to be a lie.
    Don't believe your own ears.

Suffer agitation calmly.
   Bother with nothing under the sun.
The wisest thing to be
   is a witless harmless fool.

Eat your meat and sleep your fill,
   don't let her see your wretched pain,
cross the mire in a single leap,
   nor care a straw for your woman's moods.

You that are jealous and cannot help but love her
   don't care a straw for that empty woman's moods.
If you can't manage that, for honour's sake
   outclimb all idiots to the peak of madness.

88   Sir, so suspicious,
            your case makes fine gossip
       and all quite uncalled for
         —it's odd you should worry.

Sour twisted women
    have often lacked love;
though strange you may think it
    your wife is your own.

Such secrecy, sir!
    We find your case strange.
Guarding that woman
    —there's a fence with no field!

Not one in a hundred
    is safe as you are.
You've no need to fear
    wagging tongues at your wife.

Believe no man living
    that ever maligns her.
No need to leave home,
    sir, so suspicious.

89 *A Glance*

Black of brow, with cheeks aglow,
    blue of eye, with hair so smooth,
wind rowing through your parted locks
    —fine women at the fair are watching!

Wives, pretending not to look,
    plait their hair in front of you.
With fingers through her lovely hair
    one of them is studying you.

90   Lady of shrouding hair,
            in your thread-soft locks we see
        that whereby a man might fault
            the hair of Absolom, David's son.

        There in your bright and braided locks
            are cuckoo-curls on point of birth,
        a flock that makes no sound
            yet still distracts all men.

        Your fair long curling hair
            falls across your lovely eyes,
        eyes that are clear and crystal bright
            as the gem stones of a ring.

        A new fashion you have found,
            whatever country it came from:
        your hand without the ring required
            but a hundred rings at your throat!

        Your hair curls soft and yellow
            and circles your upright neck:
        your throat so ringed about
            it is in chains for certain . . .

91 It is far from just between us,
    myself and my beloved:
myself all eagerness
    and she without much interest.

That she'd leave me there for money
    is only the way of a woman,
while I wouldn't desert my love
    if she came to me in a shirt.

She carries the load lightly,
    the love that lies heavy on me;
nor suffers from my sickness.
    It is far from just between us.

92 No sickness worse than secret love:
    it's long, alas, since I pondered that.
No more delay: I now confess
    my secret love, so slight and slim.

I gave a love that I can't conceal
    to her hooded hair, her shy intent,
her narrow brows, her blue-green eyes,
    her even teeth and aspect soft.

I gave as well—and so declare—
    my soul's love to her soft throat,
her lovely voice, delicious lips,
    snowy bosom, pointed breast.

And may not overlook, alas,
    my cloud-hid love for her body bright,
her trim straight foot, her slender sole,
    her languid laugh, her timid hand.

Allow there was never known before
    such a love as mine for her;
there lives not, never did, nor will,
    one who more gravely stole my love.

93 Do not torment me, lady.
Let our purposes agree.
   You are my spouse on this Fair Plain:
   so let us embrace.

Set that berry-coloured mouth
on mine, O skin like foam.
   Place that smooth and lime-white limb
   —despite your quarrel—round me.

Slim and delicate, be no longer
absent from my side.
   Slender, show me to your quilts!
   Stretch our bodies side by side.

As I have put away (soft thigh)
Ireland's women for your sake
   likewise try to put away
   all other men for me.

I gave to your bright teeth
immeasurable longing.
   So it is just that you should give
   your love in the same measure.

94 Men's loving is a false affection.
   Woe to the woman does their will.
Though sweet their converse and correct
   their thoughts are hidden deep within.

Never trust their whispered secret,
   never trust their handclasp firm,
never trust their tasty kiss
   —such love as theirs has cost my health.

Never give, no more than I,
   your trust to any man on earth,
for yesterday I heard a tale
   that caused me anguish, O my God!

Gold and silver they will offer;
    wealth they will offer you as well;
law and marriage they will offer
    womanfolk, till break of day.

Not me alone have they deceived:
    many's the woman they have wronged.
The love of man will never last.
    God help who follow in my footsteps.

English

95   *Translation of an Irish song*

You and I will go to Finegall.
You and I will eat such meats as we find there.
You and I will steal such beef as we find fat.
I shall be hanged and you shall be hanged.
What shall our children do?
When teeth do grow unto themselves
as their fathers did before?

95 Finegall] lit. 'the foreigners' territory', the area of the Pale around Dublin

MAGHNAS Ó DOMHNAILL

d. 1563

96   A heart made full of thought
          I had, before you left.
       What man, however prideful,
          but lost his perfect love?

       Grief like the growing vine
          came with time upon me.
       Yet it is not through despair
          I see your image still.

       A bird lifting from clear water,
          a bright sun put out
       —such my parting, in troubled tiredness,
          from the partner of my heart.

97   A famished end to my tale this night.
          It is seldom a strong man will not cure,
       but if Dian Cecht were alive today
          this wound in my side he could not heal.

       No ebb at all in my weariness,
          like an ocean full at the harbour mouth.
       Such hard pain as I suffer now
          before this night I never knew.

       Alas that I have found this truth:
          rare is the wine without its dregs,
       and nothing tempers hard as grief,
          worse, I think, than any famine.

97 Dian Cecht] legendary healer of the Tuatha Dé Danann

98

Love, I think, is a disease,
  useless though it is to talk.
I need another heart, through love,
  for it has broken the one I had.

Yet since the fault was all its own,
  this heart of mine that offered love,
I might as well lie down with the ill
  save that I cannot bear the pain.

A pity it wasn't hate I gave,
  and hate accepted in return!
Bad luck to the one receiving love
  and worse, I think, to the one that gives.

LOCHLANN ÓG Ó DÁLAIGH

fl. mid 16th century

99
In Praise of Three Young Men

Dear these three who have come to see me,
that have played in pleasure upon me,
three of the seed of Blod's long line,
a smooth bed's load, these three come.

To bind an agreement with me
they sit about me in order,
three, blue-eyed, not sharply spoken,
young and fresh, a manly breed.

For the praise of these young men,
for each of them, I have a charge
from our graceful, modest and noble throng:
a well-made ode for them.

The family head, of Tál's tribe,
is Tadhg, the eldest noble child.
Learning honour he succeeds
Domhnall's heir, son of Brian the good.

The host of Cas, gathered about
Conchubar, shall be wisest in Munster's land.
Now from God I prophesy
there'll be no talk of foreign stock.

Third hazel-nut in the pure cluster
is Murchadh's heir, another Tadhg.
Caring for poets of ancient wisdom
this O'Brien shall fill men's mouths.

A sheltering wood about Clann Chais,
these three shoots from the native clay.
None but a poet could harm them,
these three trees of lasting fruit.

Three hawks happy in the hunt
pursuing all who would lay waste;
kindred-loving, alike in age,
swift birds of prey from the one forest.

Three bears victorious in the fray
set to protect Maicnia's walls,
the three companions together
three savage beasts shall be.

Three eaters of the salmon of knowledge,
three seeds from the gold-skinned apple,
three blossoms to help our poems,
mirrors attracting women.

Fresh hazel-nuts from the finest cluster,
three streams from a cliff's clear spring,
breed of a royal branch, generous-minded,
of princely rule, juice of the vine.

Waging war in the half of Conn
soon their javelins shall be
for our warlike, fierce and ardent throng
with spears bright-purpled from their deeds.

Maicnia's walls] the boundaries of Munster

Three curved sticks, that won the goal
from fair Maigh's teams, they shall set down
and take up ivory-hilted swords
Cobhthach's seed to save.

These young men assembled here,
these boys shall be a hero-flock,
a warhorse in each O'Brien's grip,
a steed with golden bridle.

Like spark-emitting fires
lit from a single flash
these three, in soft fair Banba
—the stuff of strife and conquest.

Their youth is no reproach.
Pure, precious gold begins
in the soft ore's glowing noble mass:
an example for Brian's line, I think.

Six bright flanks like foam,
six calves with famous steps,
six feet our prop in battle,
six hands igniting honour,

six cheeks that need not blush,
six modest far-seeing eyes,
at no request unwilling,
three fine mouths speaking peace.

Bright-sided Conchubar, two Tadhgs,
rewarding schools, caring for bards,
these are the three I choose,
not doubting they will mind me.

May the Trinity grant all three
long life upon this saintly soil,
the fair hosts' flower, with wealth unhid.
Telling of them is dear.

TADHG DALL Ó HUIGÍNN

1550–1591

100   *A Visit to Enniskillen*

God help who looks upon Enniskillen
of the shining bays and the pleasant falls.
There is danger there, for we cannot leave it
for its bright walls and gleaming lawns.

Long before I came in sight
of that bright-walled fort on the blue hills
I dreamed, if I might reach that house,
that I could never want again.

Fame I heard (and pity it was)
of a magic fort and its gems unmatched
and what enchantment lay in store
—that I might ne'er break free again.

The glorious house of the lion of Erne
(or so, indeed, all men proclaimed)
was such that none in Banba saw
ever a house the like of it,

reporting only that who should see
the bending wood or the fertile slope,
the level strand or the verdant fields,
could never take one step away.

When I had heard these things set forth
and slept on them a little while
what vision then should I behold
but that fair and ample house in splendour?

I took my way and came in course
to Enniskillen's oaken slopes.
Eager indeed was my approach
o'er the fair plain of laden fruit-stems.

Scarcely had I reached the town
when I started at all the voices calling,
swift hounds baying and hunting dogs
driving deer-flocks in from the wild.

The strand that stretched along the court,
a fairy harbour of murmuring streams,
was dense with ship-masts, like a grove
shading that strand and all its waves.

By the same enclosure, near at hand,
a beauteous plain of golden light
I saw: the bright fort's moistened lawn,
the sward of Heaven, or its like exact.

The lawn of the fortress, thus I found it:
its top turned by the hooves of horses,
no herb growing in earth or yard
from horse-herds leaping in skilful contest!

With steeds of the fort in races running
(I see them still, racing in line)
till the hills of the earth were covered over
not by mist but by horses' breath.

Then I advanced in level course
to the double fort of the branch of Liag.
That fair castle there before me
—filled it was with a wondrous people:

nobles there of the sons of Colla
in the crowded court dividing treasure;
others solving the sagas' meanings,
the racial roots of the Gaels of Greece;

a host of minstrels and of poets
also there throughout the fort
from one white shining wall to the other
—lucky the house-floor that can hold them!

In another part I found a plenty
of small-mouthed virgins in satin gowns
weaving wondrous golden fringes
on a rampart thronged with fair sleek hounds,

and many warriors about the house
taking their rest along the walls,
their warlike swords hung sharp above them
—warriors these from rich Drom Caoin;

an ample band of enchanted youth
from Síth Bodhbh or the Bruiden of Lir
—eye dared not watch them, such their beauty
on the steps of the bright, wood-woven wall;

a team of craftsmen banding goblets,
a team of smiths preparing arms,
a team of alien masons also
in that lovely pearl of murmuring streams;

rugs being dyed and blades being polished,
javelins readied, horses run,
prisoners held, their terms drawn up,
scholars guarding lists of kings;

hostages taken and released,
warriors wounded, warriors healed,
endless treasures entering, leaving
the tall smooth comely fairy fort.

Part of every day they spent
narrating feats, debating battles,
spending a while on the host of Usnech,
feasts of drinking, hearing music.

So till supper time we spent,
passing thus the pleasant day
in the green-grassed, bright and fertile court
—a single hour in length it seemed.

Then everyone began to settle
by the smooth sides of the ramparts bright:
where is the fort that held the like,
such wealth of people entering in?

Drom Caoin] Tara   Síth Bodhbh] Lough Derg, near Killaloe   the Bruiden
of Lir] Lir's dwelling on Sliab Fuait—the Fews Mountains—in Armagh

Cú Connacht Óg, Cú Connacht's son
of the lithe body, trailing smoke,
when all in his fort are settled down
seats himself in the royal chair.

I sit on the right of Tara's dragon
until our turn with the goblet comes;
although there were a share of nobles
the royal elbow ne'er disdains me.

In proper time, when the hour is come
for the fort's people to take their rest,
the choice and lively host, well-mannered,
have quilts of down prepared for them.

Before day broke on the *bruiden*'s people
a team of them was readying spears,
with harness in its place at dawn
and men going out to catch their horses.

A little while upon our waking
the pick of all I saw assembled
by Síth Truim's hawk, in warlike trappings,
in the smooth, rock-built and brightening fort.

Out they march at the dawn of day,
the valorous youth of the kingly court,
a long great company with spears
—binding peace is not their business!

It was not long before they reached us,
Colla's company, golden curled,
with every country in subjection:
happy the realm they call their own.

Many that day around Loch Erne
the foreign wife whose man lies dead.
Many the face of a wounded hostage
after the conflict entering in.

Síth Truim] on the river Boyne, near Slane

And precious treasures in that house
that were not there when the day began
and herds as well, hard by the town,
that were not near the night before!

Then were the poets of the fort rewarded
by Eachach's heir who ne'er shirked battle.
Little the cost of their poems counted
for riches were taken beyond their price.

I went to Maguire to ask permission
—myself from among the schools of art—
to leave that high bright ordered *rath*.
Alas, he allowed me to depart!

And this he said as we parted there,
the tears descending his brown cheek,
that though I might be leaving him
there was no real parting there.

I remember the day I turned my back
upon that house in the royal dwelling
such sorrow lay upon them all
no single sorrow could be seen.

I left that house, and am not recovered.
A pity I did not end my days
rather than have to live without it:
it seems a danger I will die.

So fair a house, such excellence
as in that fort, I have not known
under any sprung from the seed of Colla.
And that is every poet's judgement.

Enniskillen of shining slopes,
no one leaves by his own will.
It lures all men from no matter where.
God help who looks upon its like.

101 *A Satire on the O'Haras*

This is the satire Tadhg Dall made on the O'Haras, for which they took out his tongue, etc.

A rabble of six arrived at my house.
I will tell you of this six:
I had no milk next morning
through the thirst of those gallows-birds.

And it was a while before that
according to report
that their limbs had a bite of beef,
this two-times-three aforesaid.

It fell to me—and here's the flaw—
to bring them from death to life.
It was milk of mine they drank
parched with their own dry bread.

Their need was my bereavement.
And now I am torn in two:
it is hard to hide these verses,
though a sin for me to make them.

But concealment is bad for satire
no matter who earns the anger.
I have censured this crew of six
so I must speak it out:

The first of them I saw
a clodhopper is better clad,
his pack not worth a penny,
nor used to drink or sport.

The second as I saw him
heading the same crew
was a wretch with melted marrow.
How could I leave him out?

The third had a jaded javelin
and a gapped soft axe: himself
and that poor axe in combat
—alas for that equipment.

The fourth, as he travelled with them,
was full of flux, his fixtures
four lances across his rump
that never tore a target.

In the footsteps of these four
a fifth rogue advanced
in a short shirt not worth a penny
and a cloak, I swear, no better.

A beggar not worth a worm
followed upon that five,
a meagre man with a filthy face
—a bad risk in a battle.

I pray to God who shed His blood,
since their life itself is all decay
and scarce a state of life at all,
O spare this crew of six!

LAOISEACH MAC AN BHÁIRD

fl. late 16th century

102
    A fond greeting, hillock there,
      though I'm cheerless at your decline:
    a source of sorrow your brown thorn,
      the smooth stem we knew at your top.

    A grief to all, the gathering bush
      we knew as our assembly place:
    its boughs broken—a dismal day.
      The land is meaner now it is gone.

    The heart in my side has grown dark,
      hillock there, for your great tree.
    I have scanned, from its stem, the whole country.
      Your smooth thorn I will see no more.

    It served us all as a sign,
      the branch that is taken now.
    Far from our northern land
      we could see the distant tree.

But a blast has wrecked its root,
    that branch so long unbroken.
Many men it has sheltered,
    that ruined tree, a sore loss.

Its shapely branches of purple shade,
    my grief, are in decay.
It is right to mourn the pangs of Christ
    as I brood upon this branch.

Hacked from us in total ruin
    our lovely thorn, a barn for birds.
A like tree never grew in ground;
    a source of tears until I die.

It will hurt to the brink of death
    that it stands no more on high.
No hill of fruitful boughs I see
    but a ruined thorn to stir our grief.

The assembly hill—it troubles the schools—
    today in strangers' hands.
I am in sorrow for its slopes,
    the fair hill that held my love.

103   *Two Sons*

You follow foreign ways
and shave your thick-curled head:
O slender fist, my choice!
you are no good son of Donnchadh.

If you were, you would not yield
your hair to a foreign fashion
—the fairest feature in Fódla's land—
and your head done up in a crown.

Little you think of your yellow hair,
but that other detests their locks
and going cropped in the foreign way.
Your manners are little like.

He loved no foreign ways,
our ladies' darling, Eogan Bán,
nor bent his will to the stranger,
but took to the wilds instead.

Eogan Bán thinks little of your views.
He would give his britches gladly
and accept a rag for a cloak
and ask no coat nor hose.

He hates the jewelled spur on his boot
at the narrow of his foot,
or stockings in the foreign style,
nor allows their locks upon him.

A blunt rapier wouldn't kill a fly
holds no charm for Donnchadh's son,
nor a bodkin weighing at his rump
as he climbs to the gathering place.

Little his wish for a gold cloak
or a high Holland collar;
a golden bangle would only annoy
or a satin scarf to the heel.

He has no thought for a feather bed
but would rather lie on rushes,
more at ease—Donnchadh's good son—
in a rough-wattled hut than a tower top.

Throng of horse in the mouth of a gap,
foot-soldiers' fight, the hard fray,
are some of Donnchadh's son's delights,
and looking for fight with the foreigner.

You are not like Eogan Bán.
They laugh as you step to the mounting block.
A pity you cannot see your fault,
as you follow foreign ways.

Company in Loneliness

Hasten hither, little book,
with wholesome tales in speckled writing
and never part from me
now everyone deserts me.

Come, pure-leaved and smooth,
firm-stitched and bunched together,
and lull my grief for their loss
—that ardent-cheeked fair company.

Bring with you as you come
my radiant, ready, clean pen-case
full of sharp dart-like pens,
pliant-pointed, firm, new trimmed.

Bring paper and cushion also
for my hand, whence the writing pours
on the fluent smooth slope of leaf,
fine-lettered, jet-black, ordered.

And bring my poem-book
of noble changeless Gaelic
till I study each tale to the roots
(branches of bravery and bright knowledge)

that learned lays I may recite
with clear knowledge of branching kindreds,
the family tree of every man,
wonder feats and voyages.

Bring with you my handbook
of ordered arithmetic
till I number the points of the heavens
and the days it is since the Deluge.

And do not forget that music-bough
red-boarded, plaintive, dry,
soft-voiced, wailing sweetly
a sleepy lullaby to the mind

—bring me my fiery lyre,
grooved and shining, turbulent,
polished and tempered thoroughly,
thin-stringed, all engraved.

When I behold the skilful harp,
brown-shadowed, great, smooth-sloped,
beneath my fingers' running fire
my mind quickens of itself.

Sparkling airs I have played
with my quick keen fingertips,
close-knit, precise and grave,
calloused fingers flowing even.

Put then my lovely blade
into my bright right fist
till I put a hard battle-edge
on both its shining sides.

And give me my sweet knife-jewel,
blue-bladed, bright, sharp-tipped,
with scabbard tightly corded
—a case worthy to keep it.

In the past I have taken keen delight
in the lined and level *ficheall*-board,
pressing across it against the odds,
breaking up the ordered team,

throwing dice from dawn to dawn
in runs like a hurrying torrent
on the sleek and chequered board,
lovely, sweet, and light.

When these are gathered round me
they set my spirit soaring
and I walk in a wink of time
all the weighty sods of the world.

The more should one so love
this fair dear company
that they murmur against no man
in arrogance or reproach.

I ask their peace, and kneel to them,
this blessed dear lovely band,
and embrace this orphan over all
who never leaves me lonely.

English

ANONYMOUS

105   from *The Praise of Waterford*

God of his goodnes, praysed that he be,
    For the daylie increase of thy good fame,
O pleasant Waterford, thow loyal citie
    That five hundred yeres receavest thy name
    Er the later conquest unto thee came,
In Ireland deservest to be peereless—
Quia tu semper intacta manes.

. . . Henry the Valiant, famous of memorye,
    Well did he know by true experyence
Thy true fydelytie in tyme of victorye
    When Lambert was crowned by false advertence
    And Parkin allso, with no lesse reverens,
Then only of this land thow were empresse—
Quia tu semper intacta manes.

... Now God we pray, that three art in one,
　Preserve his high grace in royal estate
And kepe this cytie from dyvysyon
　In true allegiaunce, without debate,
　And our hartes in the same to sociate;
Then Waterford true shall never decrease—
Quam diu vere intacta manes.

106　　　　　*A Postscript to Verses on the
　　　　　　　　History of France*

　　　The Lords do crave all.
　　　The King accords all.
　　　The Parliament passeth all.
　　　The Chancellor doth seal all.
　　　Queen Mother doth rule all.
　　　The Cardinals do bless all.
　　　The Pope doth pardon all.
　　　And without God's help
　　　the divill will have all.

ANONYMOUS

107   *The Scholar's Life*

Sweet is the scholar's life,
  busy about his studies,
the sweetest lot in Ireland
  as all of you know well.

No king or prince to rule him
  nor lord however mighty,
no rent to the chapterhouse,
  no drudging, no dawn-rising.

Dawn-rising or shepherding
  never required of him,
no need to take his turn
  as watchman in the night.

He spends a while at chess,
  and a while with the pleasant harp
and a further while wooing
  and winning lovely women.

His horse-team hale and hearty
  at the first coming of spring;
the harrow for his team
  is a fistful of pens.

108   There are three who await my death
  and are always close at hand
(I wish them hung on a gibbet!)
  —Devil, Family, Maggot.

None of that cunning three
  would give to the other two
an armful out of his share
  in exchange for theirs combined:

the Devil—a gloomy visage
   that wishes only ill—
wouldn't take my wealth and body
   for my sweet and gentle soul;

my Family would rather
   my wealth this very night,
for all our bonds of blood,
   than my body and my soul;

while Maggot (God help us all)
   if my head were stretched in soil
would much prefer my body
   to my poor soul and my wealth.

O Christ who was hanged on tree
   and lanced by the ignorant Blind-man
now as they wait my ruin
   I wish them choked, all three!

109   *Three Epigrams*

Gold priests, wooden chalices
in Ireland in Patrick's time.
   Golden chalices, wooden priests,
   as the wretched world stands now.

*   *   *

Broad and ample he warms himself,
   a son in his father's house.
A father's warmth in his son's house:
   his own two knees to his chest.

*   *   *

Heat goes deep as cold.
   Hate goes deep as love.
But envy strikes to the marrow
   and sticks there for ever.

EOCHAIDH Ó HEOGHUSA

fl. late 16th–early 17th century

A Change in Style

Give thanks for this turn for the better,
   now that I have discovered
a fortunate mean little swap
   that works to my advantage.

I've deserted the stricter ranks
   of a discipline sharp and clear
for an average soft sort of work
   that earns me better attention.

My dark and fine-wrought work
   brought me only complaint.
My poems didn't merit much favour
   in the mind of the multitude.

I renounce, though it's bitter to say it,
   every groat of my earnings in future
if a single verse of my poems
   proves awkward for anyone.

Easy verse on the open road:
   if that's what they want from me
I'll be able to pay my debts
   (by leave of the Earl of Clann Conaill).

In the easy, the empty, I promise
   I'll outmanage the fools of the world.
I've got sense, and I'm out at last
   in the weather with everyone else.

I've forsaken—and it's a pleasure—
   my dark and difficult paths,
though when he hears some of my poems
   the Earl will be forced to laugh.

But for fear I might lose the patrons
    that gave me my qualifications
I won't have the Prince of Uí Chonaill
    take a place on the judging committee.

This year, with my falsified poetry,
    I have plenty to love me well,
and could better my reputation
    if it wasn't for thoughts of the Earl.

But Aodh's son, of the steadfast mind,
    who could solve my cruxes simply,
is off among the Saxons.
    No wonder I am getting on well!

Every poem composed in the past,
    it almost broke my heart.
But this new fashion amongst us
    should prove very good for the health.

If the Prince of Bearnas finds fault
    with any stanza I make
he'll have plenty to speak against him.
    Give thanks for this turn for the better.

111   *Mag Uidhir's Winter Campaign*

I feel the cold this night for Aodh.
A cause of misery, its heavy shower drops.
A woeful chance for my friend,
the night's venomous cold.

And a venom tonight in my heart
how the fiery downpours fall.
Meeting the spears of frost, as he does,
is terrible to the mind.

110 Bearnas] the modern Barnesmore in Co. Donegal

Over the cloud breasts, the sky
has opened its watery doors.
It has made seas out of little pools.
The firmament spews out ruin.

Now even for a wild hare in the woods,
or a salmon in a sea estuary,
or a birdflock, it would be fearful
to go out wandering.

I suffer for Aodh Mag Uidhir
in a strange land tonight,
in a red glare of showering thunderbolts
under edged clouds in blood-red anger.

Misery, that our beloved man
is in the province of Clann Dáire
on a cold soaking grass track
under a raging and mocking sky.

On his cheerful cheeks I feel the cold
of the fury of the winter blasts
driving the storm winds of the stars
at the pale-limbed royal Gaileang warrior.

It hurts, it wounds our spirit,
that the soft curve of his fine-formed flank
is bruised by the rough sullen night
under his full suit of cold iron.

His gentle palm—in strife ungentle—
is stitched by the icy storm
to the thin shaft of the cold-tipped pike.
It is icy for Aodh this night.

I hope neither he nor I
will regret this circuit of Ireland . . .
I sense danger in it:
may it pass—let my fear not come.

Aodh Mag Uidhir] Anglicized 'Hugh Maguire'   Clann Dáire] the people of west
Munster   Gaileang] a scattered tribe settled in parts of Connaught and in Meath

If his travels turn out ill,
this traverse of Maicnia's Fold
(such a march as none have seen),
will the thread of life not break?

The low banks of the source streams
flood in the warriors' path.
The meadows are under a frozen cloak;
it keeps the horses from their feed.

People in their homes cannot see
that the river-banks are drowned,
the soaked margins of once clear streams.
We cannot get our tents dry.

He is worried, it is a great unease,
he may lose the horses and wagons
before crossing the quiet Lee westward
to the roads in Maicnia's level Fold.

But it is not these losses
I think about on his journey;
what pierces to the heart
are the cold pangs of the weather.

And yet—there is something to warm
his honest and noble face:
all the castle walls blue-burning
in a pall of wind-tossed fire!

Their flaming blaze will thaw
the ice film from his firm clear eye.
The ruddy sheets of flame will melt
the frost that grips his smooth brown hand!

All over Munster of the bright walls
many courts, stripped bare, are covered in ashes
by our slaughterer in the land of the Gael
to wrap them from the cold air!

Maicnia's Fold] bardic name for Munster; Dáire was Maicnia's father

FEAR FLATHA Ó GNÍMH

fl. early 17th century

After the Flight of the Earls

God rest the soul of Ireland,
   island of faltering steps.
The soft-voiced people of Brian
   are heavy with grief, I think.

Denial of faith and justice
   are to Fódla the same as death
and disgrace to her sons and sages,
   if the stories and songs are true.

How can Banba not perish
   now her gallant herd of heroes
have taken their way to Spain?
   Alas for the heirs of Ulster.

For fear of an alien law
   I may not discuss her plight:
the level land of Niall the king
   bathed in righteous blood.

No regard for the festivals
   nor for the clergy's decisions;
her bard-schools' pleasure is past
   and her maidens are no more modest.

They live without act or energy,
   a heavy weight upon Ireland,
no courage, no crowd of heroes
   on Féilim's fair-grassed isle.

I mourn for her youth destroyed,
   a free-handed, valorous troop.
Fierce drinking drowns their senses.
   By that you will know them all.

people of Brian] people of Ireland   Fódla, Banba, land of Niall, Féilim's fair-
grassed isle] Ireland

Conall's race is dead,
   a host hungry for fame,
and the seed of Eoghan the smiter.
   Great shame to the men of Ireland.

Only their leavings linger:
   the blood of the earls of Seanaid,
heroes from the Maigue and Méin.
   So much for the Geraldines' best.

Clann Carthy is leaderless,
   hard though it hurts to say it.
And the winds have grown perverse:
   it is dangerous even to talk.

And there was a great forgetting:
   not a trace of Blod's old honour,
a victorious force, high minded,
   though nobody knows them now.

In place of Ó Ruairc and Mag Uidhir
   —soldiers who shirked no danger—
a craven host, foul-hearted,
   that I drown with a passing tear.

Conchubar's seed (a hard saying)
   the kings of Connacht in times past
though their heirs are a noble swarm
   ill-luck is their only kingdom.

The race of Murchadh and Ó Mordha,
   warriors brave in battle,
scarce one of that noble seed
   holds a sod of his native land.

The seed of Béarra's high clan,
   heroes who shirked no fight,
have put me on a troubled path,
   with Ó Cearrbhail and Ó Ceallaigh.

Conall's race . . . the seed of Eoghan] the northern families of Donegal (Tyrconnell) and
Tyrone   the Maigue and Méin] rivers in Limerick   Blod's old honour] the
O'Briens

Her nobles and freemen dead,
    she cannot cure her shame.
It is a shameful step for the Gael,
    if we dare presume to say it.

By a blow of Balor's eye
    her lovely land is sickened,
her corn blossomless in the clay
    —and I pray God rest her soul.

113   *The Passing of the Poets*

God help who follows his father's craft!
On Banba's fresh plain it happens
a father's trade is best no longer,
in the cool green fields of Ireland.

It seems that the poets' order
no longer, North or South,
may speak of their elders' work.
Let us turn to a different task,

not spinning the threads of wisdom
nor tracing our branching peoples
nor weaving a graceful verse
—nor talking of poetry.

The first who took to versing
might have turned to something else,
for he chose no lasting honour.
The arts reproach the scholar.

His teachers would better have shown him
horse training, or steering a ship,
or roping a plough to a bullock,
than manufacturing verse.

Balor's eye] the Fomorian monster whose mere glance could kill
113   Banba's . . . plain] a bardic name for Ireland

A pity that sage couldn't find
some craft more free from blame
—nailing planks or making buckets—
ere he came to the use of learning.

Men of base trade look down
on our woven rhetorical songs.
There's nothing for slaves, I think,
in our wise works' delicate ore.

The honour of verse is faded
and esteem for its guardians gone.
The schools of the land of Ireland
would do better to dig in the dirt.

And let them not think the scorn
is for poets and fine verse only.
It shames not them alone
but the glory of all the Gael.

It's not thought for the alien, either,
makes them spare Freamhann's peoples' jewels.
Rich men not sharing their wealth
will soon be left to famish.

And because their riches are wasted,
the wealth whole and entire
of Brega's youth, by goblets cheered,
these too have nothing to offer:

the waves of their courage are ebbed,
their games and their sports forbidden,
the hearts of Brega's fathers
concealed—soft cloaked in satin—

and kingly sons diminished
and poems made meaningless,
the rights of past kings hidden,
the feats of the Gael obscured.

Freamhann's people, Brega's youth, Brega's fathers] bardic names for the people of
Ireland

The Gael are blamed for their poetry.
Who now will prove best in friendship
and who prove best in defence?
Who will protect the right?

Need has descended upon them,
and our learned ones must take
the path they took of old
in search of Irial's people.

With them, among Banba's hosts,
our art had its beginning,
the seed of Rogh, in the oldest places.
So let it end with them.

In token, once, of which
twelve hundred druids were driven
to go in search of justice
to the great Clan of Rudhraig;

now the schools of Séadna's fair land,
such the demands upon them,
must make a similar journey
to visit Fear Dorcha's son.

Achieving our goal is left
in the power of a single hand,
the honeysuckle of Cobha Plain,
sole head of all our hope.

Mac Aonghusa has offered
to save the school at Tara.
Let others be cruel or gentle
to him men turn for succour.

As he holds the crown above all
through sternness of the ancient Gael,
so Art will be most generous
in time of greatest giving.

Irial] son of Conall Cernach, an ancient Ulster hero   Banba's hosts] a bardic
name for the people of Ireland   the seed of Rogh] Fergus, son of Rogh, grandson
of Rudhraig   Clan of Rudhraig] the ancestral family of Conall Cernach and other
Ulster heroes

Fear Dorcha's son scatters jewels,
others hoard their riches;
others' wealth is locked away,
he showers forth the flower of the world.

The lavishness that deserted
the hearts of Créidhe's high clan
stands fast in Art's sole heart
for all London's troops can say.

Like the Hound of Feats, he summons
the order of poets to his home.
Today as in the past
our hopes are with the blood of Rogh.

MATHGHAMHAIN Ó HIFEARNÁIN

fl. early 17th century

114   I ask, who will buy a poem?
        It holds right thoughts of scholars.
     Who needs it? Will anyone take it?
        A fine poem to make him immortal.

     A poem of close-knit skill,
        I have walked all Munster with it
     from market cross to cross
        for a year, and I'm no better off.

     Not a man or a woman would give me
        down-payment, no tiniest groat.
     And no one would tell me why
        —ignored by Gael and stranger.

     What use is a craft like this,
        a shame though it has to die?
     Making combs would earn more honour.
        Why would anyone take to verse?

113 the Hound of Feats] Cúchulainn

Corc of Cashel is dead, and Cian,
    who hoarded no cattle or cash,
men happy to pay their poets.
    So goodbye to the seed of Éibhear.

They kept the palm for giving
    until Cobhthach was lost, and Tál.
Many I leave unmentioned
    that I might have made poems for still.

I'm a ship with a ruined cargo
    now the famous Fitzgeralds are gone.
No answer. A terrible case.
    It is all in vain that I ask.

SEATHRÚN CÉITINN

1580–c. 1644

115 At the news from Fál's high plain I cannot sleep.
I am sick till doom at the plight of its faithful folk.
Long have they stood as a hedge against hostile trash
but a lot of the cockle has grown up through them at last.

O brazen Fódla, it is shameful you do not see
it were fitter to nourish Míle's sweet high race.
Not a drop is left in the plain of your smooth bright breast
—drained dry by the litter of every alien sow.

Any worthless crew that thought to cross the sea
to the fair, gold, age-old *lios* of Cobhthach 'the just',
theirs without struggle of hands our mighty mansions
and the choicest swards of our lovely-bordered places.

There's a new sort growing in the plain of Lugh the lithe
who are base by right, though they flourish their 'rolls' on high
—Eoghan's seed exhausted, Tál's blood troubled and broken,
and the youth of Bántsrath scattered in foreign lands.

Fál's high plain, Fódla, Míle's sweet high race, *lios* of Cobhthach, the plain of Lugh]
bardic names for Ireland and the Irish people

From the worthy chiefs of Nás not a stir of strength,
though fierce that awesome army's fire in battle,
manœuvring often under the nose of the State.
(Not theirs the shame that the law is honoured by none.)

If that high prince lived, of Áine and Drom Daoile,
or the great gift-generous lions of the Máigh,
this horde would have no place in the bend of the Bríde,
smashed, driven out, with outcry and loud wails.

If the Craftsman of Stars protect not Ireland's people
from violent vengeful enemies, bold and ready,
better gather and winnow them now without delay
and sail them out wandering safe on the waves of Clíona.

116

O lady full of guile,
    take away your hand.
Though you sicken for my love,
    I am not an active man.

Consider my grey hairs.
    Consider my slack body.
Consider my tired blood.
    What is it you want?

Don't think I am perverse.
    You need not tilt your head.
Let's love without the deed
    for ever, spirit slender.

Take your mouth from mine:
    grave is your condition.
Touch not skin to skin:
    the heat leads on to lust.

Your branching curly hair,
    your eye as grey as dew,
your sweet pale rounded breast
    excite the eye alone.

All deeds but that of the flesh
    —and lying in your quilt—
I will do for love of you,
    O lady full of guile.

PÁDRAIGÍN HAICÉAD

c. 1600–1654

117 *On Hearing it has been Ordered in the Chapterhouses of*
Ireland that the Friars make no more Songs or Verses

I heard from a decent man the other day
a piece of news from the 'spouse of Conn and Corc':
that the Church condemns our Gaelic's subtle paths,
the polished pleasure of our noble fathers.

I will not spring at the flank of their argument
now that the time is past when I could utter
each thought erupting from the scope of my mind,
when the edge of my intellect was a thing to fear

showering with no loss of pliant force
into the general flank of those arrogant priests
or down on top of their bald malignant skulls
a hard sharp fistful of accomplished darts.

I will stitch my mouth up with a twisted string
and say no word about their mean complaining,
merely condemn the herd of narrow censors
and the hate they bear my people, O my God.

PIARAS FEIRITÉAR

c. 1600–1653

118   Lay your weapons down, young lady.
               Do you want to ruin us all?
           Lay your weapons down, or else
               I'll have you under royal restraint.

---

117 spouse of Conn and Corc] Ireland

These weapons put behind you:
   hide henceforth your curling hair;
do not bare that white breast
   that spares no living man.

Lady, do you believe
   you've never killed, to North or South?
Your mild eye-glance has killed at large
   without the need of knife or axe.

You may think your knee's not sharp
   and think your palm is soft:
to wound a man, believe me,
   you need no knife or spear!

Hide your lime-white bosom,
   show not your tender flank.
For love of Christ let no one see
   your gleaming breast, a tuft in bloom.

Conceal those eyes of grey
   if you'd go free for all you've killed.
Close your lips, to save your soul;
   let your bright teeth not be seen.

Not few you have done to death:
   do you think you're not mortal clay?
In justice, put your weapons down
   and let us have no further ruin.

If you've terrified all you want,
   lady who seek my downfall,
now—before I am sunk in soil—
   your weapons, lay them down.

What your surname is, young lady,
   I leave to puzzle the world.
But add an 'a' or an 'é'
   and it gives your Christian name away . . .

DÁIBHÍ Ó BRUADAIR

*c.*1625–1698

119   *Adoramus Te, Christe*

Ghost of our blood, I worship You,
    Hero on Heaven's rampart,
Who left for love a mighty Father
    by Mary's grace to save us.
You made a leap like sun through glass
    to abolish Adam's evil
and saved with a cross Man and his tribe
    at Eastertime from Hell.

Harbour-candle that lulls to rest
    the quarrel of deadly dangers,
the poor man's soul, I beg of You,
    save, and restrain Satan.
Your broken side is all my fault,
    and the tracks of the three nails,
but do not shut Your calm bright eye
    upon me—make me welcome.

We regard Your nurse the more, God's son,
    that she was of David's line:
a virgin with milk, to prove the Law,
    with a mother's looks and grace,
bright, noble, fair to nurture You,
    Child, in a holy nook.
Pure like her never grew in womb
    nor will till the end of time.

120   O it's best be a total boor
                (though it's bad be a boor at all)
            if I'm to go out and about
                among these stupid people.

It's best to be, good people,
   a stutterer among you
since that is what you want,
   you blind ignorant crew.

If I found me a man to swap
   I'd give him my lovely skill.
He'd find it as good as a cloak
   around him against the gloom.

Since a man is respected more
   for his suit than for his talents
I regret what I've spent on my art,
   that I haven't it now in clothes.

Since happy in word and deed is each boorish clod
without music or metre or motherwit on his tongue,
I regret what I've wasted struggling with hard print
since the prime of life—that I might have spent as a boor.

121   *For the Family of Cúchonnacht Ó Dálaigh*

The high poets are gone
   and I mourn for the world's waning,
the sons of those learned masters
   emptied of sharp response.

I mourn for their fading books,
   reams of no earnest stupidity,
lost, unjustly abandoned,
   begotten by drinkers of wisdom.

After those poets, for whom art and knowledge were wealth,
   alas to have lived to see this fate befall us:
their books in corners greying into nothing
   and their sons without one syllable of their secret treasure.

122 A shrewish, barren, bony, nosy servant
refused me when my throat was parched in crisis.
May a phantom fly her starving over the sea,
the bloodless midget that wouldn't attend my thirst.

If I cursed her crime and herself, she'd learn a lesson.
The couple she serves would give me a cask on credit
but she growled at me in anger, and the beer nearby.
May the King of Glory not leave her long at her barrels.

A rusty little boiling with a musicless mouth,
she hurled me out with insult through the porch.
The Law requires I gloss over her pedigree
—but little the harm if she bore a cat to a ghost.

She's a club-footed slut and not a woman at all,
with the barrenest face you would meet on the open road,
and certain to be a fool to the end of the world.
May she drop her dung down stupidly into the porridge!

attributed to
TOMÁS 'LÁIDIR' MAC COISDEALBHAIGH
fl. mid 17th century

123 *Úna Bhán*

Úna fair, my flower of the amber tresses,
who have found your death on account of evil counsel,
see now, my caged love, which of the two counsels
was the better, and I in a ford in the Donogue river.

Úna fair, you have left me knotted in sorrow,
but what use talking about it again for ever?
Ringleted locks, with the melted gold ascending,
I would rather be near you than all the glory of Heaven.

Úna fair, it was you that upset my senses.
Úna, you came between me and my God, and deeply.
Úna, my fragrant branch, little coiling curl,
I'd better have been without eyes than ever have seen you.

A piercing pain: young Úna Nic Dhiarmada!
Fragrant branch, sweet-mannered, with speech like music;
sugar-sweet mouth, milk-fresh, like ale or wine;
foot supple of step and easy inside a shoe.

Úna, my heart, my limb, of the soft fresh breasts,
tempting green eyes, fine hair flowing yellow and thick,
let your dowry be a hundred cows—five hundred horses!—
I would choose yourself above all you might bring of treasure.

I had travelled, and hard the journey, through every province,
but her parents refused my hand, though fine and open.
The choicest flower of the Búille, and generous with cattle,
what good was it guarding her from me, and letting her perish?

Úna fair, like a rose you were in a garden
or a candlestick of gold on a queenly table.
You were song and music upon the way before me.
Ruin—bitter dawn: you not wed to your dark belovĕd.

English

LUKE WADDING
1588–1657

124   *For Innocents Day*

The Angell said to Joseph mild
Fly with the Mother and the Child
Out of this Land to Aegipt goe
The heavenly Babe will have it soe.
For that his hower is not yet come,
To dy for mans Redemption.

Proud Herod he doth froth and frowne
Feareth to loose Kingdome and Crown
Full of disdane and full of scorn
He must destroy this younge King borne.
But stay, his hower is not yet come
To dy for mans Redemption.

Herod foreb'are this cruell flood
Of the most pure Innocent blood
To thee a Crown this Child doth bring
To make thee happier than a King.
From highest heavens along he's come
To dy for mans Redemption.

125   *On the Circumsision: New Years Day*

To the tune of Neen Major Neale

This first day of the year
Jesus to us doth give
His pure and precious blood
That we in him may live
A most rare new-years gift
A greater none can have
A gift more rich and precious
None can desire or Crave.

This gift brings us great Joy,
And makes us all admire,
It proves His love for us
To be all flames and fire
And for our sake this day
Jesus is His sweet name,
A name which cost him deare
His blood's spilt for the same.

This name doth cost him deare
By Circumsision knife
For it this day he bleeds
And after gives his life

176

Coverd with costly Red
In his own blood He lies
Prepared to give the rest
When on the Cross he dyes.

Both heaven and earth admire.
And doe adore Jesus
To Himself this day severe,
And mercyfull to us
As soon as he's made man
And being but eight dayes Old
For us he gives his blood
More precious than all gold.

But how can Circumsision
With Jesus's name agree
The true marke of a sinner
To saviour Joyned be
If circumsis'd how saviour
If saviour why circumsis'd
Why should this marke of sinners
To saviour be apply'd.

What's done on this great day
By circumsis'd Jesus,
Is comfort and delight
Wonder and Joy to us
Who never had beginning
He by whom all begun
Begins this day the worke
Of our Salvation

Bless'd be this new years day
Bless'd be this name Jesus
Bless'd be this day of grace
And mercy unto us
Let's all put on new hearts
To give to our Jesus
No other new years gift
Doth he require from us.

Two Ballads of the Williamite Wars

Lilli Burlero

Ho! brother Teague, dost hear de decree
    Lilli burlero bullen a la
Dat we shall have a new debittie
    Lilli burlero bullen a la.
Lero, lero, lero, lero,
    Lilli burlero bullen a la
Lero, lero, lero, lero,
    Lilli burlero bullen a la.

Ho! by my shoul it is a Talbot
    [*refrain*]
And he will cut all the Englishmen's throat
    [*refrain*]

Though by my shoul de English do prat
De law's on dare side, and Chreist knows what

But if dispense do come from the Pope
We'll hang Magno Carto and demselves on a rope

And the good Talbot is made a lord
And he with brave lads is coming aboard

Who all in France have taken a swear
Dat dey will have no Protestant heir

Ara! but why does King James stay behind?
Ho! by my shoul 'tis a Protestant wind

But see de Tyrconnell is now come ashore
And we shall have commissions galore

And he that will not go to de mass
Shall be turned out and look like an ass

Now, now de heretics all go down
By Christ and St Patrick de nation's our own

There was an old prophecy found in a bog
That Ireland should be rul'd by an ass and a dog

And now this prophecy is come to pass
    Lilli burlero bullen a la
For Talbot's the dog and Tyrconnell's the ass
    Lilli burlero bullen a la.
Lero, lero, lero, lero,
    Lilli burlero bullen a la
Lero, lero, lero, lero,
    Lilli burlero bullen a la.

127   *The Boyne Water*

July the first, of a morning clear, one thousand six hundred and ninety,
King William did his men prepare—of thousands he had thirty—
To fight King James and all his foes, encamped near the Boyne Water;
He little feared, though two to one, their multitude to scatter.

King William called his officers, saying: 'Gentlemen, mind your station,
And let your valour here be shown before this Irish nation;
My brazen walls let no man break, and your subtle foes you'll scatter,
Be sure you show them good English play as you go over the water.'

Both foot and horse they marched on, intending them to batter,
But the brave Duke Schomberg he was shot as he crossed over the
    water.
When that King William did observe the brave Duke Schomberg
    falling,
He reined his horse with a heavy heart, on the Enniskillenes calling:

'What will you do for me, brave boys—see yonder men retreating?
Our enemies encouraged are, and English drums are beating.'
He says, 'My boys feel no dismay at the losing of one commander,
For God shall be our King this day, and I'll be general under.'

Within four yards of our fore-front, before a shot was fired,
A sudden snuff they got that day, which little they desired;
For horse and man fell to the ground, and some hung on their saddle:
Others turned up their forked ends, which we call coup de ladle.

Prince Eugene's regiment was the next, on our right hand advanced
Into a field of standing wheat, where Irish horses pranced;
But the brandy ran so in their heads, their senses all did scatter,
They little thought to leave their bones that day at the Boyne Water.

Both men and horse lay on the ground, and many there lay bleeding,
I saw no sickles there that day—but, sure, there was sharp shearing.
Now, praise God, all true Protestants, and heaven's and earth's Creator,
For the deliverance he sent our enemies to scatter.

The Church's foes will pine away, like churlish-hearted Nabal,
For our deliverer came this day like the great Zorobabal.
So praise God, all true Protestants, and I will say no further,
But had the Papists gained that day, there would have been open
    murder.
Although King James and many more were ne'er that way inclined,
It was not in their power to stop what the rabble they designed.

EIGHTEENTH CENTURY

SÉAMAS DALL MAC CUARTA
c. 1650–1733

(Translated from the Irish)

128   The houses of Corr an Chait are cold
      and cold their men and women.
Not for gold or wine
      would one of them come to greet you.

They wouldn't come to greet you
      for the whole world, East and West,
for the world from Earth to Heaven.
      And that is the badger's habit.

It's the badger's habit to burrow down
      night and day in the dark.
For the world from Earth to Heaven
      he wouldn't come to greet you.

King-badger loves not gaiety, sport nor pleasure;
these love not sage nor druid nor music-maker,
nor Seamus blind, nor Niall Óg's company.
So let them bide, burrowing in the dirt.

JONATHAN SWIFT
1667–1745

129   *On Stella's Birthday*

           Written AD 1718–[19]

Stella this day is thirty-four
(We shan't dispute a year or more),
However Stella, be not troubled,
Although thy size and years are doubled,

Since first I saw thee at sixteen
The brightest virgin on the green,
So little is thy form declin'd
Made up so largely in thy mind.
Oh, would it please the gods to split
Thy beauty, size, and years, and wit,
No age could furnish out a pair
Of nymphs so graceful, wise and fair
With half the lustre of your eyes,
With half your wit, your years and size:
And then before it grew too late,
How should I beg of gentle Fate
(That either nymph might have her swain)
To split my worship too in twain.

130   *The Description of an Irish Feast, translated
almost literally out of the original Irish*

Translated in the year 1720

O Rourk's noble fare
    Will ne'er be forgot,
By those who were there,
    Or those who were not.
His revels to keep,
    We sup and we dine,
On seven score sheep,
    Fat bullocks and swine.
Usquebagh to our feast
    In pails was brought up,
An hundred at least,
    And a madder our cup.
O there is the sport,
    We rise with the light,
In disorderly sort,
    From snoring all night.
O how was I trick'd,
    My pipe it was broke,
My pocket was pick'd,
    I lost my new cloak.

130 Usquebagh] whiskey   madder] wooden vessel

I'm rifled, quoth Nell,
  Of mantle and kercher,
Why then fare them well,
  The De'il take the searcher.
Come, harper, strike up,
  But first by your favour,
Boy, give us a cup;
  Ay, this has some savour:
O Rourk's jolly boys
  Ne'er dreamt of the matter,
Till rous'd by the noise,
  And musical clatter,
They bounce from their nest,
  No longer will tarry,
They rise ready dressed,
  Without one *Ave Mary*.
They dance in a round,
  Cutting capers and ramping,
A mercy the ground
  Did not burst with their stamping.
The floor is all wet
  With leaps and with jumps,
While the water and sweat,
  Splish, splash in their pumps.
Bless you late and early,
  Laughlin O Enagin,
By my hand, you dance rarely,
  Margery Grinagin.
Bring straw for our bed,
  Shake it down to the feet,
Then over us spread,
  The winnowing sheet.
To show, I don't flinch,
  Fill the bowl up again,
Then give us a pinch
  Of your sneezing; *a Yean*.
Good Lord, what a sight,
  After all their good cheer,
For people to fight
  In the midst of their beer:
They rise from their feast,

a Yean (recte: *A bhean*)] woman

And hot are their brains,
A cubit at least
   The length of their skeans.
What stabs and what cuts,
   What clatt'ring of sticks,
What strokes on the guts,
   What bastings and kicks!
With cudgels of oak,
   Well harden'd in flame,
An hundred heads broke,
   An hundred struck lame.
You churl, I'll maintain
   My father built Lusk,
The castle of Slane,
   And Carrickdrumrusk:
The Earl of Kildare,
   And Moynalta, his brother,
As great as they are,
   I was nurs'd by their mother.
Ask that of old Madam,
   She'll tell you who's who,
As far up as Adam,
   She knows it is true,
Come down with that beam,
   If cudgels are scarce,
A blow on the weam,
   Or a kick on the arse.

131   *The Progress of Poetry*

The farmer's goose, who in the stubble,
Has fed without restraint, or trouble;
Grown fat with corn and sitting still,
Can scarce get o'er the barn-door sill:
And hardly waddles forth, to cool
Her belly in the neighb'ring pool:
Nor loudly cackles at the door;
For cackling shews the goose is poor.

130 skeans (*recte*: *scian*)] knives, or daggers

But when she must be turn'd to graze,
And round the barren common strays,
Hard exercise, and harder fare
Soon make my dame grow lank and spare:
Her body light, she tries her wings,
And scorns the ground, and upward springs,
While all the parish, as she flies,
Hear sounds harmonious from the skies.

Such is the poet, fresh in pay
(The third night's profits of his play);
His morning-draughts till noon can swill,
Among his brethren of the quill:
With good roast beef his belly full,
Grown lazy, foggy, fat, and dull:
Deep sunk in plenty, and delight,
What poet e'er could take his flight?
Or stuff'd with phlegm up to the throat,
What poet e'er could sing a note?
Nor Pegasus could bear the load,
Along the high celestial road;
The steed, oppress'd, would break his girth,
To raise the lumber from the earth.

But, view him in another scene,
When all his drink is Hippocrene,
His money spent, his patrons fail,
His credit out for cheese and ale;
His two-year's coat so smooth and bare,
Through ev'ry thread it lets in air;
With hungry meals his body pin'd,
His guts and belly full of wind;
And, like a jockey for a race,
His flesh brought down to flying-case:
Now his exalted spirit loathes
Encumbrances of food and clothes;
And up he rises like a vapour,
Supported high on wings of paper;
He singing flies, and flying sings,
While from below all Grub Street rings.

132   *Clever Tom Clinch Going to be Hanged*
                    Written in the year 1726

As clever Tom Clinch, while the rabble was bawling,
Rode stately through Holborn, to die in his calling;
He stopt at the George for a bottle of sack,
And promis'd to pay for it when he'd come back.
His waistcoat and stockings, and breeches were white,
His cap had a new cherry ribbon to tie't.
The maids to the doors and the balconies ran,
And said, lack-a-day! he's a proper young man.
But, as from the windows the ladies he spied,
Like a beau in the box, he bow'd low on each side;
And when his last speech the loud hawkers did cry,
He swore from his cart, it was all a damn'd lie.
The hangman for pardon fell down on his knee;
Tom gave him a kick in the guts for his fee.
Then said, I must speak to the people a little,
But I'll see you all damn'd before I will whittle.
My honest friend Wild, may he long hold his place,
He lengthen'd my life with a whole year of grace.
Take courage, dear comrades, and be not afraid,
Nor slip this occasion to follow your trade.
My conscience is clear, and my spirits are calm,
And thus I go off without Pray'r-Book or Psalm.
Then follow the practice of clever Tom Clinch,
Who hung like a hero, and never would flinch.

133   *Holyhead. Sept. 25, 1727*

                Lo here I sit at Holyhead
                With muddy ale and mouldy bread
                All Christian victuals stink of fish
                I'm where my enemies would wish
                Convict of lies is every sign,
                The inn has not one drop of wine
                I'm fasten'd both by wind and tide
                I see the ship at anchor ride

        132 *whittle*] turn informer, 'peach'

The Captain swears the sea's too rough
He has not passengers enough.
And thus the Dean is forc'd to stay
Till others come to help the pay
In Dublin they'd be glad to see
A packet though it brings in me.
They cannot say the winds are cross
Your politicians at a loss
For want of matter swears and frets,
Are forced to read the old gazettes.
I never was in haste before
To reach that slavish hateful shore
Before, I always found the wind
To me was most malicious kind
But now, the danger of a friend
On whom my fears and hopes depend
Absent from whom all climes are curst
With whom I'm happy in the worst
With rage impatient makes me wait
A passage to the land I hate.
Else, rather on this bleaky shore
Where loudest winds incessant roar
Where neither herb nor tree will thrive,
Where nature hardly seems alive,
I'd go in freedom to my grave,
Than rule yon isle and be a slave.

134   from *The Life and Character of Dean Swift*

The day will come, when't shall be said,
'D'ye hear the news—? the Dean is dead—!
Poor man! he went, all on a sudden—!'
Ha's dropp'd, and giv'n the crow a pudden!
What money was behind him found?
'I hear about two thousand pound—
'Tis own'd he was a man of wit—,'
Yet many a foolish thing he writ—;
'And, sure he must be deeply learn'd—!'
That's more than ever I discern'd—;
'I know his nearest friends complain,
He was too airy for a dean—.

He was an honest man I'll swear—:'
Why Sir, I differ from you there,
For, I have heard another story,
He was a most confounded Tory—!
'Yet here we had a strong report,
That he was well-receiv'd at Court—.'
Why, then it was, I do assert,
Their goodness, more than his desert—.
He grew, or else his comrades lied,
Confounded dull—, before he died—.

. . . . . .

'Must we the Drapier then forget?
Is not our nation in his debt?
'Twas he that writ the Drapier's Letters—!'
He should have left them for his betters;
We had a hundred abler men,
Nor need depend upon his pen—.
Say what you will about his reading,
You never can defend his breeding!
Who, in his satires running riot,
Could never leave the world in quiet—;
Attacking, when he took the whim,
Court, city, camp, all one to him—.

. . . . . .

What scenes of evil he unravels,
In satires, libels, lying travels!
Not sparing his own clergy-cloth,
But, eats into it, like a moth—!

. . . . . .

I envy not the wits who write
Merely to gratify their spite;
Thus did the Dean: his only scope
Was, to be held a misanthrope.
This into gen'ral odium drew him,
Which if he lik'd, much good may do him:
This gave him enemies in plenty,
Throughout two realms nineteen in twenty.
His zeal was not to lash our crimes,
But, discontent against the times;

For, had we made him timely offers,
To raise his post, or fill his coffers,
Perhaps he might have truckled down,
Like other brethren of his gown,
For party he would scarce have bled—:
I say no more—, because he's dead—.

    .   .   .   .   .   .

What writings had he left behind—?
'I hear, they're of a diff'rent kind:
A few, in verse; but most, in prose—.'
Some high-flown pamphlets, I suppose—:
All scribbled in the worst of times,
To palliate his friend Oxford's crimes,
To praise Queen Anne, nay more, defend her,
As never fav'ring the Pretender—:
Or libels yet conceal'd from sight—,
Against the Court to shew his spite—.
Perhaps, his Travels, Part the Third;
A lie, at ev'ry second word:
Offensive to a loyal ear—:
But—not one sermon, you may swear—.

'Sir, our accounts are diff'rent quite,
And your conjectures are not right;
'Tis plain, his writings were design'd
To please, and to reform mankind;
And, if he often miss'd his aim,
The world must own it, to their shame;
The praise is his, and theirs the blame.

'Then, since you dread no further lashes,
You freely may forgive his ashes.'

135   from *Verses on the Death of Dr Swift*

The time is not remote, when I
Must by the course of nature die:
When I foresee my special friends,
Will try to find their private ends:
Tho' it is hardly understood,
Which way my death can do them good:

Yet, thus methinks, I hear 'em speak;
See, how the Dean begins to break:
Poor gentleman, he droops apace,
You plainly find it in his face:

.

For poetry, he's past his prime,
He takes an hour to find a rhyme:
His fire is out, his wit decay'd,
His fancy sunk, his muse a jade.
I'd have him throw away his pen;
But there's no talking to some men.

.   .   .   .   .

Behold the fatal day arrive!
'How is the Dean?' 'He's just alive.'
Now the departing prayer is read:
He hardly breathes. The Dean is dead.
Before the passing-bell begun,
The news thro' half the town has run.

.   .   .   .   .

From Dublin soon to London spread,
'Tis told at Court, the Dean is dead.
Kind Lady Suffolk in the spleen,
Runs laughing up to tell the Queen.
The Queen, so gracious, mild, and good,
Cries, 'Is he gone? 'Tis time he should.'

.   .   .

My female friends, whose tender hearts
Have better learn'd to act their parts,
Receive the news in doleful dumps,
'The Dean is dead, (and what is trumps?)
Then Lord have mercy on his soul.
(Ladies I'll venture for the Vole.)
Six deans they say must bear the pall.
(I wish I knew what king to call.)
Madam, your husband will attend
The funeral of so good a friend.
No madam, 'tis a shocking sight,
And he's engag'd tomorrow night!

My Lady Club would take it ill,
If he should fail her at quadrille.
He lov'd the Dean. (I lead a heart.)
But dearest friends, they say, must part.
His time was come, he ran his race;
We hope he's in a better place.'

Why do we grieve that friends should die?
No loss more easy to supply.
One year is past; a different scene;
No further mention of the Dean;
Who now, alas, no more is miss'd,
Than if he never did exist.
Where's now this fav'rite of Apollo?
Departed; and his works must follow:
Must undergo the common fate;
His kind of wit is out of date.
Some country squire to Lintot goes,
Enquires for Swift in verse and prose:
Says Lintot, 'I have heard the name:
He died a year ago.' The same.
He searcheth all his shop in vain;
'Sir you may find them in Duck Lane:
I sent them with a load of books,
Last Monday to the pastry-cooks.
To fancy they could live a year!
I find you're but a stranger here.
The Dean was famous in his time;
And had a kind of knack at rhyme:
His way of writing now is past;
The town hath got a better taste:
I keep no antiquated stuff;
But, spick and span I have enough.
Pray, do but give me leave to show 'em;
Here's Colley Cibber's Birthday Poem.
This ode you never yet have seen,
By Stephen Duck, upon the Queen.
Then, here's a letter finely penn'd
Against the craftsman and his friend;
It clearly shows that all reflection
On Ministers, is disaffection.
Next, here's Sir Robert's Vindication,
And Mr Henley's last oration:

The hawkers have not got 'em yet,
Your Honour please to buy a set?

    .   .   .   .   .

Suppose me dead; and then suppose
A club assembled at the Rose;
Where from discourse of this and that,
I grow the subject of their chat:
And, while they toss my name about,
With favour some, and some without;
One quite indiff'rent in the cause,
My character impartial draws:

'The Dean, if we believe report,
Was never ill receiv'd at Court:
As for his works in verse and prose,
I own myself no judge of those:
Nor, can I tell what critics thought 'em;
But, this I know, all people bought 'em;
As with a moral view design'd
To cure the vices of mankind:
His vein, ironically grave,
Expos'd the fool, and lash'd the knave:
To steal a hint was never known,
But what he writ was all his own.

'He never thought an honour done him,
Because a duke was proud to own him:
Would rather slip aside, and choose
To talk with wits in dirty shoes:

    .   .   .   .   .

'With princes kept a due decorum,
But never stood in awe before 'em:
And to her Majesty, God bless her,
Would speak as free as to her dresser,
She thought it his peculiar whim,
Nor took it ill as come from him.
He follow'd David's lesson just,
In princes never put thy trust.
And, would you make him truly sour;
Provoke him with *a slave in power*:
The Irish Senate, if you nam'd,
With what impatience he declaim'd!

Fair Liberty was all his cry;
For her he stood prepar'd to die;
For her he boldly stood alone;
For her he oft expos'd his own.
Two kingdoms, just as faction led,
Had set a price upon his head;
But, not a traitor could be found,
To sell him for six hundred pound.

'Had he but spar'd his tongue and pen
He might have rose like other men:
But, power was never in his thought;
And, wealth he valu'd not a groat:

. . . . . .

'His friends in exile, or the Tower,
Himself within the frown of power;
Pursu'd by base envenom'd pens,
Far to the land of slaves and fens;
A servile race in folly nurs'd,
Who truckle most, when treated worst.

. . . . . .

'The Dean did by his pen defeat
An infamous destructive cheat.
Taught fools their int'rest how to know;
And gave them arms to ward the blow.
Envy hath own'd it was his doing,
To save that helpless land from ruin,
While they who at the steerage stood,
And reap'd the profit, sought his blood.

. . . . . .

'But Heav'n his innocence defends,
The grateful people stand his friends:
Not strains of law, nor judges' frown,
Nor topics brought to please the Crown,
Nor witness hir'd, nor jury pick'd,
Prevail to bring him in convict.

'In exile with a steady heart,
He spent his life's declining part;

Where, folly, pride, and faction sway,
Remote from St John, Pope, and Gay.

'His friendship there to few confin'd,
Were always of the middling kind:
No fools of rank, a mongrel breed,
Who fain would pass for lords indeed:
Where titles give no right or power,
And peerage is a wither'd flower,
He would have held it a disgrace,
If such a wretch had known his face.
On rural squires, that kingdom's bane,
He vented oft his wrath in vain:
Biennial squires, to market brought,
Who sell their souls and votes for naught;
The nation stripp'd, go joyful back,
To rob the Church, their tenants rack,
Go snacks with thieves and rapparees,
And keep the peace to pick up fees:
In every job to have a share,
A jail or barrack to repair;
And turn the tax for public roads
Commodious to their own abodes.

'Perhaps I may allow, the Dean
Had too much satire in his vein;
And seem'd determin'd not to starve it,
Because no age could more deserve it.
Yet, malice never was his aim;
He lashed the vice but spar'd the name.
No individual could resent,
Where thousands equally were meant.
His satire points at no defect,
But what all mortals may correct;
For he abhorr'd that senseless tribe,
Who call it humour when they jibe:
He spar'd a hump or crooked nose,
Whose owners set not up for beaux.
True genuine dullness mov'd his pity,
Unless it offer'd to be witty.
Those, who their ignorance confess'd,
He ne'er offended with a jest;

But laugh'd to hear an idiot quote,
A verse from Horace, learn'd by rote.

'He knew an hundred pleasant stories,
With all the turns of Whigs and tories:
Was cheerful to his dying day,
And friends would let him have his way.

'He gave the little wealth he had,
To build a house for fools and mad:
And show'd by one satiric touch,
No nation wanted it so much:
That kingdom he hath left his debtor,
I wish it soon may have a better.'

AOGÁN Ó RATHAILLE

*c.*1675–1729

(Translated from the Irish)

136   Brightness most bright I beheld on the way, forlorn.
Crystal of crystal her eye, blue touched with green.
Sweetness most sweet her voice, not stern with age.
Colour and pallor appeared in her flushed cheeks.

Curling and curling, each strand of her yellow hair
as it took the dew from the grass in its ample sweep;
a jewel more glittering than glass on her high bosom
—created, when she was created, in a higher world.

True tidings she revealed me, most forlorn,
tidings of one returning by royal right,
tidings of the crew ruined who drove him out,
and tidings I keep from my poem for sheer fear.

Foolish past folly, I came to her very presence
bound tightly, her prisoner (she likewise a prisoner . . .).
I invoked Mary's Son for succour: she started from me
and vanished like light to the fairy dwelling of Luachair.

Heart pounding, I ran, with a frantic haste in my race,
by the margins of marshes, through swamps, over bare moors.
To a powerful palace I came, by paths most strange,
to that place of all places, erected by druid magic.

All in derision they tittered—a gang of goblins
and a bevy of slender maidens with twining tresses.
They bound me in bonds, denying the slightest comfort,
and a lumbering brute took hold of my girl by the breasts.

I said to her then, in words that were full of truth,
how improper it was to join with that drawn gaunt creature
when a man the most fine, thrice over, of Scottish blood
was waiting to take her for his tender bride.

On hearing my voice she wept in high misery
and flowing tears fell down from her flushed cheeks.
She sent me a guard to guide me out of the palace
—that brightness most bright I beheld on the way, forlorn.

The Knot

Pain, disaster, downfall, sorrow and loss!
Our mild, bright, delicate, loving, fresh-lipped girl
with one of that black, horned, foreign, hate-crested crew
and no remedy near till our lions come over the sea.

137 The drenching night drags on: no sleep or snore,
no stock, no wealth of sheep, no horned cows.
This storm on the waves nearby has harrowed my head
—I who ate no winkles or dogfish in my youth!

If that guardian King from the bank of the Leamhan lived on,
with all who shared his fate (and would pity my plight)
to rule that soft, snug region, bayed and harboured,
my people would not stay poor in Duibhne country.

137 the Leamhan] the river Laune   Duibhne country] in the Dingle Peninsula,
Co. Kerry

Great Carthy, fierce and fine, who loathed deceit;
with Carthy of the Laoi, in yoke unyielding, faint;
and Carthy King of Ceann Toirc with his children, buried;
it is bitterness through my heart they have left no trace.

My heart has dried in my ribs, my humours soured,
that those never-niggardly lords, whose holdings ranged
from Caiseal to Clíona's Wave and out to Thomond,
are savaged by alien hordes in land and townland.

You wave down there, lifting your loudest roar,
the wits in my head are worsted by your wails.
If help ever came to lovely Ireland again
I'd wedge your ugly howling down your throat!

138   *The Vision*

One morning ere Titan had thought to stir his feet,
on the top of a fine high hill I had laboured up,
I chanced on a pleasant flock of joyous girls,
a troop from Sídh Seanadh's bright mansions to the north.

A film of enchantment spread, of aspect bright,
from the shining boulders of Galway to Cork of the harbours:
clusters of fruit appearing in every treetop,
acorns in woods, pure honey upon the stones.

Three candles they lit, of indescribable light,
on Cnoc Fírinne's lofty summit in Conallach Rua.
Then I followed the flock of cloaked women as far as Thomond
and questioned them on their diligent round of tasks.

Then answered the lady Aoibhill, of aspect bright,
they had cause to light three candles above the harbours:
in the name of the faithful king who is soon to come
to rule and defend the triple realm for ever.

137 the Laoi] the river Lee   Ceann Toirc] Kanturk, Co. Cork

I started up—soft, sudden—out of my dream
believing the good news Aoibhill told me was true,
but found that I was nerve-shaken, downcast and morose
that morning ere Titan had thought to stir his feet.

139   *Valentine Browne*

A mist of pain has covered my dour old heart
since the alien devils entered the land of Conn;
our Western Sun, Munster's right ruler, clouded
—there's the reason I'd ever to call on you, Valentine Browne.

First, Cashel's company gone, its guest-houses and youth;
the gabled palace of Brian flooded dark with otters;
Ealla left leaderless, lacking royal Munster sons
—there's the reason I'd ever to call on you, Valentine Browne.

The deer has altered her erstwhile noble shape
since the alien raven roosted in Ros's fastness;
fish fled the sunlit stream and the quiet current
—there's the reason I'd ever to call on you, Valentine Browne.

Dairinis in the West with no Earl of the noble race;
in Hamburg, to our cost, that Earl over gay peaceful hawks;
and these old grey eyes weeping for both these things
—there's the reason I'd ever to call on you, Valentine Browne.

Feathers of the swift bird-flock drift on the wind
tattered like a cat's fur in a waste of heather;
cattle deny the flow of milk to their calves
—since 'Sir Val' walked into the rights of the gentle Carthy.

Into the uplands Pan directed his gaze
to see where that Mars vanished, who left us to die.
Dwarf monsters have taken up the Blade of the Three
and hacked our dead across from heel to top.

140   No help I'll call till I'm put in the narrow coffin.
By the Book, it would bring it no nearer if I did!
Our prime strong-handed prop, of the seed of Eoghan
—his sinews are pierced and his vigour is withered up.

Wave-shaken is my brain, my chief hope gone.
There's a hole in my gut, there are foul spikes through my
    bowels.
Our land, our shelter, our woods and our level ways
are pawned for a penny by a crew from the land of Dover.

The Sionainn, the Life, the musical Laoi, are muffled
and the Biorra Dubh river, the Bruice, the Bríd, the Bóinn.
Reddened are Loch Dearg's narrows and the Wave of Tóim
since the Knave has skinned the crowned King in the game.

Incessant my cry; I spill continual tears;
heavy my ruin; I am one in disarray.
No music is nigh as I wail about the roads
except for the noise of the Pig no arrows wound.

That lord of the Rinn and Cill, and the Eoghanacht country
—want and injustice have wasted away his strength.
A hawk now holds those places, and takes their rent,
who favours none, though near to him in blood.

Our proud royal line is wrecked; on that account
the water ploughs in grief down from my temples,
sources sending their streams out angrily
to the river that flows from Truipeall to pleasant Eochaill.

I will stop now—my death is hurrying near
now the dragons of the Leamhan, Loch Léin and the Laoi are
    destroyed.
In the grave with this cherished chief I'll join those kings
my people served before the death of Christ.

      the seed of Eoghan] a Munster noble family

CATHAL BUÍ MAC GIOLLA GHUNNA

c. 1680–1756

(Translated from the Irish)

The Yellow Bittern

Bittern, I'm sorry to see you stretched
   with your bones decayed and eaten away.
Not want of food but need of a drink
   has brought you so to lie face up.
I feel it worse than the ruin of Troy
   to see you stretched on the naked stones,
who caused no hurt nor harm in the world,
   as happy with boghole water as wine.

It hurts, fair bittern, a thousandfold
   —your fallen head on the open road,
whose honk I heard in the early mornings
   out on the mud as you took your drink.
Everyone tells your brother Cathal
   that's certainly how I'm going to die.
Not so. Behold this handsome bird
   so lately dead for want of a drop.

Sorrow, young bittern, a thousandfold
   to see you before me among the clumps,
and the big rats travelling toward your wake,
   taking part in the fun and games.
If only you'd sent me word in time
   that you were in trouble and needed a drink
I'd have dealt a blow at Vesey's lake
   would have wetted your mouth and your innards too.

Your other birds I don't lament,
   blackbird, thrush, or the grey crane,
but my yellow bittern full of heart
   so like myself in face and hue.
He was for ever taking a drink
   and they say I'm the same from time to time
—but I'll leave undrunk no drop I find
   for fear I'd catch my death of thirst.

200

My darling said give up the drink
    or I've only a little while to live
but I told her that she told a lie,
    the selfsame drink prolongs my life.
Have ye not seen this smooth-necked bird
    that died of thirst a while ago?
So wet your lips, my neighbours dear.
    There won't be a drop when you're dead and gone.

OLIVER GOLDSMITH

1728–1774

142   from *The Traveller*

On Freedom and Ambition

Ye powers of truth, that bid my soul aspire,
Far from my bosom drive the low desire;
And thou, fair Freedom, taught alike to feel
The rabble's rage, and tyrant's angry steel;
Thou transitory flower, alike undone
By proud contempt, or favour's fostering sun,
Still may thy blooms the changeful clime endure,
I only would repress them to secure:
For just experience tells, in every soil,
That those who think must govern those that toil;
And all that freedom's highest aims can reach,
Is but to lay proportion'd loads on each.
Hence, should one order disproportion'd grow,
Its double weight must ruin all below.

O then how blind to all that truth requires,
Who think it freedom when a part aspires!
Calm is my soul, nor apt to rise in arms,
Except when fast-approaching danger warms:
But when contending chiefs blockade the throne,
Contracting regal power to stretch their own;
When I behold a factious band agree
To call it freedom when themselves are free;

Each wanton judge new penal statutes draw,
Laws grind the poor, and rich men rule the law;
The wealth of climes, where savage nations roam,
Pillag'd from slaves to purchase slaves at home;
Fear, pity, justice, indignation start,
Tear off reserve, and bare my swelling heart;
Till half a patriot, half a coward grown,
I fly from petty tyrants to the throne.

Yes, brother, curse with me that baleful hour,
When first ambition struck at regal power;
And thus polluting honour in its source,
Gave wealth to sway the mind with double force.
Have we not seen, round Britain's peopled shore,
Her useful sons exchang'd for useless ore?
Seen all her triumphs but destruction haste,
Like flaring tapers bright'ning as they waste;
Seen opulence, her grandeur to maintain,
Lead stern depopulation in her train,
And over fields where scatter'd hamlets rose,
In barren solitary pomp repose?
Have we not seen, at pleasure's lordly call,
The smiling long-frequented village fall?
Beheld the duteous son, the sire decay'd,
The modest matron, and the blushing maid,
Forc'd from their homes, a melancholy train,
To traverse climes beyond the western main;
Where wild Oswego spreads her swamps around,
And Niagara stuns with thund'ring sound?

E'en now, perhaps, as there some pilgrim strays
Through tangled forests, and through dangerous ways;
Where beasts with man divided empire claim,
And the brown Indian marks with murd'rous aim;
There, while above the giddy tempest flies,
And all around distressful yells arise,
The pensive exile, bending with his woe,
To stop too fearful, and too faint to go,
Casts a long look where England's glories shine,
And bids his bosom sympathise with mine.

Vain, very vain, my weary search to find
That bliss which only centres in the mind:

Why have I stray'd from pleasure and repose,
To seek a good each government bestows?
In every government, though terrors reign,
Though tyrant kings, or tyrant laws restrain,
How small, of all that human hearts endure,
That part which laws or kings can cause or cure.
Still to ourselves in every place consign'd,
Our own felicity we make or find:
With secret course, which no loud storms annoy,
Glides the smooth current of domestic joy.
The lifted axe, the agonising wheel,
Luke's iron crown, and Damien's bed of steel,
To men remote from power but rarely known,
Leave reason, faith, and conscience, all our own.

143   from *The Deserted Village*

Sweet smiling village, loveliest of the lawn,
Thy sports are fled, and all thy charms withdrawn;
Amidst thy bowers the tyrant's hand is seen,
And desolation saddens all thy green:
One only master grasps the whole domain,
And half a tillage stints thy smiling plain:
No more thy glassy brook reflects the day,
But chok'd with sedges, works its weedy way.
Along thy glades, a solitary guest,
The hollow-sounding bittern guards its nest;
Amidst thy desert walks the lapwing flies,
And tires their echoes with unvaried cries.
Sunk are thy bowers in shapeless ruin all,
And the long grass o'ertops the mould'ring wall;
And trembling, shrinking from the spoiler's hand,
Far, far away, thy children leave the land.

Ill fares the land, to hast'ning ills a prey,
Where wealth accumulates, and men decay:
Princes and lords may flourish, or may fade;
A breath can make them, as a breath has made;
But a bold peasantry, their country's pride,
When once destroy'd, can never be supplied.

A time there was, ere England's griefs began,
When every rood of ground maintain'd its man;
For him light labour spread her wholesome store,
Just gave what life requir'd, but gave no more:
His best companions, innocence and health;
And his best riches, ignorance of wealth.

But times are alter'd; trade's unfeeling train
Usurp the land and dispossess the swain;
Along the lawn, where scatter'd hamlets rose,
Unwieldy wealth, and cumbrous pomp repose;
And every want to opulence allied,
And every pang that folly pays to pride.

   .   .   .   .   .

Sweet Auburn! parent of the blissful hour,
Thy glades forlorn confess the tyrant's power.
Here as I take my solitary rounds,
Amidst thy tangling walks, and ruin'd grounds,
And, many a year elaps'd, return to view
Where once the cottage stood, the hawthorn grew,
Remembrance wakes with all her busy train,
Swells at my breast, and turns the past to pain.

   .   .   .   .   .

Sweet was the sound, when oft at evening's close
Up yonder hill the village murmur rose;
There, as I pass'd with careless steps and slow,
The mingling notes came soften'd from below;
The swain responsive as the milk-maid sung,
The sober herd that low'd to meet their young;
The noisy geese that gabbled o'er the pool,
The playful children just let loose from school;
The watchdog's voice that bay'd the whisp'ring wind,
And the loud laugh that spoke the vacant mind;
These all in sweet confusion sought the shade,
And fill'd each pause the nightingale had made.
But now the sounds of population fail,
No cheerful murmurs fluctuate in the gale,
No busy steps the grass-grown foot-way tread,
For all the bloomy flush of life is fled.
All but yon widow'd, solitary thing
That feebly bends beside the plashy spring;

She, wretched matron, forc'd, in age, for bread,
To strip the brook with mantling cresses spread,
To pick her wintry faggot from the thorn,
To seek her nightly shed, and weep till morn;
She only left of all the harmless train,
The sad historian of the pensive plain.

Near yonder copse, where once the garden smil'd,
And still where many a garden flower grows wild;
There, where a few torn shrubs the place disclose,
The village preacher's modest mansion rose.
A man he was to all the country dear,
And passing rich with forty pounds a year;
Remote from towns he ran his godly race,
Nor e'er had chang'd, nor wished to change his place;
Unpractis'd he to fawn, or seek for power,
By doctrines fashion'd to the varying hour;
Far other aims his heart had learned to prize,
More skill'd to raise the wretched than to rise.
His house was known to all the vagrant train,
He chid their wand'rings, but reliev'd their pain;
The long-remember'd beggar was his guest,
Whose beard descending swept his aged breast;
The ruin'd spendthrift, now no longer proud,
Claim'd kindred there, and had his claims allow'd;
The broken soldier, kindly bade to stay,
Sat by his fire, and talk'd the night away;
Wept o'er his wounds, or tales of sorrow done,
Shoulder'd his crutch, and show'd how fields were won.
Pleas'd with his guests, the good man learn'd to glow,
And quite forgot their vices in their woe;
Careless their merits, or their faults to scan,
His pity gave ere charity began.

.   .   .   .   .   .

Beside yon straggling fence that skirts the way,
With blossom'd furze unprofitably gay,
There, in his noisy mansion, skill'd to rule,
The village master taught his little school;
A man severe he was, and stern to view;
I knew him well, and every truant knew;
Well had the boding tremblers learn'd to trace
The day's disasters in his morning face;

Full well they laugh'd, with counterfeited glee,
At all his jokes, for many a joke had he;
Full well the busy whisper, circling round,
Convey'd the dismal tidings when he frown'd;
Yet he was kind; or if severe in aught,
The love he bore to learning was in fault;
The village all declar'd how much he knew;
'Twas certain he could write, and cipher too;
Lands he could measure, terms and tides presage,
And e'en the story ran that he could gauge.
In arguing too, the parson own'd his skill,
For e'en though vanquish'd, he could argue still;
While words of learned length and thund'ring sound
Amazed the gazing rustics rang'd around,
And still they gaz'd, and still the wonder grew,
That one small head could carry all he knew.

But past is all his fame. The very spot
Where many a time he triumph'd, is forgot.
Near yonder thorn, that lifts its head on high,
Where once the sign-post caught the passing eye,
Low lies that house where nut-brown draughts inspir'd,
Where grey-beard mirth and smiling toil retir'd,
Where village statesmen talk'd with looks profound,
And news much older than their ale went round.
Imagination fondly stoops to trace
The parlour splendours of that festive place;
The white-wash'd wall, the nicely sanded floor,
The varnish'd clock that click'd behind the door;
The chest contriv'd a double debt to pay,
A bed by night, a chest of drawers by day;
The pictures plac'd for ornament and use,
The twelve good rules, the royal game of goose;
The hearth, except when winter chill'd the day,
With aspen boughs, and flowers, and fennel gay;
While broken tea-cups, wisely kept for show,
Rang'd o'er the chimney, glisten'd in a row.

. . . .

Thither no more the peasant shall repair
To sweet oblivion of his daily care;
No more the farmer's news, the barber's tale,
No more the wood-man's ballad shall prevail;

No more the smith his dusky brow shall clear,
Relax his pond'rous strength, and lean to hear;
The host himself no longer shall be found
Careful to see the mantling bliss go round;
Nor the coy maid, half willing to be press'd,
Shall kiss the cup to pass it to the rest.

  . . . . . .

Ye friends to truth, ye statesmen, who survey
The rich man's joys increase, the poor's decay,
'Tis yours to judge, how wide the limits stand
Between a splendid and a happy land.

  . . . . . .

Yet count our gains. This wealth is but a name
That leaves our useful products still the same.
Not so the loss. The man of wealth and pride
Takes up a space that many poor supplied;
Space for his lake, his park's extended bounds,
Space for his horses, equipage, and hounds;
The robe that wraps his limbs in silken sloth
Has robb'd the neighbouring fields of half their growth,
His seat, where solitary sports are seen,
Indignant spurns the cottage from the green;
Around the world each needful product flies,
For all the luxuries the world supplies:
While thus the land adorn'd for pleasure, all
In barren splendour feebly waits the fall.

  . . . . . .

Where then, ah! where, shall poverty reside,
To 'scape the pressure of contiguous pride?
If to some common's fenceless limits stray'd,
He drives his flock to pick the scanty blade,
Those fenceless fields the sons of wealth divide,
And e'en the bare-worn common is denied.

If to the city sped—What waits him there?
To see profusion that he must not share;
To see ten thousand baneful arts combin'd
To pamper luxury, and thin mankind;
To see those joys the sons of pleasure know
Extorted from his fellow creature's woe.

Here, while the courtier glitters in brocade,
There the pale artist plies the sickly trade;
Here, while the proud their long-drawn pomps display,
There the black gibbet glooms beside the way.
The dome where Pleasure holds her midnight reign
Here, richly deck'd, admits the gorgeous train;
Tumultuous grandeur crowds the blazing square,
The rattling chariots clash, the torches glare.
Sure scenes like these no troubles e'er annoy!
Sure these denote one universal joy!
Are these thy serious thoughts?—Ah, turn thine eyes
Where the poor houseless shiv'ring female lies.
She once, perhaps, in village plenty bless'd,
Has wept at tales of innocence distress'd;
Her modest looks the cottage might adorn,
Sweet as the primrose peeps beneath the thorn;
Now lost to all; her friends, her virtue fled,
Near her betrayer's door she lays her head,
And, pinch'd with cold, and shrinking from the shower,
With heavy heart deplores that luckless hour,
When idly first, ambitious of the town,
She left her wheel and robes of country brown.

Do thine, sweet Auburn, thine, the loveliest train,
Do thy fair tribes participate her pain?
E'en now, perhaps, by cold and hunger led,
At proud men's doors they ask a little bread!

Ah, no. To distant climes, a dreary scene,
Where half the convex world intrudes between,
Through torrid tracts with fainting steps they go,
Where wild Altama murmurs to their woe.
Far different there from all that charm'd before,
The various terrors of that horrid shore;
Those blazing suns that dart a downward ray,
And fiercely shed intolerable day;
Those matted woods where birds forget to sing,
But silent bats in drowsy clusters cling;
Those pois'nous fields with rank luxuriance crown'd,
Where the dark scorpion gathers death around;
Where at each step the stranger fears to wake
The rattling terrors of the vengeful snake;

Where crouching tigers wait their hapless prey,
And savage men more murd'rous still than they;
While oft in whirls the mad tornado flies,
Mingling the ravag'd landscape with the skies.
Far different these from every former scene,
The cooling brook, the grassy-vested green,
The breezy covert of the warbling grove,
That only shelter'd thefts of harmless love.

    .   .   .   .

E'en now the devastation is begun,
And half the business of destruction done;
E'en now, methinks, as pond'ring here I stand,
I see the rural virtues leave the land:
Down where yon anchoring vessel spreads the sail,
That idly waiting flaps with ev'ry gale,
Downward they move, a melancholy band,
Pass from the shore, and darken all the strand.
Contented toil, and hospitable care,
And kind connubial tenderness, are there;
And piety, with wishes plac'd above,
And steady loyalty, and faithful love.
And thou, sweet Poetry, thou loveliest maid,
Still first to fly where sensual joys invade;
Unfit in these degenerate times of shame,
To catch the heart, or strike for honest fame;
Dear charming nymph, neglected and decried,
My shame in crowds, my solitary pride;
Thou source of all my bliss, and all my woe,
That found'st me poor at first, and keep'st me so;
Thou guide by which the nobler arts excel,
Thou nurse of every virtue, fare thee well!
Farewell, and Oh! where'er thy voice be tried,
On Torno's cliffs, or Pambamarca's side,
Whether where equinoctial fervours glow,
Or winter wraps the polar world in snow,
Still let thy voice, prevailing over time,
Redress the rigours of th' inclement clime;
Aid slighted truth; with thy persuasive strain
Teach erring man to spurn the rage of gain;
Teach him, that states of native strength possess'd,
Though very poor, may still be very bless'd;

That trade's proud empire hastes to swift decay,
As ocean sweeps the labour'd mole away;
While self-dependent power can time defy,
As rocks resist the billows and the sky.

144   *A Sonnet*

        Weeping, murmuring, complaining,
            Lost to every gay delight;
        Myra, too sincere for feigning,
            Fears th' approaching bridal night.

        Yet, why impair thy bright perfection?
            Or dim thy beauty with a tear?
        Had Myra followed my direction,
            She long had wanted cause of fear.

145   *Translation of a South American Ode*

        In all my Enna's beauties blest,
            Amidst profusion still I pine;
        For though she gives me up her breast,
            Its panting tenant is not mine.

146   *Elegy on the Death of a Mad Dog*

            from *The Vicar of Wakefield*

        Good people all, of every sort,
            Give ear unto my song;
        And if you find it wond'rous short,
            It cannot hold you long.

        In Islington there was a man,
            Of whom the world might say,
        That still a godly race he ran,
            Whene'er he went to pray.

A kind and gentle heart he had,
   To comfort friends and foes;
The naked every day he clad,
   When he put on his clothes.

And in that town a dog was found,
   As many dogs there be,
Both mongrel, puppy, whelp, and hound,
   And curs of low degree.

This dog and man at first were friends;
   But when a pique began,
The dog, to gain some private ends,
   Went mad and bit the man.

Around from all the neighbouring streets
   The wond'ring neighbours ran,
And swore the dog had lost his wits,
   To bite so good a man.

The wound it seem'd both sore and sad
   To every Christian eye;
And while they swore the dog was mad,
   They swore the man would die.

But soon a wonder came to light,
   That show'd the rogues they lied:
The man recover'd of the bite,
   The dog it was that died.

147   *Song*

from *The Vicar of Wakefield*

When lovely woman stoops to folly,
   And finds too late that men betray,
What charm can soothe her melancholy,
   What art can wash her guilt away?

The only art her guilt to cover,
   To hide her shame from every eye,
To give repentance to her lover,
   And wring his bosom, is—to die.

148 *Song*

from *She Stoops to Conquer*

Let school-masters puzzle their brain,
   With grammar, and nonsense, and learning;
Good liquor, I stoutly maintain,
   Gives *genus* a better discerning.
Let them brag of their heathenish gods,
   Their Lethes, their Styxes, and Stygians:
Their Quis, and their Quaes, and their Quods,
   They're all but a parcel of Pigeons.
               Toroddle, toroddle, toroll.

When Methodist preachers come down
   A-preaching that drinking is sinful,
I'll wager the rascals a crown
   They always preach best with a skinful.
But when you come down with your pence,
   For a slice of their scurvy religion,
I'll leave it to all men of sense,
   But you, my good friend, are the pigeon.
               Toroddle, toroddle, toroll.

Then come, put the jorum about,
   And let us be merry and clever;
Our hearts and our liquors are stout;
   Here's the Three Jolly Pigeons for ever.
Let some cry up woodcock or hare,
   Your bustards, your ducks, and your widgeons;
But of all of the birds in the air,
   Here's a health to the Three Jolly Pigeons.
               Toroddle, toroddle, toroll.

149 from *Retaliation*

A Poem

Of old, when Scarron his companions invited,
Each guest brought his dish, and the feast was united;
If our landlord supplies us with beef, and with fish,
Let each guest bring himself, and he brings the best dish:

Our Dean shall be venison, just fresh from the plains;
Our Burke shall be tongue, with a garnish of brains;
Our Will shall be wild-fowl, of excellent flavour,
And Dick with his pepper shall heighten their savour:
Our Cumberland's sweet-bread its place shall obtain,
And Douglas is pudding, substantial and plain:
Our Garrick's a salad; for in him we see
Oil, vinegar, sugar, and saltness agree:
To make out the dinner, full certain I am,
That Ridge is anchovy, and Reynolds is lamb;
That Hickey's a capon, and by the same rule,
Magnanimous Goldsmith a gooseberry fool.
At a dinner so various, at such a repast,
Who'd not be a glutton, and stick to the last?
Here, waiter! more wine, let me sit while I'm able,
Till all my companions sink under the table;
Then, with chaos and blunders encircling my head,
Let me ponder, and tell what I think of the dead.

Here lies the good Dean, re-united to earth,
Who mix'd reason with pleasure, and wisdom with mirth:
If he had any faults, he has left us in doubt,
At least, in six weeks, I could not find 'em out;
Yet some have declar'd, and it can't be denied 'em,
That sly-boots was cursedly cunning to hide 'em.

Here lies our good Edmund, whose genius was such,
We scarcely can praise it, or blame it too much;
Who, born for the universe, narrow'd his mind,
And to party gave up what was meant for mankind.
Though fraught with all learning, yet straining his throat
To persuade Tommy Townshend to lend him a vote;
Who, too deep for his hearers, still went on refining,
And thought of convincing, while they thought of dining;
Though equal to all things, for all things unfit,
Too nice for a statesman, too proud for a wit:
For a patriot, too cool; for a drudge, disobedient;
And too fond of the *right* to pursue the *expedient*.
In short, 'twas his fate, unemploy'd, or in place, Sir,
To eat mutton cold, and cut blocks with a razor.

.   .   .   .

Here lies David Garrick, describe me, who can,
An abridgment of all that was pleasant in man;

As an actor, confess'd without rival to shine:
As a wit, if not first, in the very first line:
Yet, with talents like these, and an excellent heart,
The man had his failings, a dupe to his art.
Like an ill-judging beauty, his colours he spread,
And beplaster'd with rouge his own natural red.
On the stage he was natural, simple, affecting;
'Twas only that when he was off he was acting.
With no reason on earth to go out of his way,
He turn'd and he varied full ten times a day.
Though secure of our hearts, yet confoundedly sick
If they were not his own by finessing and trick,
He cast off his friends, as a huntsman his pack,
For he knew when he pleas'd he could whistle them back.
Of praise a mere glutton, he swallow'd what came,
And the puff of a dunce he mistook it for fame;
Till his relish grown callous, almost to disease,
Who pepper'd the highest was surest to please.
But let us be candid, and speak out our mind,
If dunces applauded, he paid them in kind.
Ye Kenricks, ye Kellys, and Woodfalls so grave,
What a commerce was yours, while you got and you gave!
How did Grub Street re-echo the shouts that you rais'd,
While he was be-Roscius'd, and you were be-prais'd!
But peace to his spirit, wherever it flies,
To act as an angel, and mix with the skies:
Those poets, who owe their best fame to his skill,
Shall still be his flatterers, go where he will.
Old Shakespeare, receive him, with praise and with love,
And Beaumonts and Bens be his Kellys above.

. . . .

Here Reynolds is laid, and, to tell you my mind,
He has not left a better or wiser behind:
His pencil was striking, resistless, and grand;
His manners were gentle, complying, and bland;
Still born to improve us in every part,
His pencil our faces, his manners our heart:
To coxcombs averse, yet most civilly steering,
When they judg'd without skill he was still hard of hearing:
When they talk'd of their Raphaels, Correggios, and stuff,
He shifted his trumpet, and only took snuff.

EOGHAN RUA Ó SÚILLEABHÁIN

1748–1784

(Translated from the Irish)

150   from 'Séamas, light-hearted and loving
              friend of my breast'

To Séamas Fitzgerald

Séamas, light-hearted and loving friend of my breast,
Greek-Geraldine-blooded, valiant and terrible in arms,
supply in good order one smooth clean shaft for my spade
and, to finish the show, add tastefully one foot-piece.

When you have done, and my weapon's in elegant order,
since the learning won't pay in a lifetime to drown my thirst
I'll not pause in my going till I've brought my spade to Galway
where daily I'll get my pay: my keep and a sixpence.

At the end of the day, if my bones be weary or weak,
and the foreman consider my spadecraft less than heroic,
I'll discourse serenely upon *The Adventure of Death*
or the wars of the Greeks at Troy, that exhausted princes.

Then I will speak in due course of Samson the hero,
Alexander the mighty, hungry to face the foe,
of the reign of the Caesars, valiant and terrible in arms,
or Hector the hero who left hundreds dead on the field,

of Caitcheann Mac Tréin who wrought slaughter and loss on
    Fianna,
and the doings of Deirdre, in body and beauty supreme;
to finish, deceiving and rambling, I'll chant him a poem
—and there for you, Séaras, is how I will spend the day.

Passing the day in such manner, I'll take my pay
and tie it with hempen rope in the front of my shirt.
Then in the best of good humour I'll come to town
and not squander a part of a sixpence until we meet.

For you're one like myself, tormented by thirst in your time.
In the pub by the road let us look for excitement together:
'Ale!' I will lavishly order, and drinks to the counter,
and I'll save not a halfpenny pay till the day I die!

151   *A Magic Mist*

Through the deep night a magic mist led me
    like a simpleton roaming the land,
no friends of my bosom beside me,
    an outcast in places unknown.
I stretched out dejected and tearful
    in a nut-sheltered wood all alone
and prayed to the bright King of Glory
    with 'Mercy!' alone on my lips.

My heart, I declare, full of turmoil
    in that wood with no human sound nigh,
the thrush's sweet voice the sole pleasure,
    ever singing its tunes on each bough.
Then a noble *sídh*-girl sat beside me
    like a saint in her figure and form:
in her countenance roses contended
    with white—and I know not which lost.

Furrowed thick, yellow-twisting and golden
    was the lady's hair down to her shoes,
her brows without flaw, and like amber
    her luring eye, death to the brave.
Sweet, lovely, delicious—pure music—
    the harp-notes of the *sídh* from her lips,
breasts rounded, smooth, chalk-white, most proper,
    never marred by another, I swear.

Though lost to myself till that moment,
    with love for the lady I throbbed
and I found myself filled with great pleasure
    that she was directed my way.
How it fell, I write out in these verses,
    how I let my lips speak unrestrained,
the sweet things that I told the fair maiden
    as we stretched on the green mountain-slope:

216

'Are you, languid-eyed lady who pierced me
   with love for your face and your form,
the Fair-One caused hordes to be slaughtered
   as they write in the Battle of Troy?
Or the mild royal girl who let languish
   the chief of Boru and his troop?
Or the queen who decreed that the great prince
   from Howth follow far in pursuit?'

Delicious, sweet, tender, she answered,
   ever shedding tears down in her pain:
'I am none of those women you speak of,
   and I see that you don't know my clan.
I'm the bride wed in bliss for a season,
   under right royal rule, to the King
over Caiseal of Conn and of Eoghan
   who ruled undisputed o'er Fódla.

'Gloomy my state, sad and mournful,
   by horned tyrants daily devoured,
and heavy oppressed by grim blackguards
   while my prince is set sailing abroad.
I look to the great Son of Glory
   to send my lion back to his sway
in his strong native towns, in good order,
   to flay the swarth goats with his blades.'

'Mild, golden-haired, courteous fair lady,
   of true royal blood, and no lie,
I mourn for your plight among blackguards,
   sad and joyless, dark under a pall.
If your King to his strong native mansions
   the Son of Glory should send, in His aid,
those swarth goats—swift, freely and willing—
   with shot would I joyfully flay!

'If our Stuart returned o'er the ocean
   to the lands of Inis Áilge in full course
with a fleet of Louis' men, and the Spaniard's,
   by dint of joy truly I'd be
on a prancing pure steed of swift mettle
   ever sluicing them out with much shot
—after which I'd not injure my spirit
   standing guard for the rest of my life.'

ANONYMOUS

(Translated from the Irish)

152   *Two Epigrams*

The world laid low, and the wind blew like a dust
Alexander, Caesar, and all their followers.
Tara is grass; and look how it stands with Troy.
And even the English—maybe they might die.

*   *   *

Loss of our learning brought darkness, weakness and woe
on me and mine, amid these unrighteous hordes.
Oafs have entered the places of the poets
and taken the light of the schools from everyone.

EIBHLÍN DHUBH NÍ CHONAILL

fl. 1770

(Translated from the Irish)

153   from *The Lament for Art Ó Laoghaire*

My steadfast love!
When I saw you one day
by the market-house gable
my eye gave a look
my heart shone out
I fled with you far
from friends and home.

And never was sorry:
you had parlours painted
rooms decked out
the oven reddened
and loaves made up
roasts on spits

and cattle slaughtered;
I slept in duck-down
till noontime came
or later if I liked.

My steadfast friend!
It comes to my mind
that fine Spring day
how well your hat looked
with the drawn gold band,
the sword silver-hilted,
your fine brave hand
and menacing prance,
and the fearful tremble
of treacherous enemies.
You were set to ride
your slim white-faced steed
and Saxons saluted
down to the ground,
not from goodwill
but by dint of fear
—though you died at their hands,
my soul's beloved.

     .   .   .   .   .

My steadfast friend!
I didn't credit your death
till your horse came home
and her reins on the ground,
your heart's blood on her back
to the polished saddle
where you sat—where you stood . . .
I gave a leap to the door,
a second leap to the gate
and a third on your horse.

I clapped my hands quickly
and started mad running
as hard as I could,
to find you there dead
by a low furze-bush
with no Pope or bishop
or clergy or priest

to read a psalm over you
but a spent old woman
who spread her cloak corner
where your blood streamed from you
and I didn't stop to clean it
but drank it from my palms.

  . . . . . .

Long loss, bitter grief
I was not by your side
when the bullet was fired
so my right side could take it
or the edge of my shift
till I freed you to the hills,
my fine-handed horseman!

  . . . . .

Ruin and bad cess to you,
ugly traitor Morris,
who took the man of my house
and father of my young ones
—a pair walking the house
and the third in my womb,
and I doubt that I'll bear it.

My friend and beloved!
When you left through the gate
you came in again quickly,
you kissed both your children,
kissed the tips of my fingers.
You said: 'Eibhlín, stand up
and finish with your work
lively and swiftly:
I am leaving our home
and may never return.'
I made nothing of his talk
for he often spoke so.

  . . . . .

My steadfast love!
When you walked through the servile
strong-built towns,
the merchants' wives

would salute to the ground
knowing well in their hearts
a fine bed-mate you were
a great front-rider
and father of children.

Jesus Christ well knows
there's no cap on my skull
nor shift next my body
nor shoe on my foot-sole
nor stick in my house
nor reins on the brown mare
but I'll spend it on the law;
that I'll go across the ocean
to argue with the King,
and if he won't pay attention
that I'll come back again
to the black-blooded savage
that took my treasure.

.   .   .   .

My love and my beloved!
Your corn-stacks are standing,
your yellow cows milking.
Your grief upon my heart
all Munster couldn't cure,
nor the smiths of Oileán na bhFionn.
Till Art Ó Laoghaire comes
my grief will not disperse
but cram my heart's core,
shut firmly in
like a trunk locked up
when the key is lost.

Women there weeping,
stay there where you are,
till Art Mac Conchúir summons drink
with some extra for the poor
—ere he enter that school
not for study or for music
but to bear clay and stones.

the smiths of Oileán na bhFionn] mythical fairy healers   ere he enter that school]
the darkness (see no. 80) of the churchyard in Kilcrea Abbey

BRIAN MERRIMAN

1749–1805

(Translated from the Irish)

The Midnight Court

By the brink of the river I'd often walk,
on a meadow fresh, in the heavy dew,
along the woods, in the mountain's heart,
happy and brisk in the brightening dawn.
My heart would lighten to see Loch Gréine,
the land, the view, the sky horizon,
the sweet and delightful set of the mountains
looming their heads up over each other.
It would brighten a heart worn out with time,
or spent, or faint, or filled with pain
—or the withered and sour, without means or wealth—
to gaze for a while across the woods
at the shoals of ducks on the cloudless bay
and a swan between them, sailing with them,
at fishes jumping on high for joy,
the flash of a stripe-bellied glittering perch,
the hue of the lake, the blue of the waves
heavy and strong as they rumble in.
There were birds in the trees, content and gay,
a leaping doe in the wood nearby,
sounding horns, a crowd in view,
and Reynard ahead of the galloping hounds.

Yesterday morning the sky was clear.
The sun was in Cancer, a blazing mass,
just setting to work as the night was done,
the task for the day stretched out before it.
Foliage branched on the boughs above,
the grasses close at hand were dense
with verdant growth and flowers and herbs
to drive all careworn thoughts away.
Weary I was, sleep bore me down,
and level I stretched in the verdant grass
not far from the trees, in a handy hollow,

and propped my head and stretched my limbs.
I firmly fastened shut my eyes,
securely fixed and locked in sleep,
my face contentedly covered from flies
—when I suffered in dream a swirling torment
that stripped and racked me and pierced my heart
in a heavy swoon, as I lost my wits.

I hadn't slept long when it seemed I heard
the neighbouring lands all rocking around me
and a northerly gale in a fearful blast
hammering sparks from the harbour jetty.
One glance of my eye and it seemed to me
by the harbour's edge I saw advancing
a frightful, fierce, fat, full-bummed female,
thick-calved, bristling, bony and harsh,
her height exact—if I guessed it right—
six yards or seven, with something over.
An even perch of her cloak trailed off
away in the mud, bemired and foul.
She was huge and grim; an aspect wild
sat on her scarred and eaten brow.
Incarnate horror—a fright to the land!—
was the grin of her gums, all chapped and gapped.
And, King of all heroes, her plank-like hand
grasped a pole with sinewy power
with a brazen symbol spiked on top
and a bailiff's powers inscribed across it.

She harshly spoke, in accents blunt:
'Awake, vile sleepyhead! Stir yourself
out of your misery, flat on your flank
with the Court in session and thousands flocking
—no baseless Court devoid of law,
no plundering Court of the kind you're used to,
but the Circuit Court of a gentle people,
a merciful, capable Court of maidens.
Let the seed of Éibhear now admire
these noble shapes in concord ranged
two days and a night on the mountain peak
in their palace thronged, Magh Gréine's mansion.
Hard it has galled the gracious King
and the household princes there appearing

—and all the followers in their train—
how things fall short in the land of Fáil:
for her ancient seed no land or liberty,
power or law or lease or leader,
her fields laid waste and nothing to show
where its crops have been but worts and weeds,
the finest nobles strayed abroad
and upstart cash with the upper hand,
smiling fraud, indifferent rape,
the afflicted skinned and the naked ruined.
Dreary and dire, severe and sour
—a total bondage—our laws are buried:
the poor and powerless finding chaos
on every hand, and a rush toward ruin;
lawyers' deceit, the sneer of power,
lying and fraud, neglect and favour,
Justice weak and the Law beclouded,
blinded by falsehood, fees and bribes.

'At all events (or with few left out)
a cause is sworn this day on the Book
—and bitterly sworn—not soon to fade:
with the core of our youth by palsy rotted
and a shortage of people living in Ireland;
with the human seed in our time decayed
and the land abandoned, empty and spent,
consumed without cease by war and death;
with the pride of kings gone over the brine
and none discovered to fill their place
and a shameful shortage of colts amongst us
—women in droves on land and sea,
viragos stout, in youthful pride,
bouncing staves of meat and blood,
the tiresome idle, the idle easy,
the neat and nice all going to waste
and every sort of vigorous virgin
still to be fattened in body and bust,
ready if only they're given the word
to drop from the branch (and I praise their patience!)—
the sages have judged, in consultation,
against this servitude aforesaid,
and that one of their potent company,
by a cast of the dice, be dropped in Fódla.

So Aoibheall has offered, of upright heart,
sí-woman of Craig Liath, Munster's friend,
to leave that host of learned masters
loosening bonds for a while amongst us.
Gentle and sweet, she has undertaken
to overcome false Law with force,
to stand beside the weak and needy
till the strong are made to show them mercy.
Might without right must yield with grace
and right, as is right, shall take its place.
I swear that neither tricks, compulsion,
friendship of 'miss' or 'pimp' or party,
shall walk through the Law, as once they did,
in this Court that will sit in heavenly session.
The Court is henceforth fixed in Fiacail.
Answer the summons! Set out at once.
March quick, at your peril—no more ado.
March! Or you'll drag in the muck behind me!'

She hooked her crook in the back of my collar
and started out with a fiery force.
She snatched me with her down the valley
by Mánmhuí Hill to the chapel gable.
And there I saw, by torches lit,
that lovely building, glowing and fair,
sturdy and shining, bristling, bright,
brilliant and strong, fine-doored and firm.
I saw the *sí*-woman, civil and mild,
sit strong on the bench of Right and Freedom.
I saw the powerful guard, attentive,
haughty and huge, drawn up beside her.
I saw, as well, a crowded household,
women and men, from floor to ceiling.
And I saw a slow-eyed, noble lady,
moist-lipped, delicate-fingered, soft,
sweet, winning, agreeable, curled and fair,
standing on high at the bench of oaths.
Her hair was loose and tumbled down,
care in her looks was firmly fixed,
there was force in her stare, and fire in her eyes
boiling with anger for argument
but her utterance blocked by a burning breast
—mute, not a whisper, impulse choked—

such that she would rather death
and a flow in freedom issuing out
as she stood like a dart on the platform, rigid,
beating her hands and wringing her claws.
At last great cisternfuls she wept.
After some sobs her voice returned.
Her misery passed, her aspect altered,
she wiped her face, and spoke as follows:

'Joy from the heart, a thousand welcomes,
wise, ancient Aoibheall come from Craig Liath
—light of the day, untrammelled moon,
worldly treasure locked in bondage,
winning queen of the hosts of bliss,
in Thomond and Tír Luirc greatly missed.
The base of my case and my complaint,
the cause of my torment and fatigue,
why I've lost my bearings, sailing senseless,
worn like a mist with burning pains,
is the handsome maids in this world below
thrown meanly aside without guilt or crime
or guide or goal, and wasting in hosts
into dirty hags without husbands' love.
In my travels already I've met, myself,
a hundred and one would not have refused
(and myself among them, more's the pity)
that are sunk like sods without child or man.
It is hurt and hardship, grieved as I am,
without coin or comfort, profit or peace,
dejected, destitute, dreary and dark
without rest or sleep or nightly joy,
by sorrow insulted, stretched uneasy
on a lukewarm bed with my pounding thoughts.

'Respectable people of Craig, look lively
on the women of Banba bound in hardship.
O weakened heart, if the men go on
the way they are going we'll have to steal them!
By the time it strikes them to take a partner
there isn't a person left would have them
—limp, sucked dry, exhausted ancients.
If it happens at all, in the heat of youth,
that a man out of seven, on feeling his beard,

goes out with a girl, it's never some mild one
nicely settled in seed and breed,
well-mannered, gentle, soft, and shapely,
who can seat herself or make an entrance,
but an icy dullard or woeful ghost
with an ill-fitting dowry gathered in pain.
It's a scald to my heart and drives me wild
with my brain worn out and all its broodings
ill, at an ebb, in pain, exhausted,
lamenting and wailing—a pitiful leavings—
when I see a courageous, cordial man,
busy and bouncing, alive and alert,
knowing and skilful, sturdy and warm,
sweet-cheeked, laughing, loving and fine,
or a firm-footed boy, well-balanced and brisk,
commanding and proper, well-fashioned and fair,
bargained and bought and in wedlock bound
to a worm or a fool, a hag or a half-wit
slovenly slut of an indolent girl,
sullen and sulky, a whinge and a shame,
ignorant, fussy, a gossipy nag,
nosy and nasty, ill-tempered, inert.
Destruction and ruin! Some ignorant sulk,
some trollop all feet, with her hair unfixed,
is being bound this night, and it burns me sore
—for where is my fault I'm not chosen first?

'Where is the cause I remain unloved
and I so slender, fine and shy?
My mouth so good, and my teeth and smile?
I've a glowing complexion, a tender brow.
I have delicate eyes and a forelock fine,
curled and plaited and looped and twined.
My features, free from dirt or grime,
are fine-drawn, shapely, timid and bright.
My throat and bosom, hands and fingers,
seize between them beauty's prize.
Observe my waist! How slight the bones.
No baldness here. Am I bent, or stiff?
Bum, body and limbs: no cause for shame.
And safe under cover my nameless gem.
I'm no slut of a girl, no slug of a woman,
but handsome and good, delightful and fair,

no sloven or slattern or streel in a mess,
no ill-mannered heap you can't ease or please,
no useless hussy or festering mope,
but a maiden as choice as choice can be!

'If my spirits were sagging like some of the neighbours,
stupid and slow, without wisdom or wit
or vision or verve in the use of my looks,
I'd have cause to be crying, and fall in despair.
But I never went out in the public gaze,
at weddings or wakes, with old or young,
off at the sports or a dance or the races,
mixing with people all over the plain,
but I dressed at my ease and with never a flaw
in the finest of garments from head to foot,
my hair wound round, with its share of powder,
the back of my bonnet starched and set,
with a shiny hood and no shortage of ribbons,
a gown all speckled and finished with frills;
and never was missing an airy facing,
handsome and fine, on my crimson cloak,
or flowers and fruits and birds in plenty
on my striped and queenly cambric slip,
or shaped and slender dainty heels,
shiny and high, screwed under my shoes,
or buckles and rings and silken gloves,
bracelets and hoops or the dearest lace.

'Careful, then; I'm not fearful or shy,
a sheepish child or a witless fool,
lonely and worried or crying in fear,
feeble or touched, unbalanced or blind.
I won't be dodging the people's gaze;
my face and my brow are proud and high.
And I'm certainly always on display
at every field where the game's fought hard,
at dances, hurling, races, courting,
bone-fires, gossip and dissipation,
at fairs and markets and Sunday Mass
to see and be seen, and choose a man.
But I've wasted my sense in the hopeless hunt;
they deceived me ever and wrung my guts
after my wooing and lapse and love

and all I've suffered of awful anguish,
and all I spent on tossing the cups,
on muttering women, and hags with cards!

'There isn't a trick you can hear or read of
when the moon is new, or reaches the full,
at Shrovetide, Samhain—the whole year through—
but I've found it silly to seek for sense in it.
I never could settle me down to sleep
without fruit in a sock beneath my ear;
I found it no trouble to fast devoutly
—three vigils I'd swallow no bite or sup;
I'd rinse my shift against the stream
for a whisper in dream from my future spouse;
many a time I have swept the corn-stack,
I've left my nails and my hair in the ash,
I'd place the flail behind the fork
and quietly under my pillow, a spade;
in the kiln by the ford, I'd place my distaff,
in Raghnall's lime-kiln, my ball of thread,
out in the street, a seed of flax,
and under my bedding a head of cabbage.
There isn't a trick I have just related
but I prayed of the Devil and all his brethren!
But the point and purpose of my tale
is I've done my best and I've still no man;
hence, alas, my long recital!
In the knot of the years I am tangled tight,
I am heading hard for my days of grey
and I fear that I'll die without anyone asking.

'O Pearl of Heaven! I call and cry,
I beg and beseech! My soul upon you!
Don't let me wander and streel about,
a slovenly hag without vigour or bloom,
stale and unwanted at stingy hearths,
without family, friends, relief or rest.
Thunder and lightning! Jesus' blood!
I was fooled—an idiot: whole, entire—
while the pick of the worst and the fools of Fódla
got their hands on the goods before my eyes:
Sadhbh has a rich and restful brute,
Muireann is merry, her face to her mate,

Mór and Marcella are buried in comfort,
jeering between them and joking about me.
Sláine and Síle are skittish and easy
and Áine and Cecily, their litters around them;
and more, likewise, of the nation's women,
and me as I am, without issue or milk,
a long time useless, worn by weakness.

'But grant me time—the cure is at hand:
a matter of herbs decayed and devilish
and magical charms, to gain me yet
a handsome boy, some elegant heir,
and win me over his love and affection.
A lot of the kind I have seen employed
and I could make use of the same devices . . .
A sterling aid in arranging pairs
is the bite of an apple, or powdered herbs
—little Balls-of-Joy or Lumps-of-Dung,
the Shining Splicer, or Hammer-the-Hole,
Nannygoat's-Bait or Maiden's Dart,
Goldenlove—all lustful spells,
the burning up of leaves in secret,
and more of the like that shouldn't be learned.
It's a thing of great wonder, Thomond over,
that the maiden yonder obtained a spouse
—but she told me at Shrove, in confidence
(and the wedding occurred on the verge of Samhain!)
that she ate and drank, this lady fair,
nothing but bog-flies burnt in ale!
I'm a long time waiting. I need release.
Enough delay. Spur on with speed!
If your circuit-round can't cure my colic
serious measures I'll have to take!'

Then up there leaped a mangy elder
in venomous haste, all fire and fuss
with shivering limbs and palpitations
and fury and frenzy in all his bones
—a woeful sight for the Court, in truth—
and I heard him say at the witness table:

'Hurt and harm and perpetual heart-scald!
You infamous slut of a line of beggars!

No wonder, I say, that the sun shines weak,
no wonder the horrors that happen in Ireland
—no law nor order, Justice blighted,
our milch cows giving no milk or calves,
and the rest of the ruin that's over the land—
with these latest fashions on Mór and Síle!
Slovenly slut, don't we all remember
your own descent from an evil people?
There's nothing to praise in your ugly elders
—pedlars, beggars and useless louts.
We know the crawler you had for a father
without friend or fame or backing or cash,
a grey-haired slob without sense or learning,
plate or pleasure, or food or sauce,
not a rag to his crotch, and a coatless back,
a twig round his waist, and soleless shoes.
O people, believe, if himself and his lot
were sold at a fair, 'twould be all he could do
after paying their debts—by the saintly dead!—
to buy a good tankard of drink with the leavings!

'It's a terrible scandal and show for the people
that a wretch like yourself, without cattle or sheep,
should have shoes with a buckle, a silken cloak,
and a pocket hanky a-flap on the breeze!
You can baffle the world with the show you put on
but I know what you are by the cut of your cap.
I am nearly speechless—I know you have nothing:
it's a while since your back had the help of a shift
but it's only the wicked would know it was missing
with the fancy cuff on your cambric sleeve.
Canvas in plenty you have on your waist
and nobody knows it's not stays that hold you.
Frillies and rings you show to the world
while your rashes and cracks are by gloves disguised.
Confess to the Court—or I'll tell it myself—
how long since you drank a good drop with your meal!
A wretched soft heap, with dirty feet,
you are hard on your body, with Bucks and no meat!
It's easy enough get your hair to gleam,
but my eyes have seen the hutch where you lie
with nothing stretched under you (smooth or rough,
the crudest tow, or wheel-spun linen)

but a rubbishy mat without cover or quilt,
not a plaid or a rug or a stitch, stripped bare
in the back of a hut with no place to sit
but the soot dripping wet and the rising damp,
weeds appearing in great profusion
and the signs of hens inscribed across it,
a weakened ridge and bending beams
and a brown downpour profusely falling.

'O Fates' Beloved! How tall she talks!
How highly and mightily she proceeds
at large in her colours and silken cloak,
a sight for ever. But where was it got?
Tell where you found your fancy show.
Tell how you earned these senseless rags.
A lawful source would be hard to prove
—for since when have you owned an inch of earth?
The cost of your cowl, will you tell where it came from,
and tell where you came on the cost of your dress
and (leaving aside how the coat was got)
tell how you came on the cost of the shoes?

'Aoibheall, lofty, loving and powerful,
I pray and adjure: O answer and aid!
For it's true, I admit, that the wards of Fódla
are pinned in their place by these plunderers' ilk.
On the hand of a friend: I know of a neighbour
near to our village, not far from home,
a simple boy, naïve and trusting,
who met one once that became his wife.
It sours my heart when I behold her,
her flash and her finish, her flourish and pomp,
with her herd of cows and her barley growing,
money in pocket and gold in hand.
Yesterday there on the side of the street
I saw her: the spit of a powerful woman!
Fat in her force; a jeer; unreliable;
hardened with nagging and brimming with cheek.
Except that I'd sooner not waken scandal,
spread slander abroad or get lost in gossip
I could easy repeat what I heard—verbatım—
on foot of her tattered and battered condition,
dragged to the ground with their roars around her,

flung on the street, stretched out in a stable.
Her fame will live, there'll be talk for ever
of her name and her shame and her dirty doings
in Íbh Breacáin, of the bread and wine,
in the level plains of Mac Callán country,
in Bainis and Inis with noble and mean
and Cill Bhreacáin and Cláir and Cuinche,
with the baleful bean-growing brutes of Tradrai
and the skulking cut-throats out in Creatlach.
Oh, the twist was there . . . But for all I've said
I could still believe her free from guilt
except for that pestilent day that I found her
spreadeagled not far from Garas, stretched out
on the open road, not an inch beneath her,
by a gang from the bog, on the way from Dubhdhoire.
Astonishment, then, to strain the mind
(and I weakly twitch at the awful tale)
how she stayed so slim while filled by all,
but could start a child when she so desired.
There's a wondrous force in the words prescribed:
for she didn't require one moment's grace
—from the *Ego vos* that Jesus ordered
read on the boards before the candles
till her breasts inflated full with milk—
but a clear nine months, with a week to spare!

'It is dangerous, then, for a single man
to be bound till death by the obligation,
gripped by regret and by envy tossed.
I didn't learn that, alas, for nothing.
The neighbours know the way that I was
in my former days and my first career:
a powerful swaggerer flush with cash,
with a courteous house, and all appointments,
friends in court and legal aid,
help from the knowing, and much goodwill,
with a force in my speech, respect and weight,
and land and means at my free disposal,
my spirit at peace and my mind content.
But I lost through a woman my health and strength.
A fine, slim, capable woman she was,
with a stance and waist and a body and bones,
with a wave in her hair, all twisted and curled

and a light on her features gleaming bright
—the ease of laughter, the signs of youth,
and her aspect inviting a kiss, and welcome!
Ah, thoughtless, restless, I shook with desire
from top to toe, and by love was taken.
Vengeance it was, barbaric and dark,
on account of my deeds, no doubt in the world,
that rained down hard with hate from Heaven
to drive me wild and net me at last.

'The clergy's knot was firmly tied
and we were bound in bonds as one.
I cleared at once the sums demanded
on account of the day's benighted doings.
And fair enough—I couldn't be faulted:
I quelled all strife among the rabble
(beggars the lot), the clerk was happy,
the priest well pleased (with plenty of reason),
the locals gathered, we kindled torches,
food in plenty was spread on the tables
with clatter of music and endless drink
and a powerful party was had by all.

'My total loss that I failed to choke
on the night I was christened!—or ere I lusted
to bed with that woman who turned me grey
and drove me wild, without friend or wits.
Everyone, old and young, could tell me
how game she was in the country pubs
to drink and buy, as they beat the tables,
and relax on her back for married or single.
Her name and fame were long chewed over
but I couldn't for long believe a word.
Every couple that heard it went in fear
I'd go mad in my skin and be found no more.

'But I wouldn't give in, half blind as I was.
All their warnings were sound and fury,
mockery, futile talk in vain,
till her womb confirmed the tales for sure.
No busy-bodying false reports
—says she to me and says she to her—
but the deed itself spoke firm and true.

In gruesome fact, she gave me a son
(no sinew of mine!) before its time;
I'd a fireside family after a night!

'What a scalding, stormy, fierce commotion
—the baby swaddled, the housewife sick,
the porridge perched on the burning embers,
a canister heating hard with milk,
and a dish heaped high with goody and sugar
for the greedy midwife Muireann Ní Cháimlia.
Some more of the neighbours gathered in council,
hushed for my benefit round the fire
exchanging whispers in my hearing:
"A thousand praises, Light of Lights!
The flesh is barely formed, and yet
the father stands in all its features!
Sadhbh, will you look at the lie of the limbs,
the shape so straight, the organs and fingers,
the power in those hands—they'll be fighter's fists!—
the shape of the bones, and the meaty growth."
They judged for certain his nature sprang
from the cut of my face and handsome features,
the turn of my nose, my gleaming brow,
my elegant frame, my hue and appearance,
the set of my eyes, and my smile, indeed
—from heel to head they traced it all!
But sight nor light could I get of the wretch.
"Sure a draught would ruin him past recovery"
(says the crowd assembled, trying to fool me)
"—the merest puff would melt the creature."

'But I roughly spoke and sued to Jesus,
I rasped and I tore, with a threat of the embers,
proclaiming my rage in furious words.
All the hags in the house, you would swear they trembled,
but they handed him over to save upset.
"Handle with care now, mind don't bruise him,
he's easily shaken, rock him gently.
She took a fall, and it brought him early.
Mind don't squeeze him; leave him lie,
he's near his death, with not long to go.
If we keep him alive till dawn, for the priest,
he'd be better off dead than the state he's in."

I opened the knot of his swaddling clothes,
and examined him closely spread on my knee
and bedamn but I saw he was tight and strong!
I found him lusty and supple, well-set,
and broad and strong for a babe in the shoulders,
with sturdy heels and plenty of hair,
and compact ears and nails full grown.
His elbows clenched, his grip and his bones,
his eyes lit up and his nostrils flared
and I noted his hardy and vigorous knees
—a powerful, muscular, handsome pup,
healthy, well-fleshed, hard and fiery!

'So I call aloud, in the clearest terms,
and place in your presence the people's cause.
Consider with care and all compassion
their hornèd heads and their whole complaint.
Amend this law—this clamp of the clergy—
and save the few not fettered so far.
If the needful population fails
in the green and lovely fields of Ireland
we soon can fill the land with heroes.
What need of feeble and futile prayer?
Where is the need for a noisy wedding
with quarts of spirits and paying the music
and boastful brutes at the table roaring,
hullabaloo and the booze spilled over
—when the seed bestowed by God grew ripe
with no earthly priest at the first conjunction?
Full and far-flung, broad and strong
you will find this independent brood.
I see them often, wealthy and well,
ample and able in tone and heart,
and I see no blemish or blink or blindness
in these jump-the-guns brought up by women,
their stamp and their wit as fast and as fine,
as strong and as tight, as a legal one's.

'I have said so much, and the proof is simple.
There is one of them here about the house.
—Do you see him there, so tame and gentle?
But settle him down beside a table
and study him close: although he is young

he's a fully established piece of flesh,
a bouncer in bulk and body and bone!
Where could you fault him, hand or foot?
No feeble reed, no wizened antique,
no fool with a hump, no goose with a belly,
nor shapeless lump nor stunted pup,
but a lively lad, erect and vigorous!
Easy to see no lifeless stick
you would fasten on as a scourge for woman
—boneless and slack, with no middle or might
or love or affection or urge or drive—
would spray in the womb of a lovely woman
with furious heat this handsome stallion!
He settles for certain, at once and no lie,
by the power of his parts and the cut of his limbs,
the urge of his blood and his howling health
—without flicker or fault—he's a titan born.

'Seek not, therefore, starry Queen,
to ruin us all with a useless law.
Set loose in bed, without shackle or tie,
seed of the lout and the brazen noble;
release together, as Nature bids,
the seed supreme and the vulgar drop.
Declare at large, to old and young,
licence to breed throughout the nation.
The Gael will find it a source of strength
and force return like the ancient heroes
with fists and waists and backs again
on the men of the world like Goll Mac Morna.
There'll be light in the sky and fish in the nets
and the soil of the hills will groan with growth,
and women and men thereby for ever
will chant your praises in blissful joy.'

The maiden listened a while, and then
leaped to her feet in swift impatience.
She made response with her eyes on fire
and filled with a torrent of terrible rage:

'By the Crown of Craig! if I didn't allow
for your troubled condition and want of sense,

and out of respect for the gentle Court,
I'd behead with my nail your scrawny neck,
I'd knock you clattering under the table
and there'd long be talk of my thrusts against you.
With a right delight I'd rip your life-strings
and steer your soul towards Acheron's floods.

'A considered reply isn't worth my while,
you cankered crawler of horrible tongue,
but I've more to tell to the Court grandees
—how the girl that you didn't deserve was lost.
Poor she was, without cattle or cash,
and lived for long without warmth or shelter,
tired of life and steered astray
from pillar to post—no kith nor kin,
no rest nor ease, by day or by night,
but begging her bread from women she scorned.
This man here promised an easy spell
—this no-good promised her warmth and shelter,
honest dealing, and cows to milk,
and sleeping late in a feather bed,
blazing hearths and turf in plenty,
earthen walls without a draught,
roof and protection from weather and sky
and flax and wool to spin for clothing.
We knew from the start, and this maggot as well,
not warmth nor affection nor love in the least
could catch him this noble pearl of women,
but her desperate need, crying out for comfort.
It was gloomy doings, the nightly joy
—oppression and burden, trouble and fright:
legs of lead and skinny shoulders,
iron knees as cold as ice,
shrunken feet by embers scorched,
an old man's ailing, wasting body.
What handsome woman would not go grey
at the thought of being wed to a bundle of bones
that wouldn't inquire, not twice in the year,
was she half-grown boy or meat or fish?
—this dry cold thing stretched out across her
surly and spent, without power or bounce.
O what to her was a lively hammering
hard as the Devil, and twice a night!

'It won't, I hope, be thought *she* was guilty
or might fall down weak, worn out by the like,
this vigorous, handsome, kind, sweet girl.
She certainly met with the opposite rearing:
she'd never complain at a night of work
but give a brave slasher as good as she got.
She'd never refuse, any time or place,
on bone of her back with her eyes shut tight,
with never a balk or immoderate sulk
nor attack like a cat, nor scrape nor scratch,
but stretched her all like a sheaf beside him
flank on flank, with her legs around him,
coaxing his thoughts by easy stages,
fingering down on him, mouth on mouth,
putting her leg across him often,
rubbing her brush from waist to kncc,
or snatching the blanket and quilt from his loins
to fiddle and play with the juiceless lump.
But useless to tickle or squeeze or rub
or attack with her elbows, nails or heels.
I'm ashamed to relate how she passed the night
squeezing the sluggard, shuddering, sprawling,
tossing her limbs and the bedding beneath her,
her teeth and her members all a-shiver,
not sleeping a wink till the dawn of day,
performing and tossing from side to side.
Lightly this leper may talk of women
with no force in his spine and no power in his bones. . . !

'If this gentle, so deep in need, should leave,
the crime committed, I'd take her side.
Is there fox on a hill, or fish in the sea
or stalking eagle or stag in the wild,
foolish enough to pass a year
—or a day—without feed, and the prey to hand?
Can anyone show me where in the world
is the beast perverse or the aimless bird
that will peck in the clay or the heather or ditch
with the greenwood lush and the grass nearby?
Answer me now, you grievous rogue,
and let there be sense in whatever you say.
Is your appetite less when you sit to the table
after a month in a house of plenty?

Is a corner more crowded, a space any less,
because millions of men passed through for a season?
Alas for your brains, you plump antique,
do you fear you'll run short in your time of need!
Do you think, in your ravings, that there is a danger
of draining the Shannon or drinking it dry?
Can you empty the sea, dry up the brine
or exhaust with a ladle the ocean floor?
Consider in time your tasteless thoughts
and fasten a halter about your head.
Let the whole world handle her night and day
—there would still be more than your fill to spare.
Some timely advice: don't lose your mind
through fear of a woman being overkind!

'Trouble and strife! I could understand
such jealousy out of an elegant swain
or a bouncer bright, ferocious and firm,
grasping, gamy, happy and hard,
prancing, prodigal, galloping, gallant,
tough in the torso, a fancy kicker
—but withered and worn, a stunted ancient,
a feeble stud with an empty stick!

'No wonder my heart is filled with strain,
riddled by all these empty thoughts. . .
Yet what keeps free from shackle of spouse
all our ancient Church's clergy?
I am strong in patience and slight in rage,
but a fatal grief, a grinding pain,
the men that are missing, with all we need,
and our hearts' desires locked up in the cloth!
A pitiful sight for a fervent maiden
the size and shape of their lovely limbs,
the blush of their brows, the light of their smiles,
bums, bellies and bodies a-tremble softly,
their beauty, moistness, youth and bloom,
the bulk of their bone and weight of flesh,
the ponderous stern and tireless back,
the burning wish, and the strength assured!
At the highest tables, every comfort,
gold and means for their pleasure and drink;
then to feather bed, on bacon fed,

with cakes and wine and sweets and song;
plenty and power, youth often as not,
and we know for ourselves that they're flesh and blood!

'I wouldn't be grudging at gelded gossips
or blinded colts, or creeps diseased
—but lusty lads and powerful gougers
sluggish in sleep with the work to do!
Though I truly believe there are some would choose
domestic bliss—so I won't be hard.
It's not right, in fairness, the Order entire
should be taken, condemned and hanged on high.
Death of the lot I won't require,
nor drowning the ship to the final man.
Though many among them were scoundrels ever,
and lacking in rule or principle,
merciless misers cruel and hard,
with a fearful cold and hate toward maidens,
yet there are some that are kinder than others,
flooded with love and the generous graces.
Goods and herds you will often find,
and a flowing churn, where a priest has passed.
I have often heard their skills admired,
the range of their shrewd and salty deeds,
and often heard throughout the land
a lively whisper oft discussed
—and their prodigal practice plainly seen,
with their offspring acting under an alias.
But it wrings my bosom to the core
how they spend their vigour on ageing women.
A blow to the land, and its virgins' loss,
this senseless waste of the holy seed.

'Bleak pain in Ireland's bitter fields
the loss we owe this futile rule
but, heart of wisdom, I leave to you
the cure of the case and the clergy's crux.
In doubt and in error they take the vow
or I'm totally blind—enlighten me!
Bearing in mind the words of the prophets
and the Lord's apostles, strongly spoken,
say what power deflects their nature
and blocks their flesh in this dismal pen.

Paul, I believe, has ordered no one
to flinch from marriage, but turn from lust
—to leave your kin, how great the love,
enter the world and clasp a wife.
But it's pointless work for a woman like me
to set these legal texts before you.
You know the Spirit yourself, my pearl,
all tales in their settings shine clear to you:
the power of the Word; the Voice eternal;
the speech of the Lamb that is not gainsaid;
God who agreed to unite with a mother;
the laws of the prophets that favour maidens.

'*Sí*-prophetess, I adjure aloud
—O breed of Heaven, O regal crest,
O light of glory and crown of hosts—
attend my voice, protect and help.
Weigh in your mind the maidens' needs,
the single girls' desires, in thousands,
falling across each others' necks,
flocking in throngs, like broods of geese.
The tiniest gaggle that roams the street,
of dirty urchins, plain and whingeing,
soon (if only they're fed their fill
of juice and vegetables and milk)
swell like a shot with the signs of growth,
their breasts arrive, and bounce, and bubble!

'But scald my heart! How vain my thoughts
to talk of a mate in that boiling mass.
It is hard indeed to hope for comfort
—not a man in three for the women in Munster,
a place so poor and sore in need,
all faint and feeble, these hapless times,
in an Ireland empty, with thriving weeds,
and the country's youth growing bent and grey.
No one should suffer long singleness,
and that is for sure: let me find a man
and I'll harness him gentle straight away
and so be off—but keep him subject.'

The gracious one on the bench arose,
the day shone out, and the place all round.

Young, lovely, her shape and her delicate mien.
Her voice was high and alive and thrilling
as she wrung her fists and firmly told
a table-bailiff to order 'Silence!'
Her lips spoke forth, exhaling light,
and the Court entire paid grave attention:

'I find at once a will to win,
a force, in your speech, my mournful maid.
I see (and I think it a dismal sight)
this seed of Órla, Mór and Meadhbh
—a thin contriver, a shady creature,
an artful spy, a baleful beggar,
the juice of shame and the milk of meanness—
claiming the sages' noble blood!

'We enact hereby as a law for women:
a man, twenty-one and not yoked to a mate,
to be forcibly dragged by the head, without pity,
and tied to this tree beside the tomb.
There strip him bare of jacket and vest
and flay with a rope his waist and back.
All such persons brimming with years
who basely conceal their under-spike,
letting go to waste, with joy toward none,
clout of their balls and vigour of limb
—hoarding their maleness, with women available
hanging unplucked on the branch above—
lascivious ladies, dark with lust,
I leave it to you to handle their pains!
Invent ordeals of fires and nails,
spend womanly thoughts and brains upon it,
assemble your counsels all together
and I'll sanction you for the use of force.
Exact these grown men's pangs at once:
only death with the direst pains will do me.

'But the aim of my speech does not extend
to our stale, unstrung and abject elders
with dreary crotch and dismal hole,
fruitless womb and phantom labour.
So long, indeed, as the young may breed
old men will do to give concealment.

Sluggish old fools I have often seen
settled to housework (Heaven be thanked!),
tied all night and day to their women
and cloaking their deeds, protecting their names
—eager to help, though good for little.
Put their name to the family, I'm content!'

With the following words, she made an end
(I hate an over-talkative woman):

'Speak easy, now, your voices soft;
a hand to your lips, there's peril in talk
—but watch for these powerful passionate lads . . .
Some day (whoe'er sees it) they'll have to wed;
the time will come, with the Council's sanction
and the Pope applying his potent hand;
a committee will sit on the country's ills
and release to you all, under binding bonds,
a torrent of blood, a storm of flesh,
those ardent slashers—your heart's desire!
As do all other men reared up by woman
(mark what I say; let me see you respond)
you'll answer to me if you suffer at all
any useless wretches, or Muireanns in pants!
Off, now, in pursuit of those shrivelling seniors.
Get rid of this sort of weed from Fódla.

'I must be moving, and leave you now.
I've a lengthy circuit to make in Munster.
The journey ahead—delay won't help,
with so much of my business still not heard.
But I'll come once more, though without much warmth
from some that won't relish my return
—those among you mean in thought,
the kind that trumpet forth their fame
boasting aloud of maidens mastered;
the people will know your winks and whispers!
The scandal of girls both married and single
they deem heroic, it gives them pleasure.
Not drive of desire spurs on their sin,
the reek of blood or boiling lust,
delight in the act or the organ's itch,

but exploits bragged to the jeers of thousands.
Not need for ease attracts the like
but shout and talk and boastful pride,
unbridled uproar, crowds and jokes,
themselves gone feeble, lax and limp,
faltering, frail-arsed, slack in the flesh,
and a fury of need in the ladies after . . .
I acknowledge your case upon the spot;
I note your need, and must accept.
I will have this crew in bonds and fetters
next month when I return once more.'

She studied me close, the starry queen.
She finished, and my poor heart grew faint.
I felt some kind of a terrible fit
and a mortal trance in my bones and senses.
I saw the ground and the people reeling;
the force of their wailing beat in my ears.
A beam-sized bailiff came in power,
reached out her hand, and I lost my colour.
Sullen and savage, she pulled my ear
and dragged me up to the top of the table.

That Babe so maddened by spinsterhood
sprang up and clapped her hands on high
and ripely spoke: 'You ancient crust,
I have long been hoping to comb your locks!
You were often urged, O unnatural heart:
it is time to submit to the ladies' law.
What case can you find against the charge?
You deserve not a word, you listless tatter!
Your great achievements: where are they?
Or the ladies obliged for all your deeds?
Majestic Maid, observe this organ:
no blemish rules it out for women.
Closely examine his looks and limbs
from the top of his head to his spindly sole.
I grant he's a most misshapen beast
but I've seen no better yoked with a "Yes".
The grey I don't like—I would sooner yellow.
And bony, too, but I won't complain.
And a man with a bend in his back, or a hump?
Good men have had slants to their shoulderblades.

O the gammiest leg is the liveliest often,
with the crookedest knee on a vigorous wreck.
It was having to bury some blemish or other
that left this relic so sullen and single
—held high in esteem by the country's best,
with a lifetime full of the people's friendship,
music-playing and pleasure and sport,
cards and drink at the wise men's table
and in to the end with the riot and revel.
The crawler! I'd happily yield respect
to a good-looking, likeable, fertile, talented,
blithesome and gay merry man of the name!
But the Lord didn't order your sort of beast:
a virgin still and the grey increasing.
I shake to my soul with the urge to judge!
Soon we will settle your empty talk,
with your crime writ clear across your brow:
three decades without a spouse's shackles!
Renowned for patience, hear me now.
Grant help in this calamitous case.
The pangs and desires that stifle me,
lovely woman, I'll make him pay for!
Help, I say to you! Capture him! Take him,
Úna, I summon you, fetch me the rope.
Where are you, Áine? Don't be left out.
Máire, fasten his hands behind him.
Muireann and Meadhbh and Sadhbh and Síle,
put in effect, with fires of zeal,
those heights of torment the lady ordered:
bury in flesh the woven cords,
give generous measure of cruellest pains
to his bum and his rump; show Brian no mercy.
Lift your arms, raise up the scourge.
He's a fine example, ladies dear.
Cut into him deep, he has earned no favour;
take off his hide from head to heel,
let the peals resound o'er Éibhear's lands
and the hearts of all aged bachelors shake!

'I believe it's a decent and good Decree:
it is meet we record the date it passed
—as follows: take off, subtract in a flurry,
exactly a hundred and ten from a thousand;

precisely double the sum remaining;
then add one week from the Son's descent.'

She seizes the pen. My head is distracted
by fear of flaying and terror of flogging.
And then as she wrote the number down,
with the household nobles sitting on guard,
I ended my dream, I opened my eyes
and sprang from my pangs in a leap—awake!

RICHARD BRINSLEY SHERIDAN
1751–1816

155   *Drinking Song*

from *The School for Scandal*

Here's to the maiden of bashful fifteen,
    Here's to the widow of fifty;
Here's to the flaunting extravagant quean,
    And here's to the housewife that's thrifty:
      Chorus. Let the toast pass,
        Drink to the lass,
I'll warrant she'll prove an excuse for the glass.

Here's to the charmer, whose dimples we prize,
    And now to the maid who has none, sir,
Here's to the girl with a pair of blue eyes,
    And here's to the nymph with but one, sir.
       Let the toast pass, etc.

Here's to the maid with a bosom of snow,
    And to her that's as brown as a berry;
Here's to the wife with a face full of woe,
    And now to the girl that is merry:
       Let the toast pass, etc.

For let 'em be clumsy, or let 'em be slim,
    Young or ancient, I care not a feather;
So fill a pint bumper quite up to the brim,
    And let us e'en toast them together:
       Let the toast pass, etc.

156 *Song*

from *The Duenna*

Give Isaac the nymph who no beauty can boast;
But health and good humour to make her his toast,
If strait, I don't mind whether slender or fat,
And six feet or four—we'll ne'er quarrel for that.

Whate'er her complexion, I vow I don't care,
If brown it is lasting, more pleasing if fair;
And tho' in her cheeks I no dimples should see,
Let her smile, and each dell is a dimple to me.

Let her locks be the reddest that ever were seen,
And her eyes may be e'en any colour but green,
For in eyes, tho' so various in lustre and hue,
I swear I've no choice, only let her have two.

'Tis true I'd dispense with a throne on her back,
And white teeth I own, are genteeler than black,
A little round chin too's a beauty I've heard,
But I only desire she mayn't have a beard.

SEVENTEENTH TO NINETEENTH CENTURIES

FOLK POETRY

Folk Poems and Songs, Prayers and Charms from the Irish

157 It is well for small birds that can rise up on high
and warble away on the one branch together.
Not so with myself and my millionfold love
that so far from each other must rise every day.

She's more white than the lily and lovely past Beauty,
more sweet than the violin, more bright than the sun,
with a mind and refinement surpassing all these . . .
O God in Your Heaven give ease to my pain!

158 My own dark head (my own, my own)
your soft pale arm place here about me.
Honeymouth that smells of thyme
he would have no heart who denied you love.

There are girls in the town enraged and vexed,
they tear and loosen their hair on the wind
for the dashingest man in this place—myself!
But I'd leave them all for my secret heart.

Lay your head, my own (my own, my own)
your head, my own, lay it here upon me.
Honeymouth that smells of thyme
he would have no heart who denied you love.

159   My grief on the ocean
it is surely wide
stretched between me
and my dearest love.

I am left behind
to make lament
—not expected for ever
beyond the sea.

My sorrow I'm not
with my fond fair man
in the province of Munster
or County Clare.

My grief I am not
with my dearest love
on board of a ship
for America bound.

On a bed of rushes
I lay last night,
and I shook it out
in the heat of the day.

My love came near
up to my side
shoulder to shoulder
and mouth on mouth.

160   Remember that night
   and you at the window
with no hat or glove
   or coat to cover you?
I gave you my hand
   and you took and clasped it
and I stayed with you
   till the skylark spoke.

Remember that night
   when you and I
were under the rowan
   and the night was freezing?

Your head on my breasts
and your bright-pipe playing . . .
I little thought then
that our love could sever.

My heart's beloved
come some night soon
when my people sleep,
and we'll talk together.
I'll put my arms round you
and tell you my story.
O your mild sweet talk
took my sight of Heaven!

The fire is unraked
and the light unquenched.
The key's under the door
—close it softly.
My mother's asleep
and I am awake
my fortune in hand
and ready to go.

161   *Yourself and Myself*

If you come at all
come only at night
and walk quietly
—don't frighten me.
You'll find the key
under the doorstep
and me by myself
—don't frighten me.

There's no pot in the way
no stool or can
or rope of straw
—nothing at all.
The dog is quiet
and won't say a word.
It's no shame to him:
I've trained him well.

My mammy's asleep
and my daddy is coaxing her
kissing her mouth
 and kissing her mouth.
Isn't she lucky!
Have pity on me
lying here by myself
 in the feather bed.

162   *Little Black Rose*

Róisín, have no sorrow for all that has happened you:
the Friars are out on the brine, they are travelling the sea,
your pardon from the Pope will come, from Rome in the East,
and we won't spare the Spanish wine for my Róisín Dubh.

Far have we journeyed together, since days gone by.
I've crossed over mountains with her, and sailed the sea.
I have cleared the Erne, though in spate, at a single leap,
and like music of strings all about me, my Róisín Dubh.

You have driven me mad, fickle girl—may it do you no good!
My soul is in thrall, not just yesterday nor today.
You have left me weary and weak in body and mind,
O deceive not the one who loves you, my Róisín Dubh.

I would walk the dew beside you, or the bitter desert,
in hopes I might have your affection, or part of your love.
Fragrant small branch, you have given your word you love me,
the choicest flower of Munster, my Róisín Dubh.

If I had six horses I would plough against the hill—
I'd make Róisín Dubh my Gospel in the middle of Mass—
I'd kiss the young girl who would grant me her maidenhead
and do deeds behind the *lios* with my Róisín Dubh!

The Erne will be strong in flood, the hills be torn,
the ocean be all red waves, the sky all blood,
every mountain valley and bog in Ireland will shake
one day, before she shall perish, my Róisín Dubh.

Cill Chais

Now what will we do for timber,
    with the last of the woods laid low?
There's no talk of Cill Chais or its household
    and its bell will be struck no more.
That dwelling where lived the good lady
    most honoured and joyous of women
—earls made their way over wave there
    and the sweet Mass once was said.

Ducks' voices nor geese do I hear there,
    nor the eagle's cry over the bay,
nor even the bees at their labour
    bringing honey and wax to us all.
No birdsong there, sweet and delightful,
    as we watch the sun go down,
nor cuckoo on top of the branches
    settling the world to rest.

A mist on the boughs is descending
    neither daylight nor sun can clear.
A stain from the sky is descending
    and the waters receding away.
No hazel nor holly nor berry
    but boulders and bare stone heaps,
not a branch in our neighbourly haggard,
    and the game all scattered and gone.

Then a climax to all of our misery:
    the prince of the Gael is abroad
oversea with that maiden of mildness
    who found honour in France and Spain.
Her company now must lament her,
    who would give yellow money and white
—she who'd never take land from the people
    but was friend to the truly poor.

I call upon Mary and Jesus
    to send her safe home again:
dances we'll have in long circles
    and bone-fires and violin music;

that Cill Chais, the townland of our fathers,
will rise handsome on high once more
and till doom—or the Deluge returns—
we'll see it no more laid low.

164   *The Widow's Curse*

Gerald the Bitter, with your polished smile,
may all be desert up to your door,
two-headed brambles infest your land
with a lake of green all over your hall,
a hawk's nest at your chimney-hole
and a goat's den at the head of your bed
—for you took my son and you took his father,
you took my dozen cows and the bull.
Your heir, Gerald, may he never inherit!

165   *To the Holy Trinity*

Three folds in cloth, yet there is but the one cloth.
Three joints in a finger, yet there is but the one finger.
Three leaves in a shamrock, yet there is but the one shamrock.
Frost, snow and ice ... yet the three are only water.
Three Persons in God likewise, and but the one God.

166   *A Charm for Lighting the Fire*

I will build my fire today
in the presence of Heaven's holy angels
in the presence of Airíl shapely in form
in the presence of Uiríl of all the beauties
with no hatred, no envy, no jealousy,
no fear or terror of anyone under the sun
for my refuge is the Holy Son of God.
God, kindle inside my heart the spark of love
for my enemies, my kin, my friends,
for the wise, the foolish, the slave
(Son of Mary, gentle and bright)
from the thing of humblest lot
up to the loftiest name.

167   *A Charm for Love and Lasting Affection*

> The charm Mary put on the butter
> is the charm for love and lasting affection:
> May your body not cease
> to pay me attention
> may your love follow my face
> as the cow follows her calf
> from today till the day I die.

Ballads in English

168   *The Blackbird*

Once on a morning of sweet recreation
  I heard a fair lady a-making her moan
With sighing and sobbing and sad lamentation
  And singing: 'My Blackbird most royal is flown.
He's all my heart's treasure, my joy and my pleasure,
  So justly, my love, my heart follows thee;
And I am resolved, in fair or foul weather,
  To seek out my Blackbird wherever he be.

'I will go, though a stranger, into peril and danger,
  My heart is so loyal in every degree,
For he's constant and kind, and courageous of mind,
  And good luck to my Blackbird wherever he be.
In Scotland he's loved and dearly approved,
  In England a stranger he seemeth to be,
But his name I'll advance in Ireland or France,
  And good luck to my Blackbird wherever he be.

'The birds of the forest, they all flock together,
  The turtle has chosen to dwell with the dove,
And I am resolved in fair or foul weather
  Once more in the springtime to seek out my love.
But since fickle Fortune, which still proves uncertain,
  Hath caused this parting between him and me
His right I'll proclaim, and who dares me blame?
  So good luck to my Blackbird wherever he be.'

The Shan Van Vocht

Oh! the French are on the sea,
  Says the *Shan Van vocht*;
The French are on the sea,
  Says the *Shan Van vocht*;
Oh! the French are in the bay,
They'll be here without delay,
And the Orange will decay,
  Says the *Shan Van vocht*.

Chorus

Oh! the French are in the bay,
They'll be here by break of day,
And the Orange will decay,
  Says the *Shan Van vocht*.

And where will they have their camp?
  Says the *Shan Van vocht*;
Where will they have their camp?
  Says the *Shan Van vocht*;
On the Currach of Kildare,
The boys they will be there
With their pikes in good repair,
  Says the *Shan Van vocht*.

To the Currach of Kildare
The boys they will repair,
And Lord Edward will be there,
  Says the *Shan Van vocht*.

Then what will the yeomen do?
  Says the *Shan Van vocht*;
What *will* the yeomen do?
  Says the *Shan Van vocht*;
What *should* the yeomen do,
But throw off the red and blue,
And swear that they'll be true
  To the *Shan Van vocht*.

What *should* the yeomen do
But throw off the red and blue,
And swear that they'll be true
  To the *Shan Van vocht*.

And what colour will they wear?
  Says the *Shan Van vocht*;
What colour will they wear?
  Says the *Shan Van vocht*;
What colour should be seen
Where our fathers' homes have been,
But their own immortal Green?
  Says the *Shan Van vocht*.

What colour should be seen
Where our fathers' homes have been,
But their own immortal Green?
  Says the *Shan Van vocht*.

And will Ireland then be free?
  Says the *Shan Van vocht*;
Will Ireland then be free?
  Says the *Shan Van vocht*;
Yes! Ireland SHALL be free,
From the centre to the sea;
Then hurra for Liberty!
  Says the *Shan Van vocht*.

Yes! Ireland SHALL be free,
From the centre to the sea;
Then hurra for Liberty!
  Says the *Shan Van vocht*.

170   *The Wearin' o' the Green*

Oh, Paddy dear! and did ye hear the news that's goin' round?
The shamrock is forbid by law to grow on Irish ground!
No more St Patrick's day we'll keep; his colour can't be seen,
For there's a cruel law ag'in' the Wearin' o' the Green!

I met with Napper Tandy, and he took me by the hand,
And he said, 'How's poor ould Ireland, and how does she stand?'
'She's the most distressful country that ever yet was seen,
For they're hanging men and women for the Wearin' o' the Green.'

An' if the colour we must wear is England's cruel red,
Let it remind us of the blood that Ireland has shed;
Then pull the shamrock from your hat, and throw it on the sod,
An' never fear, 'twill take root there, though under foot 'tis trod.

When law can stop the blades of grass from growin' as they grow,
An' when the leaves in summer time their colour dare not show,
Then I will change the colour, too, I wear in my caubeen;
But till that day, plaise God, I'll stick to the Wearin' o' the Green.

171   *The Croppy Boy*

It was early, early in the spring,
The birds did whistle and sweetly sing,
Changing their notes from tree to tree
And the song they sang was 'Old Ireland Free'.

It was early, early in the night,
The Yeoman cavalry gave me a fright,
The Yeoman cavalry was my downfall
And I was taken by Lord Cornwall.

It was in the coach house that I was laid
And in the parlour that I was tried.
My sentence passed and my courage low
As to Duncannon I was forced to go.

As I was going up Wexford Street
My own first cousin I chanced to meet.
My own first cousin did me betray
And for one bare guinea swore my life away.

As I was passing my father's door
My brother William stood in the door,
My aged father stood there before
And my own dear mother her hair she tore.

As I was going up Wexford Hill
Oh who would blame me to cry my fill?
I looked behind and I looked before
And my own dear mother I shall ne'er see more.

As I was standing on the scaffold high
My own dear father was standing nigh.
My own dear father did me deny
And the name he gave me was 'The Croppy Boy'.

It was in Duncannon this young man died
And in Duncannon his body was laid.
Now all good people that do pass by
O spare a tear for 'The Croppy Boy'.

172

General wonder in our land,
   And general consternation;
General gale on Bantry strand,
   For general preservation.

General rich he shook with awe
   At general insurrection;
General poor his sword did draw,
   With general disaffection.

General blood was just at hand,
   As General Hoche appeared;
General woe fled through our land,
   As general want was feared.

General gale our fears dispersed,
   He conquered general dread;
General joy each heart has swelled,
   As General Hoche has fled.

General love no blood has shed,
   He left us general ease,
General horror he has fled,
   Let God get general praise.

To that great General of the skies,
   That sent us general gale,
With general love our voices rise
   In one great general peal.

173

The Orange Lily

My dear Orange brothers, have you heard of the news,
How the treacherous Frenchmen our gulls to amuse,
The troops that last April they promised to send,
At length at Killala they ventured to land.
　Good Croppies, but don't be too bold now,
　Lest you should be all stow'd in the hold now,
　Then to Bot'ny you'd trudge, I am told now,
　　And a sweet orange lily for me.

But now that they're landed they find their mistake,
For in place of the Croppies they meet the brave Lake;
He soon will convince them that our orange and blue
Can ne'er be subdued by their plundering crew.
　Good Croppies, then don't, etc.

That false traitor Emmet, more ungrateful than hell,
With McNevin and Arthur, though fast in their cell;
What they formerly swore they have dar'd to deny,
And the Secret Committee have charg'd with a lie!
　Good Croppies, then don't, etc.

But as, by this falsehood, it is clear they intend
To induce us poor peasants the French to befriend;
We shall soon, I hope, see them high dangling in air,
'Twould be murd'ring the loyal such miscreants to spare.
　Good Croppies, then don't, etc.

On the trees at the camp Crop Lawless intended,
To hang up all those who their country defended;
As the scene is reversed, a good joke it will be,
In the place of dear Camden to put up those three.
　Good Croppies then don't, etc.

that false traitor Emmet] Thomas Addis Emmet, brother of Robert　　McNevin,
Arthur [O'Connor], Lawless] members of the United Irishmen　　Camden] the
Marquis Camden

Judgement being entered on that bloody Bond,
Execution should follow, the people contend;
Why stay it, say they, when engagements they've broken?
The Direct'ry deny ev'ry word they had spoken.
    Good Croppies, then don't, etc.

Then gird on your sabres, my brave Orangemen all,
For the Croppies are down, and the Frenchmen shall fall;
Let each lodge sally forth, from one to nine hundred.
Those freebooters ere long with the dead shall be number'd.
    Good Croppies, then don't, etc.

174   *The Night Before Larry was Stretched*

The night before Larry was stretched,
The boys they all paid him a visit;
A bait in their sacks, too, they fetched;
They sweated their duds till they riz it:
For Larry was ever the lad,
When a boy was condemned to the squeezer,
Would fence all the duds that he had
To help a poor friend to a sneezer,
And warm his gob 'fore he died.

The boys they came crowding in fast,
They drew all their stools round about him,
Six glims round his trap-case were placed,
He couldn't be well waked without 'em.
When one of us asked could he die
Without having truly repented,
Says Larry, 'That's all in my eye;
And first by the clargy invented,
To get a fat bit for themselves.'

'I'm sorry, dear Larry,' says I,
'To see you in this situation;
And blister my limbs if I lie,
I'd as lieve it had been my own station.'

173 that bloody Bond] Oliver Bond, another member of the conspiracy

'Ochone! it's all over,' says he,
'For the neck-cloth I'll be forced to put on,
And by this time tomorrow you'll see
Your poor Larry as dead as a mutton,
Because, why, his courage was good.

'And I'll be cut up like a pie,
And my nob from my body be parted.'
'You're in the wrong box, then,' says I,
'For blast me if they're so hard-hearted;
A chalk on the back of your neck
Is all that Jack Ketch dares to give you;
Then mind not such trifles a feck,
For why should the likes of them grieve you?
And now, boys, come tip us the deck.'

The cards being called for, they played,
Till Larry found one of them cheated;
A dart at his napper he made
(The boy being easily heated);
'Oh, by the hokey, you thief,
I'll scuttle your nob with my daddle!
You cheat me because I'm in grief,
But soon I'll demolish your noddle,
And leave you your claret to drink.'

Then the clergy came in with his book,
He spoke him so smooth and so civil;
Larry tipped him a Kilmainham look,
And pitched his big wig to the devil;
Then sighing, he threw back his head,
To get a sweet drop of the bottle,
And pitiful sighing, he said:
'Oh, the hemp will be soon round my throttle,
And choke my poor windpipe to death.

'Though sure it's the best way to die,
Oh, the devil a better a-living!
For, sure when the gallows is high
Your journey is shorter to heaven:

But what harasses Larry the most,
And makes his poor soul melancholy,
Is to think on the time when his ghost
Will come in a sheet to sweet Molly—
Oh, sure it will kill her alive!'

So moving these last words he spoke,
We all vented our tears in a shower;
For my part, I thought my heart broke,
To see him cut down like a flower.
On his travels we watched him next day,
Oh, the throttler! I thought I could kill him;
But Larry not one word did say,
Nor changed till he came to 'King William'—
Then, musha! his colour grew white.

When he came to the nubbling chit,
He was tucked up so neat and so pretty,
The rumbler jogged off from his feet,
And he died with his face to the city;
He kicked, too—but that was all pride,
But soon you might see 'twas all over;
Soon after the noose was untied.
And at darky we waked him in clover,
And sent him to take a ground sweat.

BOOK III

—

THE NINETEENTH AND
TWENTIETH CENTURIES

ANTOINE RAIFTEIRÍ

1784–1835

(Translated from the Irish)

175   I am Raifteirí, the poet, full of courage and love,
my eyes without light, in calmness serene,
taking my way by the light of my heart
feeble and tired to the end of the road:
look at me now, my face toward Balla,
playing my music to empty pockets!

THOMAS MOORE

1779–1852

176   She is far from the land where her young hero sleeps,
    And lovers are round her, sighing:
But coldly she turns from their gaze, and weeps,
    For her heart in his grave is lying.

She sings the wild song of her dear native plains,
    Every note which he lov'd awaking;—
Ah! little they think who delight in her strains,
    How the heart of the Minstrel is breaking.

He had liv'd for his love, for his country he died,
    They were all that to life had entwin'd him;
Nor soon shall the tears of his country be dried,
    Nor long will his love stay behind him.

Oh! make her a grave where the sunbeams rest,
    When they promise a glorious morrow;
They'll shine o'er her sleep, like a smile from the West,
    From her own lov'd island of sorrow.

177

'Tis the last rose of summer
   Left blooming alone;
All her lovely companions
   Are faded and gone;
No flower of her kindred,
   No rose-bud is nigh,
To reflect back her blushes,
   Or give sigh for sigh.

I'll not leave thee, thou lone one!
   To pine on the stem;
Since the lovely are sleeping,
   Go, sleep thou with them.
Thus kindly I scatter
   Thy leaves o'er the bed,
Where thy mates of the garden
   Lie scentless and dead.

So soon may *I* follow,
   When friendships decay,
And from Love's shining circle
   The gems drop away.
When true hearts lie wither'd,
   And fond ones are flown,
Oh! who would inhabit
   This bleak world alone?

178

Dear Harp of my Country! in darkness I found thee,
   The cold chain of silence had hung o'er thee long,
When proudly, my own Island Harp, I unbound thee,
   And gave all thy chords to light, freedom, and song!

The warm lay of love and the light note of gladness
   Have waken'd thy fondest, thy liveliest thrill;
But, so oft hast thou echo'd the deep sigh of sadness,
   That ev'n in thy mirth it will steal from thee still.

Dear Harp of my Country! farewell to thy numbers,
   This sweet wreath of song is the last we shall twine!
Go, sleep with the sunshine of Fame on thy slumbers,
   Till touch'd by some hand less unworthy than mine;

If the pulse of the patriot, soldier, or lover,
   Have throbb'd at our lay, 'tis thy glory alone;
I was *but* as the wind, passing heedlessly over,
   And all the wild sweetness I wak'd was thy own.

179   *The Meeting of the Waters*

There is not in the wide world a valley so sweet
As that vale in whose bosom the bright waters meet;
Oh! the last rays of feeling and life must depart,
Ere the bloom of that valley shall fade from my heart.

Yet it *was* not that Nature had shed o'er the scene
Her purest of crystal and brightest of green;
'Twas *not* her soft magic of streamlet or hill,
Oh! no,—it was something more exquisite still.

'Twas that friends, the belov'd of my bosom, were near,
Who made every dear scene of enchantment more dear,
And who felt how the best charms of nature improve,
When we see them reflected from looks that we love.

Sweet vale of Avoca! how calm could I rest
In thy bosom of shade, with the friends I love best,
Where the storms that we feel in this cold world should cease,
And our hearts, like thy waters, be mingled in peace.

180   Oh! blame not the bard, if he fly to the bowers,
   Where pleasure lies carelessly smiling at fame;
He was born for much more, and in happier hours,
   His soul might have burn'd with a holier flame.
The string that now languishes loose on the lyre,
   Might have bent a proud bow to the warrior's dart;
And the lip which now breathes but the song of desire,
   Might have pour'd the full tide of the patriot's heart!

But alas! for his country—her pride is gone by,
   And that spirit is broken which never would bend;
O'er the ruin her children in secret must sigh,
   For 'tis treason to love her, and death to defend.

Unpriz'd are her sons, till they've learn'd to betray;
  Undistinguish'd they live, if they shame not their sires;
And the torch that would light them through dignity's way,
  Must be caught from the pile where their country expires.

Then blame not the bard, if in pleasure's soft dream
  He should try to forget what he never can heal;
Oh! give but a hope—let a vista but gleam
  Through the gloom of his country, and mark how he'll feel!
That instant, his heart at her shrine would lay down
  Every passion it nurs'd, every bliss it ador'd;
While the myrtle, now idly entwin'd with his crown,
  Like the wreath of Harmodius, should cover his sword.

But though glory be gone, and though hope fade away,
  Thy name, lov'd Erin! shall live in his songs:
Not even in the hour when his heart is most gay,
  Will he lose the remembrance of thee and thy wrongs.
The stranger shall hear thy lament on his plains,
  The sigh of thy harp shall be sent o'er the deep,
Till thy masters themselves, as they rivet thy chains,
  Shall pause at the song of their captive and weep!

181   Oh! where's the slave so lowly,
           Condemn'd to chains unholy,
               Who, could he burst
               His bonds at first,
           Would pine beneath them slowly?
           What soul, whose wrongs degrade it,
           Would wait till time decay'd it,
               When thus its wing
               At once may spring
           To the throne of him who made it?
               Farewell, Erin! farewell all,
               Who live to weep our fall!

           Less dear the laurel growing,
           Alive, untouch'd and blowing,
               Than that whose braid
               Is pluck'd to shade
           The brows with victory glowing!

We tread the land that bore us,
Our green flag glitters o'er us,
　　The friends we've tried
　　Are by our side,
And the foe we hate before us.
　　Farewell, Erin! farewell all,
　　Who live to weep our fall!

182　　*The Petition of the Orangemen of Ireland*

To the People of England, the humble Petition
　　Of Ireland's disconsolate Orangemen, showing—
That sad, very sad, is our present condition;—
　　Our jobbing all gone, and our noble selves going;—

That, forming one seventh—within a few fractions—
　　Of Ireland's seven millions of hot heads and hearts,
We hold it the basest of all base transactions
　　To keep us from murd'ring the other six parts;—

That, as to laws made for the good of the many,
　　We humbly suggest there is nothing less true;
As all human laws (and our own, more than any)
　　Are made *by* and *for* a particular few;—

That much it delights ev'ry true Orange brother,
　　To see you, in England, such ardour evince,
In discussing *which* sect most tormented the other,
　　And burn'd with most *gusto*, some hundred years since;—

That we love to behold, while old England grows faint,
　　Messrs Southey and Butler nigh coming to blows,
To decide whether Dunstan, that strong-bodied Saint,
　　Ever truly and really pull'd the Devil's nose;*

Whether t'other Saint, Dominic, burnt the Devil's paw—
　　Whether Edwy intrigued with Elgiva's old mother—†
And many such points, from which Southey can draw
　　Conclusions most apt for our hating each other.

---

* 'Devil' here and in stanza 6 should be read as a monosyllable; subsequent footnotes are Moore's own.

† To such important discussions as these the greater part of Dr Southey's *Vindiciæ Ecclesiæ Anglicanæ* is devoted.

That 'tis very well known this devout Irish nation
    Has now, for some ages, gone happily on,
Believing in two kinds of Substantiation,
    One party in *Trans* and the other in *Con*;*

That we, your petitioning *Cons*, have, in right
    Of the said monosyllable, ravaged the lands,
And embezzled the goods, and annoy'd, day and night,
    Both the bodies and souls of the sticklers for *Trans*;—

That we trust to Peel, Eldon, and other such sages,
    For keeping us still in the same state of mind;
Pretty much as the world used to be in those ages,
    When still smaller syllables madden'd mankind;—

When the words *ex* and *per*† did as well, to annoy
    One's neighbours and friends with, as *con* and *trans* now;
And Christians, like Southey, who stickled for *oi*,
    Cut the throats of all Christians, who stickled for *ou*.‡

That, relying on England, whose kindness already
    So often has help'd us to play this game o'er,
We have got our red coats and our carabines ready,
    And wait but the word to show sport, as before.

That, as to the expense—the few millions, or so,
    Which for all such diversions John Bull has to pay—
'Tis, at least, a great comfort to John Bull to know
    That to Orangemen's pockets 'twill all find its way.
    For which your petitioners ever will pray,
                            &c. &c. &c. &c. &c.

---

    * Consubstantiation—the true Reformed belief; at least, the belief of Luther, and, as
Mosheim asserts, of Melanc[h]thon also.
    † When John of Ragusa went to Constantinople (at the time this dispute between 'ex'
and 'per' was going on), he found the Turks, we are told, 'laughing at the Christians for
being divided by two such insignificant particles'.
    ‡ The Arian controversy. Before that time, says Hooker, 'in order to be a sound
believing Christian, men were not curious what syllables or particles of speech they used'.

JAMES CLARENCE MANGAN
1803–1849

183   *Dark Rosaleen*

(From the Irish of Costello)

O my Dark Rosaleen,
    Do not sigh, do not weep!
The priests are on the ocean green,
    They march along the Deep.
There's wine ... from the royal Pope
    Upon the ocean green;
And Spanish ale shall give you hope,
    My Dark Rosaleen!
    My own Rosaleen!
Shall glad your heart, shall give you hope,
Shall give you health, and help, and hope,
    My Dark Rosaleen.

Over hills and through dales,
    Have I roamed for your sake;
All yesterday I sailed with sails
    On river and on lake.
The Erne ... at its highest flood
    I dashed across unseen,
For there was lightning in my blood,
    My Dark Rosaleen!
    My own Rosaleen!
Oh! there was lightning in my blood,
Red lightning lightened through my blood,
    My Dark Rosaleen!

All day long in unrest
    To and fro do I move,
The very soul within my breast
    Is wasted for you, love!
The heart ... in my bosom faints
    To think of you, my Queen,
My life of life, my saint of saints,
    My Dark Rosaleen!

273

My own Rosaleen!
To hear your sweet and sad complaints,
My life, my love, my saint of saints,
   My Dark Rosaleen!

Woe and pain, pain and woe,
   Are my lot night and noon,
To see your bright face clouded so,
   Like to the mournful moon.
But yet . . . will I rear your throne
   Again in golden sheen;
'Tis you shall reign, shall reign alone,
   My Dark Rosaleen!
   My own Rosaleen!
'Tis you shall have the golden throne,
'Tis you shall reign, and reign alone,
   My Dark Rosaleen!

Over dews, over sands
   Will I fly for your weal;
Your holy delicate white hands
   Shall girdle me with steel.
At home . . . in your emerald bowers,
   From morning's dawn till e'en,
You'll pray for me, my flower of flowers,
   My Dark Rosaleen!
   My fond Rosaleen!
You'll think of me through daylight's hours,
My virgin flower, my flower of flowers,
   My Dark Rosaleen!

I could scale the blue air,
   I could plough the high hills,
Oh, I could kneel all night in prayer,
   To heal your many ills!
And one . . . beamy smile from you
   Would float like light between
My toils and me, my own, my true,
   My Dark Rosaleen!
   My fond Rosaleen!
Would give me life and soul anew,
A second life, a soul anew,
   My Dark Rosaleen!

O! the Erne shall run red
  With redundance of blood,
The earth shall rock beneath our tread,
  And flames wrap hill and wood,
And gun-peal, and slogan cry,
  Wake many a glen serene,
Ere you shall fade, ere you shall die,
  My Dark Rosaleen!
  My own Rosaleen!
The Judgement Hour must first be nigh,
Ere you can fade, ere you can die,
  My Dark Rosaleen!

184   *The Nameless One*

Ballad

Roll forth, my song, like the rushing river,
  That sweeps along to the mighty sea;
God will inspire me while I deliver
    My soul of thee!

Tell thou the world, when my bones lie whitening
  Amid the last homes of youth and eld,
That there was once one whose veins ran lightning
    No eye beheld.

Tell how his boyhood was one drear night-hour,
  How shone for *him*, through his griefs and gloom,
No star of all heaven sends to light our
    Path to the tomb.

Roll on, my song, and to after ages
  Tell how, disdaining all earth can give,
He would have taught men, from wisdom's pages,
    The way to live.

And tell how trampled, derided, hated,
  And worn by weakness, disease, and wrong,
He fled for shelter to God, who mated
    His soul with song—

With song which alway, sublime or vapid,
    Flowed like a rill in the morning beam,
Perchance not deep, but intense and rapid—
        A mountain stream.

Tell how this Nameless, condemned for years long
    To herd with demons from hell beneath,
Saw things that made him, with groans and tears, long
        For even death.

Go on to tell how, with genius wasted,
    Betrayed in friendship, befooled in love,
With spirit shipwrecked, and young hopes blasted,
        He still, still strove.

Till, spent with toil, dreeing death for others,
    And some whose hands should have wrought for *him*
(If children live not for sires and mothers),
        His mind grew dim.

And he fell far through that pit abysmal
    The gulf and grave of Maginn and Burns,
And pawned his soul for the devil's dismal
        Stock of returns.

But yet redeemed it in days of darkness,
    And shapes and signs of the final wrath,
When death, in hideous and ghastly starkness,
        Stood on his path.

And tell how now, amid wreck and sorrow,
    And want, and sickness, and houseless nights,
He bides in calmness the silent morrow,
        That no ray lights.

And lives he still, then? Yes! Old and hoary
    At thirty-nine, from despair and woe,
He lives enduring what future story
        Will never know.

Him grant a grave to, ye pitying noble,
    Deep in your bosoms! There let him dwell!
He, too, had tears for all souls in trouble,
        Here and in hell.

185　　　　*O'Hussey's Ode to the Maguire*

(From the Irish of O'Hussey)

Where is my Chief, my Master, this bleak night, *mavrone*!
O, cold, cold, miserably cold is this bleak night for Hugh,
Its showery, arrowy, speary sleet pierceth one through and through,
Pierceth one to the very bone!

Rolls real thunder? Or was that red, livid light
Only a meteor? I scarce know; but through the midnight dim
The pitiless ice-wind streams. Except the hate that persecutes *him*
Nothing hath crueller venomy might.

An awful, a tremendous night is this, meseems!
The flood-gates of the rivers of heaven, I think, have been burst wide—
Down from the overcharged clouds, like unto headlong ocean's tide,
Descends grey rain in roaring streams.

Though he were even a wolf ranging the round green woods,
Though he were even a pleasant salmon in the unchainable sea,
Though he were a wild mountain eagle, he could scarce bear, he,
This sharp, sore sleet, these howling floods.

O, mournful is my soul this night for Hugh Maguire!
Darkly, as in a dream, he strays! Before him and behind
Triumphs the tyrannous anger of the wounding wind,
The wounding wind, that burns as fire!

It is my bitter grief—it cuts me to the heart—
That in the country of Clan Darry this should be his fate!
O, woe is me, where is he? Wandering, houseless, desolate,
Alone, without or guide or chart!

Medreams I see just now his face, the strawberry bright,
Uplifted to the blackened heavens, while the tempestuous winds
Blow fiercely over and round him, and the smiting sleet-shower blinds
The hero of Galang tonight!

Large, large affliction unto me and mine it is,
That one of his majestic bearing, his fair, stately form,
Should thus be tortured and o'erborne—that this unsparing storm
Should wreak its wrath on head like his!

That his great hand, so oft the avenger of the oppressed,
Should this chill, churlish night, perchance, be paralysed by frost—
While through some icicle-hung thicket—as one lorn and lost—
He walks and wanders without rest.

The tempest-driven torrent deluges the mead,
It overflows the low banks of the rivulets and ponds—
The lawns and pasture-grounds lie locked in icy bonds
So that the cattle cannot feed.

The pale bright margins of the streams are seen by none.
Rushes and sweeps along the untameable flood on every side—
It penetrates and fills the cottagers' dwellings far and wide—
Water and land are blent in one.

Through some dark woods, 'mid bones of monsters, Hugh now strays,
As he confronts the storm with anguished heart, but manly brow—
O! what a sword-wound to that tender heart of his were now
A backward glance at peaceful days.

But other thoughts are his—thoughts that can still inspire
With joy and an onward-bounding hope the bosom of Mac-Nee—
Thoughts of his warriors charging like bright billows of the sea,
Borne on the wind's wings, flashing fire!

And though frost glaze tonight the clear dew of his eyes,
And white ice-gauntlets glove his noble fine fair fingers o'er,
A warm dress is to him that lightning-garb he ever wore,
The lightning of the soul, not skies.

Avran

Hugh marched forth to the fight—I grieved to see him so depart;
And lo! to-night he wanders frozen, rain-drenched, sad, betrayed—
But the memory of the lime-white mansions his right hand hath laid
In ashes warms the hero's heart!

186   *Kathaleen Ny-Houlahan*

(From the Irish of William Heffernan)

Long they pine in weary woe, the nobles of our land,
Long they wander to and fro, proscribed, alas! and banned;
Feastless, houseless, altarless, they bear the exile's brand,
    But their hope is in the coming-to of Kathaleen Ny-Houlahan!

Think her not a ghastly hag, too hideous to be seen,
Call her not unseemly names, our matchless Kathaleen;
Young she is, and fair she is, and would be crowned a queen,
    Were the king's son at home here with Kathaleen Ny-Houlahan!

Sweet and mild would look her face, O, none so sweet and mild,
Could she crush the foes by whom her beauty is reviled;
Woollen plaids would grace herself and robes of silk her child,
    If the king's son were living here with Kathaleen Ny-Houlahan!

Sore disgrace it is to see the Arbitress of thrones,
Vassal to a *Saxoneen* of cold and sapless bones!
Bitter anguish wrings our souls—with heavy sighs and groans
    We wait the Young Deliverer of Kathaleen Ny-Houlahan!

Let us pray to Him who holds Life's issues in His hands—
Him who formed the mighty globe, with all its thousand lands;
Girding them with seas and mountains, rivers deep, and strands,
    To cast a look of pity upon Kathaleen Ny-Houlahan!

He, who over sands and waves led Israël along—
He, who fed, with heavenly bread, that chosen tribe and throng—
He, who stood by Moses, when his foes were fierce and strong—
    May He show forth His might in saving Kathaleen Ny-Houlahan.

187 *Lament over the Ruins of the Abbey
of Teach Molaga*

(*From the Irish*)

I wandered forth at night alone
Along the dreary, shingly, billow-beaten shore;
Sadness that night was in my bosom's core,
   My soul and strength lay prone.

The thin wan moon, half overveiled
By clouds, shed her funereal beams upon the scene;
While in low tones, with many a pause between,
   The mournful night-wind wailed.

Musing of Life, and Death, and Fate,
I slowly paced along, heedless of aught around,
Till on the hill, now, alas! ruin-crowned,
   Lo! the old Abbey-gate!

Dim in the pallid moonlight stood,
Crumbling to slow decay, the remnant of that pile
Within which dwelt so many saints erewhile
   In loving brotherhood!

The memory of the men who slept
Under those desolate walls—the solitude—the hour—
Mine own lorn mood of mind—all joined to o'erpower
   My spirit—and I wept!

In yonder Goshen once—I thought—
Reigned Piety and Peace: Virtue and Truth were there;
With Charity and the blessed spirit of Prayer
   Was each fleet moment fraught!

There, unity of Work and Will
Blent hundreds into one: no jealousies or jars
Troubled their placid lives: their fortunate stars
   Had triumphed o'er all Ill!

There, kneeled each morn and even
The Bell for Matin—Vesper: Mass was said or sung—
From the bright silver censer as it swung
   Rose balsamy clouds to Heaven.

Through the round cloistered corridors
A many a midnight hour, bareheaded and unshod,
Walked the Grey Friars, beseeching from their God
   Peace for these western shores.

The weary pilgrim bowed by Age
Oft found asylum there—found welcome, and found wine.
Oft rested in its halls the Paladine,
   The Poet and the Sage!

Alas! alas! how dark the change!
Now round its mouldering walls, over its pillars low,
The grass grows rank, the yellow gowans blow,
   Looking so sad and strange!

Unsightly stones choke up its wells;
The owl hoots all night long under the altar-stairs;
The fox and badger make their darksome lairs
   In its deserted cells!

Tempest and Time—the drifting sands—
The lightning and the rains—the seas that sweep around
These hills in winter-nights, have awfully crowned
   The work of impious hands!

The sheltering, smooth-stoned massive wall—
The noble figured roof—the glossy marble piers—
The monumental shapes of elder years—
   Where are they? Vanished all!

Rite, incense, chant, prayer, mass, have ceased—
All, all have ceased! Only the whitening bones half sunk
In the earth now tell that ever here dwelt monk,
   Friar, acolyte, or priest.

Oh! woe, that Wrong should triumph thus!
Woe that the olden right, the rule and the renown
Of the Pure-souled and Meek should thus go down
   Before the Tyrannous!

Where wert thou, Justice, in that hour?
Where was thy smiting sword? What had those good men done,
That thou shouldst tamely see them trampled on
   By brutal England's Power?

Alas! I rave! . . . If Change is here,
Is it not o'er the land? Is it not too in me?
Yes! I am changed even more than what I see.
    Now is my last goal near!

My worn limbs fail—my blood moves cold—
Dimness is on mine eyes—I have seen my children die;
They lie where I too in brief space shall lie—
    Under the grassy mould!

I turned away, as toward my grave,
And, all my dark way homeward by the Atlantic's verge,
Resounded in mine ears like to a dirge
    The roaring of the wave.

188   *A Vision of Connaught in the Thirteenth Century*

I walked entranced
        Through a land of Morn;
The sun, with wondrous excess of light,
        Shone down and glanced
        Over seas of corn
And lustrous gardens aleft and right.
        Even in the clime
        Of resplendent Spain,
Beams no such sun upon such a land;
        But it was the time,
        'Twas in the reign,
Of Cáhal Mór of the Wine-red Hand.

Anon stood nigh
        By my side a man
Of princely aspect and port sublime.
        Him queried I—
        'O, my Lord and Khan,
What clime is this, and what golden time?'
        When he—'The clime
        Is a clime to praise,
The clime is Erin's, the green and bland;
        And it is the time,
        These be the days,
Of Cáhal Mór of the Wine-red Hand!'

Then saw I thrones,
   And circling fires,
And a Dome rose near me, as by a spell,
   Whence flowed the tones
      Of silver lyres,
And many voices in wreathèd swell;
   And their thrilling chime
      Fell on mine ears
As the heavenly hymn of an angel-band—
   'It is now the time,
      These be the years,
Of Cáhal Mór of the Wine-red Hand!'

   I sought the hall,
      And, behold!—a change
From light to darkness, from joy to woe!
   King, nobles, all,
      Looked aghast and strange;
The minstrel-group sate in dumbest show!
   Had some great crime
      Wrought this dread amaze,
This terror? None seemed to understand
   'Twas then the time,
      We were in the days,
Of Cáhal Mór of the Wine-red Hand.

   I again walked forth;
      But lo! the sky
Showed fleckt with blood, and an alien sun
   Glared from the north,
      And there stood on high,
Amid his shorn beams, a skeleton!
   It was by the stream
      Of the castled Maine,
One Autumn eve, in the Teuton's land,
   That I dreamed this dream
      Of the time and reign
Of Cáhal Mór of the Wine-red Hand!

189 *The Woman of Three Cows*

(From the Irish)

O Woman of Three Cows, *agra*! don't let your tongue thus rattle!
O, don't be saucy, don't be stiff, because you may have cattle.
I have seen—and, here's my hand to you, I only say what's true—
A many a one with twice your stock not half so proud as you.

Good luck to you, don't scorn the poor, and don't be their despiser,
For worldly wealth soon melts away, and cheats the very miser,
And Death soon strips the proudest wreath from haughty human brows;
Then don't be stiff, and don't be proud, good Woman of Three Cows!

See where Momonia's heroes lie, proud Owen More's descendants,
'Tis they that won the glorious name, and had the grand attendants!
If *they* were forced to bow to Fate, as every mortal bows,
Can *you* be proud, can *you* be stiff, my Woman of Three Cows!

The brave sons of the Lord of Clare, they left the land to mourning;
Mavrone! for they were banished, with no hope of their returning—
Who knows in what abodes of want those youths were driven to house?
Yet *you* can give yourself these airs, O Woman of Three Cows!

O, think of Donnell of the Ships, the Chief whom nothing daunted—
See how he fell in distant Spain, unchronicled, unchanted!
He sleeps, the great O'Sullivan, where thunder cannot rouse—
Then ask yourself, should *you* be proud, good Woman of Three Cows!

O'Ruark, Maguire, those souls of fire, whose names are shrined in
    story—
Think how their high achievements once made Erin's highest glory—
Yet now their bones lie mouldering under weeds and cypress boughs,
And so, for all your pride, will yours, O Woman of Three Cows!

The O'Carrolls, also, famed when Fame was only for the boldest,
Rest in forgotten sepulchres with Erin's best and oldest;
Yet who so great as they of yore in battle or carouse?
Just think of that, and hide your head, good Woman of Three Cows!

Your neighbour's poor, and you, it seems, are big with vain ideas,
Because, *inagh*! you've got three cows—one more, I see, than *she* has.
That tongue of yours wags more at times than Charity allows,
But if you're strong, be merciful, great Woman of Three Cows!

The Summing Up

Now, there you go! You still, of course, keep up your scornful bearing,
And I'm too poor to hinder you; but, by the cloak I'm wearing,
If I had but *four* cows myself, even though you were my spouse,
I'd thwack you well to cure your pride, my Woman of Three Cows!

190   *Good Counsel*

                    (*From the Ottoman*)

Tutor not thyself in science: go to masters for perfection;
        Also speak thy thoughts aloud:
Whoso in the glass beholdeth nought besides his own reflection
        Bides both ignorant and proud.

Study not in one book only: bee-like, rather, at a hundred
        Sources gather honeyed lore:
Thou art else that helpless bird which, when her nest has once been
                plundered,
        Ne'er can build another more.

191   *To Sultan Murad II*

                    (*From the Ottoman*)

                    Earth sees in thee
                    Her Destiny:
                Thou standest as the Pole—and she
                    Resembles
                The Needle, for she turns to thee,
                    And trembles.

192
A Song from the Coptic
(Goethe)

Quarrels have long been in vogue among sages;
   Still, though in many things wranglers and rancorous,
All the philosopher-scribes of all ages
   Join, *una voce*, on one point to anchor us.
Here is the gist of their mystified pages,
Here is the wisdom we purchase with gold—
Children of Light, leave the world to its mulishness,
Things to their natures, and fools to their foolishness;
Berries were bitter in forests of old.

Hoary old Merlin, that great necromancer,
Made me, a student, a similar answer,
When I besought him for light and for lore:
Toiler in vain! leave the world to its mulishness,
Things to their natures, and fools to their foolishness;
Granite was hard in the quarries of yore.

And on the ice-crested heights of Armenia,
And in the valleys of broad Abyssinia,
Still spake the Oracle just as before:
Wouldst thou have peace, leave the world to its mulishness,
Things to their natures and fools to their foolishness;
Beetles were blind in the ages of yore.

193
Siberia

In Siberia's wastes
   The Ice-wind's breath
Woundeth like the toothèd steel;
Lost Siberia doth reveal
   Only blight and death.

Blight and death alone.
   No Summer shines.
Night is interblent with Day.
In Siberia's wastes alway
   The blood blackens, the heart pines.

In Siberia's wastes
  No tears are shed,
For they freeze within the brain.
Nought is felt but dullest pain,
  Pain acute, yet dead;

Pain as in a dream,
  When years go by
Funeral-paced, yet fugitive,
When man lives, and doth not live,
  Doth not live—nor die.

In Siberia's wastes
  Are sands and rocks.
Nothing blooms of green or soft,
But the snow-peaks rise aloft
  And the gaunt ice-blocks.

And the exile there
  Is one with those;
They are part, and he is part,
For the sands are in his heart,
  And the killing snows.

Therefore, in those wastes
  None curse the Czar.
Each man's tongue is cloven by
The North Blast, that heweth nigh
  With sharp scymitar.

And such doom each drees,
  Till, hunger-gnawn,
And cold-slain, he at length sinks there,
Yet scarce more a corpse than ere
  His last breath was drawn.

SAMUEL FERGUSON
1810–1886

194 *The Burial of King Cormac*

'Crom Cruach and his sub-gods twelve',
  Said Cormac, 'are but carven treene;
The axe that made them, haft or helve,
  Had worthier of our worship been.

'But He who made the tree to grow,
  And hid in earth the iron-stone,
And made the man with mind to know
  The axe's use, is God alone.'

Anon to priests of Crom was brought—
  Where, girded in their service dread,
They minister'd on red Moy Slaught—
  Word of the words King Cormac said.

They loosed their curse against the king;
  They cursed him in his flesh and bones;
And daily in their mystic ring
  They turn'd the maledictive stones,

Till, where at meat the monarch sate,
  Amid the revel and the wine,
He choked upon the food he ate,
  At Sletty, southward of the Boyne.

High vaunted then the priestly throng,
  And far and wide they noised abroad
With trump and loud liturgic song
  The praise of their avenging God.

But ere the voice was wholly spent
  That priest and prince should still obey,
To awed attendants o'er him bent
  Great Cormac gather'd breath to say,—

'Spread not the beds of Brugh for me
  When restless death-bed's use is done:
But bury me at Rossnaree
  And face me to the rising sun.

'For all the kings who lie in Brugh
  Put trust in gods of wood and stone;
And 'twas at Ross that first I knew
  One, Unseen, who is God alone.

'His glory lightens from the east;
  His message soon shall reach our shore;
And idol-god, and cursing priest
  Shall plague us from Moy Slaught no more.'

Dead Cormac on his bier they laid:—
  'He reign'd a king for forty years,
And shame it were', his captains said,
  'He lay not with his royal peers.

'His grandsire, Hundred-Battle, sleeps
  Serene in Brugh: and, all around,
Dead kings in stone sepulchral keeps
  Protect the sacred burial ground.

'What though a dying man should rave
  Of changes o'er the eastern sea?
In Brugh of Boyne shall be his grave,
  And not in noteless Rossnaree.'

Then northward forth they bore the bier,
  And down from Sletty side they drew,
With horsemen and with charioteer,
  To cross the fords of Boyne to Brugh.

There came a breath of finer air
  That touch'd the Boyne with ruffling wings,
It stirr'd him in his sedgy lair
  And in his mossy moorland springs.

And as the burial train came down
  With dirge and savage dolorous shows,
Across their pathway, broad and brown
  The deep, full-hearted river rose;

From bank to bank through all his fords,
  'Neath blackening squalls he swell'd and boil'd;
And thrice the wondering gentile lords
  Essay'd to cross, and thrice recoil'd.

Then forth stepp'd grey-hair'd warriors four:
  They said, 'Through angrier floods than these,
On link'd shields once our king we bore
  From Dread-Spear and the hosts of Deece.

'And long as loyal will holds good,
  And limbs respond with helpful thews,
Nor flood, nor fiend within the flood,
  Shall bar him of his burial dues.'

With slanted necks they stoop'd to lift;
  They heaved him up to neck and chin;
And, pair and pair, with footsteps swift,
  Lock'd arm and shoulder, bore him in.

'Twas brave to see them leave the shore;
  To mark the deep'ning surges rise,
And fall subdued in foam before
  The tension of their striding thighs.

'Twas brave, when now a spear-cast out,
  Breast-high the battling surges ran;
For weight was great, and limbs were stout,
  And loyal man put trust in man.

But ere they reach'd the middle deep,
  Nor steadying weight of clay they bore,
Nor strain of sinewy limbs could keep
  Their feet beneath the swerving four.

And now they slide, and now they swim,
  And now, amid the blackening squall,
Grey locks afloat, with clutching grim,
  They plunge around the floating pall.

While, as a youth with practised spear
  Through justling crowds bears off the ring,
Boyne from their shoulders caught the bier
  And proudly bore away the king.

At morning, on the grassy marge
    Of Rossnaree, the corpse was found,
And shepherds at their early charge
    Entomb'd it in the peaceful ground.

A tranquil spot: a hopeful sound
    Comes from the ever youthful stream,
And still on daisied mead and mound
    The dawn delays with tenderer beam.

Round Cormac Spring renews her buds:
    In march perpetual by his side,
Down come the earth-fresh April floods,
    And up the sea-fresh salmon glide;

And life and time rejoicing run
    From age to age their wonted way;
But still he waits the risen Sun,
    For still 'tis only dawning Day.

195   *Aideen's Grave*

They heaved the stone; they heap'd the cairn:
    Said Ossian, 'In a queenly grave
We leave her, 'mong her fields of fern,
    Between the cliff and wave.

'The cliff behind stands clear and bare,
    And bare, above, the heathery steep
Scales the clear heaven's expanse, to where
    The Danaan Druids sleep.

'And all the sands that, left and right,
    The grassy isthmus-ridge confine,
In yellow bars lie bare and bright
    Among the sparkling brine.

'A clear pure air pervades the scene,
    In loneliness and awe secure;
Meet spot to sepulchre a Queen
    Who in her life was pure.

'Here, far from camp and chase removed,
    Apart in Nature's quiet room,
The music that alive she loved
    Shall cheer her in the tomb.

'The humming of the noontide bees,
    The lark's loud carol all day long,
And, borne on evening's salted breeze,
    The clanking sea bird's song

'Shall round her airy chamber float,
    And with the whispering winds and streams
Attune to Nature's tenderest note
    The tenor of her dreams.

'And oft, at tranquil eve's decline
    When full tides lip the Old Green Plain,
The lowing of Moynalty's kine
    Shall round her breathe again,

'In sweet remembrance of the days
    When, duteous, in the lowly vale,
Unconscious of my Oscar's gaze,
    She fill'd the fragrant pail,

'And, duteous, from the running brook
    Drew water for the bath; nor deem'd
A king did on her labour look,
    And she a fairy seem'd.

'But when the wintry frosts begin,
    And in their long-drawn, lofty flight,
The wild geese with their airy din
    Distend the ear of night,

'And when the fierce De Danaan ghosts
    At midnight from their peak come down,
When all around the enchanted coasts
    Despairing strangers drown;

'When, mingling with the wreckful wail,
    From low Clontarf's wave-trampled floor
Comes booming up the burthen'd gale
    The angry Sand-Bull's roar;

'Or, angrier than the sea, the shout
   Of Erin's hosts in wrath combined,
When Terror heads Oppression's rout,
   And Freedom cheers behind:—

'Then o'er our lady's placid dream,
   Where safe from storms she sleeps, may steal
Such joy as will not misbeseem
   A Queen of men to feel:

'Such thrill of free, defiant pride,
   As rapt her in her battle car
At Gavra, when by Oscar's side
   She rode the ridge of war,

'Exulting, down the shouting troops,
   And through the thick confronting kings,
With hands on all their javelin loops
   And shafts on all their strings;

'E'er closed the inseparable crowds,
   No more to part for me, and show,
As bursts the sun through scattering clouds,
   My Oscar issuing so.

'No more, dispelling battle's gloom
   Shall son for me from fight return;
The great green rath's ten-acred tomb
   Lies heavy on his urn.

'A cup of bodkin-pencill'd clay
   Holds Oscar; mighty heart and limb
One handful now of ashes grey:
   And she has died for him.

'And here, hard by her natal bower
   On lone Ben Edar's side, we strive
With lifted rock and sign of power
   To keep her name alive.

'That while, from circling year to year,
   Her Ogham-letter'd stone is seen,
The Gael shall say, "Our Fenians here
   Entomb'd their loved Aideen."

'The Ogham from her pillar stone
   In tract of time will wear away;
Her name at last be only known
   In Ossian's echo'd lay.

'The long-forgotten lay I sing
   May only ages hence revive
(As eagle with a wounded wing
   To soar again might strive)

'Imperfect, in an alien speech,
   When, wandering here, some child of chance
Through pangs of keen delight shall reach
   The gift of utterance,—

'To speak the air, the sky to speak,
   The freshness of the hill to tell,
Who, roaming bare Ben Edar's peak
   And Aideen's briary dell,

'And gazing on the Cromlech vast,
   And on the mountain and the sea,
Shall catch communion with the past
   And mix himself with me.

'Child of the Future's doubtful night,
   Whate'er your speech, whoe'er your sires,
Sing while you may with frank delight
   The song your hour inspires.

'Sing while you may, nor grieve to know
   The song you sing shall also die;
Atharna's lay has perish'd so,
   Though once it thrill'd this sky.

'Above us, from his rocky chair,
   There, where Ben Edar's landward crest
O'er eastern Bregia bends, to where
   Dun Almon crowns the west:

'And all that felt the fretted air
   Throughout the song-distemper'd clime,
Did droop, till suppliant Leinster's prayer
   Appeased the vengeful rhyme.

'Ah me, or e'er the hour arrive
   Shall bid my long-forgotten tones,
Unknown One, on your lips revive,
   Here, by these moss-grown stones,

'What change shall o'er the scene have cross'd;
   What conquering lords anew have come;
What lore-arm'd, mightier Druid host
   From Gaul or distant Rome!

'What arts of death, what ways of life,
   What creeds unknown to bard or seer,
Shall round your careless steps be rife,
   Who pause and ponder here;

'And, haply, where yon curlew calls
   Athwart the marsh, 'mid groves and bowers
See rise some mighty chieftain's halls
   With unimagined towers:

'And baying hounds, and coursers bright,
   And burnish'd cars of dazzling sheen,
With courtly train of dame and knight,
   Where now the fern is green.

"Or, by yon prostrate altar-stone
   May kneel, perchance, and, free from blame,
Hear holy men with rites unknown
   New names of God proclaim.

'Let change as may the Name of Awe,
   Let rite surcease and altar fall,
The same One God remains, a law
   For ever and for all.

'Let change as may the face of earth,
   Let alter all the social frame,
For mortal men the ways of birth
   And death are still the same.

'And still, as life and time wear on,
   The children of the waning days
(Though strength be from their shoulders gone
   To lift the loads we raise)

'Shall weep to do the burial rites
 Of lost ones loved; and fondly found,
In shadow of the gathering nights,
 The monumental mound.

'Farewell! the strength of men is worn;
 The night approaches dark and chill:
Sleep, till perchance an endless morn
 Descend the glittering hill.'

Of Oscar and Aideen bereft,
 So Ossian sang. The Fenians sped
Three mighty shouts to heaven; and left
 Ben Edar to the dead.

196 *Deirdre's Lament for the Sons of Usnach*

    (*From the Irish*)

The lions of the hill are gone,
And I am left alone—alone—
Dig the grave both wide and deep,
For I am sick, and fain would sleep!

The falcons of the wood are flown,
And I am left alone—alone—
Dig the grave both deep and wide,
And let us slumber side by side.

The dragons of the rock are sleeping,
Sleep that wakes not for our weeping:
Dig the grave and make it ready;
Lay me on my true Love's body.

Lay their spears and bucklers bright
By the warriors' sides aright;
Many a day the Three before me
On their linkèd bucklers bore me.

Lay upon the low grave floor,
'Neath each head, the blue claymore;
Many a time the noble Three
Redden'd those blue blades for me.

Lay the collars, as is meet,
Of their greyhounds at their feet;
Many a time for me have they
Brought the tall red deer to bay.

Oh! to hear my true Love singing,
Sweet as sound of trumpets ringing:
Like the sway of ocean swelling
Roll'd his deep voice round our dwelling.

Oh! to hear the echoes pealing
Round our green and fairy sheeling,
When the Three, with soaring chorus,
Pass'd the silent skylark o'er us.

Echo now, sleep, morn and even—
Lark alone enchant the heaven!—
Ardan's lips are scant of breath,—
Neesa's tongue is cold in death.

Stag, exult on glen and mountain—
Salmon, leap from loch to fountain—
Heron, in the free air warm ye—
Usnach's Sons no more will harm ye!

Erin's stay no more you are,
Rulers of the ridge of war;
Never more 'twill be your fate
To keep the beam of battle straight.

Woe is me! by fraud and wrong—
Traitors false and tyrants strong—
Fell Clan Usnach, bought and sold,
For Barach's feast and Conor's gold!

Woe to Eman, roof and wall!—
Woe to Red Branch, hearth and hall!—
Tenfold woe and black dishonour
To the false and foul Clan Conor!

Dig the grave both wide and deep,
Sick I am, and fain would sleep!
Dig the grave and make it ready,
Lay me on my true Love's body.

197 *At the Polo-Ground*

6th May 1882

Not yet in sight.'Twere well to step aside,
Beyond the common eye-shot, till he comes.
He—I've no quarrel under heaven with him:
I'd rather it were Forster; rather still
One higher up than either; but since Fate
Or Chance has so determined, be it he.
How cool I feel; and all my wits about
And vigilant; and such a work in hand!
Yes: loitering here, unoccupied, may draw
Remark and question. How came such a one there?
Oh; I've strolled out to see the polo-players:
I'll step across to them; but keep an eye
On who comes up the highway.
                                        Here I am
Beside the hurdles fencing off the ground
They've taken from us who have the right to it,
For these select young gentry and their sport.
Curse them! I would they all might break their necks!
Young fops and lordlings of the garrison
Kept up by England here to keep us down:
All rich young fellows not content to own
Their chargers, hacks, and hunters for the field,
But also special ponies for their game;
And doubtless, as they dash along, regard
Us who stand outside as a beggarly crew.—
'Tis half-past six. Not yet. No, that's not he.—
Well, but 'tis pretty, sure, to see them stoop
And take the ball, full gallop; and when I
In gown and cocked hat once drove up Cork Hill,
Perhaps myself have eyed the common crowd,
Lining the footway, with a similar sense
Of higher station, just as these do me,
And as the man next door no doubt does them.
   'Tis very sure that grades and differences
Of rich and poor and small men and grandees
Have all along existed, and still will,—
Though many a man has risen and thriven well
By promising the Poor to make them rich
By taking from the Rich their overplus,

And putting all on a level: beggars all.
Yet still the old seize-ace comes round again;
And though my friends upon the pathway there—
No. Not he neither. That's a taller man—
Look for a general scramble and divide,
Such a partition, were it possible,
Would not by any means suit me. My share
Already earned and saved would equal ten
Such millionth quotients and sub-multiples.
No: they may follow Davitt. 'Tis Parnell
And property—in proper hands—will win.
But, say the Mob's the Master; and who knows
But some o' these days the ruffians may have votes
As good as mine or his, and pass their Act
For every man his share, and equal all?
No doubt they'd have a slice from me. What then?
I'm not afraid. I'll float. Allow the scums
Rise to the surface, something rises too
Not scum, but Carey; and will yet rise higher.
No place too high but he may look for it.
Member for Dublin, Speaker, President,
Lord Mayor for life—why not? One gentleman,
Who when he comes to deal with this day's work—
No: not in sight. That man is not so tall—
Will find, to his surprise, a stronger hand
Than his controls the rudder, sat three years
And hangs his medal on the sheriff's chain.
Yes; say Lord Mayor: my liveries green and gold,
My secretary with me in my coach,
And chaplain duly seated by my side.
My boy shall have his hack, and pony too,
And play at polo with the best of them;
Such as will then be best. He need not blush
To think his father was a bricklayer;
For laying bricks is work as reputable
As filling noggins or appraising pawns,
Or other offices of those designed
For fathers of our Dublin swells to be.
   'Tis twenty minutes now to seven o'clock.
What if he should not come at all? 'Twere then
Another—oh—*fiasco* as they call it,
Not pleasant to repeat to Number One,
But, for myself, perhaps not wholly bad.

For, if he comes, there will be consequences
Will make a stir; and in that stir my name
May come in play—well, one must run some risk
Who takes a lead and keeps and thrives by it
As I have done. But sure the risk is small.
I know those cut-throats on the pathway there
May be relied on. Theirs is work that shuts
The door against approval of both sorts.
But he who drives them, I've remarked in him
A flighty indecision in the eye,
Such as, indeed, had I a looking-glass,
I might perhaps discover in my own
When thoughts have crossed me how I should behave
In this or that conjuncture of the affair.
Him I distrust. But not from him or them
Or any present have I aught to fear.
For never have I talked to more than one
Of these executive agents at a time,
Nor let a scrap of writing leave my hand
Could compromise myself with anyone.
And should I—though I don't expect I shall—
Be brought, at any time, to book for this,
'Twill not be—or I much mistake—because
Of any indiscretion hitherto.
But, somehow, these reflections make me pause
And set me inly questioning myself,
Is it worth while—the crime itself apart—
To pull this settled civil state of life
To pieces, for another just the same,
Only with rawer actors for the posts
Of Judges, Landlords, Masters, Capitalists?
And then, the innocent blood. I've half a mind
To trip across this elm-root at my foot,
And turn my ankle.
               Oh, he comes at last!
No time for thinking now. My own life pays
Unless I play my part. I see he brings
Another with him, and, I think, the same
I heard them call Lord—something—Cavendish.
If one; two, likely. That can't now be helped.
Up. Drive on straight,—if I blow my nose
And show my handkerchief in front of them,
And then turn back, what's that to anyone?

No further, driver. Back to Island Bridge.
No haste. If some acquaintance chanced to pass,
He must not think that we are running away.
I don't like, but I can't help looking back.
They meet: my villains pass them. Gracious Powers,
Another failure! No, they turn again
And overtake; and Brady lifts his arm—
I'll see no more. On—by the Monument.
On—brisker, brisker—but yet leisurely.
By this time all is over with them both.
Ten minutes more, the Castle has the news,
And haughty Downing Street in half an hour
Is struck with palsy. For a moment there,
Among the trees, I wavered. Brady's knife
Has cut the knot of my perplexities;
Despite myself, my fortune mounts again.
The English rule will soon be overthrown,
And ours established in the place of it.
I'm free again to look, as long as I please,
In Fortune's show-box. Yes; I see the chain,
I see the gilded coach. God send the boy
May take the polish! There's but one thing now
That troubles me. These cursed knives at home
That woman brought me, what had best be done
To put them out o' the way? I have it. Yes,
That old Fitzsimon's roof's in need of repairs.
I'll leave them in his cock-loft. Still in time
To catch the tram, I'll take a seat a-top—
For no one must suppose I've anything
To hide—and show myself in Grafton Street.

198   *Lament for Thomas Davis*

I walked through Ballinderry in the spring-time,
    When the bud was on the tree;
And I said, in every fresh-ploughed field beholding
    The sowers striding free,
Scattering broadside forth the corn in golden plenty
    On the quick seed-clasping soil:
'Even such, this day, among the fresh-stirred hearts of Erin,
    Thomas Davis, is thy toil!'

I sat by Ballyshannon in the summer,
 And saw the salmon leap;
And I said, as I beheld the gallant creatures
 Spring glittering from the deep,
Through the spray, and through the prone heaps striving onward
 To the calm clear streams above,
'So seekest thou thy native founts of freedom, Thomas Davis,
 In thy brightness of strength and love!'

I stood on Derrybawn in the autumn,
 And I heard the eagle call,
With a clangorous cry of wrath and lamentation
 That filled the wide mountain hall,
O'er the bare deserted place of his plundered eyrie;
 And I said, as he screamed and soared,
'So callest thou, thou wrathful soaring Thomas Davis,
 For a nation's rights restored!'

And alas! to think but now, and thou art lying,
 Dear Davis, dead at thy mother's knee;
And I, no mother near, on my own sick-bed,
 That face on earth shall never see;
I may lie and try to feel that I am dreaming,
 I may lie and try to say, 'Thy will be done'—
But a hundred such as I will never comfort Erin
 For the loss of the noble son!

Young husbandman of Erin's fruitful seed-time,
 In the fresh track of danger's plough!
Who will walk the heavy, toilsome, perilous furrow
 Girt with freedom's seed-sheets now?
Who will banish with the wholesome crop of knowledge
 The daunting weed and the bitter thorn,
Now that thou thyself art but a seed for hopeful planting
 Against the Resurrection morn?

Young salmon of the flood-tide of freedom
 That swells round Erin's shore!
Thou wilt leap against their loud oppressive torrent
 Of bigotry and hate no more;
Drawn downward by their prone material instinct,
 Let them thunder on their rocks and foam—
Thou hast leapt, aspiring soul, to founts beyond their raging,
 Where troubled waters never come!

But I grieve not, Eagle of the empty eyrie,
   That thy wrathful cry is still;
And that the songs alone of peaceful mourners
   Are heard today on Erin's hill;
Better far, if brothers' war be destined for us
   (God avert that horrid day, I pray),
That ere our hands be stained with slaughter fratricidal
   Thy warm heart should be cold in clay.

But my trust is strong in God, who made us brothers,
   That He will not suffer their right hands
Which thou hast joined in holier rites than wedlock
   To draw opposing brands.
Oh, many a tuneful tongue that thou mad'st vocal
   Would lie cold and silent then;
And songless long once more, should often-widowed Erin
   Mourn the loss of her brave young men.

Oh, brave young men, my love, my pride, my promise,
   'Tis on you my hopes are set,
In manliness, in kindliness, in justice,
   To make Erin a nation yet,
Self-respecting, self-relying, self-advancing,
   In union or in severance, free and strong—
And if God grant this, then, under God, to Thomas Davis
   Let the greater praise belong.

THOMAS DAVIS

1814–1845

199   *Lament for the Death of Eoghan Ruadh O'Neill,*

Commonly Called Owen Roe O'Neil

'Did they dare, did they dare, to slay Owen Roe O'Neil?'
'Yes, they slew with poison him they feared to meet with steel.'
'May God wither up their hearts! May their blood cease to flow!
May they walk in living death, who poisoned Owen Roe!

'Though it break my heart to hear, say again the bitter words.'
'From Derry, against Cromwell, he marched to measure swords;
But the weapon of the Saxon met him on his way,
And he died at Cloc Uactair, upon Saint Leonard's Day.'

'Wail, wail ye for the Mighty One! Wail, wail ye for the Dead!
Quench the hearth, and hold the breath—with ashes strew the head!
How tenderly we loved him! How deeply we deplore!
Holy Saviour! but to think we shall never see him more!

'Sagest in the council was he, kindest in the hall:
Sure we never won a battle—'twas Owen won them all.
Had he lived, had he lived, our dear country had been free;
But he's dead, but he's dead, and 'tis slaves we'll ever be.

'O'Farrell and Clanrickarde, Preston and Red Hugh,
Audley and MacMahon, ye are valiant, wise, and true;
But what—what are ye all to our darling who is gone?
The rudder of our ship was he—our castle's corner-stone!

'Wail, wail him through the island! Weep, weep for our pride!
Would that on the battlefield our gallant chief had died!
Weep the victor of Beinn Burb—weep him, young men and old!
Weep for him, ye women—your Beautiful lies cold!

'We thought you would not die—we were sure you would not go,
And leave us in our utmost need to Cromwell's cruel blow—
Sheep without a shepherd, when the snow shuts out the sky—
Oh! why did you leave us, Owen? why did you die?

'Soft as woman's was your voice, O'Neil! bright was your eye!
Oh! why did you leave us, Owen? why did you die?
Your troubles are all over—you're at rest with God on high;
But we're slaves, and we're orphans, Owen!—why did you die?'

A Nation Once Again

When boyhood's fire was in my blood,
   I read of ancient freemen,
For Greece and Rome who bravely stood,
   Three Hundred men and Three men.
And then I prayed I yet might see
   Our fetters rent in twain,
And Ireland, long a province, be
   A Nation once again.

And, from that time, through wildest woe,
   That hope has shone, a far light;
Nor could love's brightest summer glow
   Outshine that solemn starlight:
It seemed to watch above my head
   In forum, field, and fane;
Its angel voice sang round my bed,
   'A Nation once again'.

It whispered, too, that 'freedom's ark
   And service high and holy,
Would be profaned by feelings dark,
   And passions vain or lowly;
For freedom comes from God's right hand,
   And needs a godly train;
And righteous men must make our land
   A Nation once again.'

So, as I grew from boy to man,
   I bent me to that bidding—
My spirit of each selfish plan
   And cruel passion ridding;
For, thus I hoped some day to aid—
   Oh! can such hope be vain?
When my dear country shall be made
   A Nation once again.

201   from *Laurence Bloomfield in Ireland*

Lord Crashton: The Absentee Landlord

Joining Sir Ulick's at the river's bend,
Lord Crashton's acres east and west extend;
Great owner here, in England greater still.
As poor folk say, 'The world's divided ill.'
On every pleasure men can buy with gold
He surfeited; and now, diseased and old,
He lives abroad; a firm in Molesworth Street
Doing what their attorneyship thinks meet.
The rule of seventy properties have they.
Wide waves the meadow on a summer day,
Far spread the sheep across the swelling hill,
And horns and hooves the daisied pasture fill;
A stout and high enclosure girdles all,
Built up with stones from many a cottage wall;
And, thanks to Phinn and Wedgely's thrifty pains,
Not one unsightly ruin there remains.
Phinn comes half-yearly, sometimes with a friend,
Who writes to Mail or Warder to commend
These vast improvements, and bestows the term
Of 'Ireland's benefactors' on the firm,
A well-earn'd title, in the firm's own mind.
Twice only in the memory of mankind
Lord Crashton's proud and noble self appear'd;
Up-river, last time, in his yacht he steer'd,
With Maltese valet and Parisian cook,
And one on whom askance the gentry look,
Altho' a pretty, well-dress'd demoiselle—
Not Lady Crashton, who, as gossips tell,
Goes her own wicked way. They stopp'd a week;
Then, with gay ribbons fluttering from the peak,
And snowy skirts spread wide, on either hand
The *Aphrodite* curtsied to the land,
And glided off. My Lord, with gouty legs,
Drinks Baden-Baden water, and life's dregs,

With cynic jest inlays his black despair,
And curses all things from his easy chair.

.   .   .   .

The Eviction

In early morning twilight, raw and chill,
Damp vapours brooding on the barren hill,
Through miles of mire in steady grave array
Threescore well-arm'd police pursue their way;
Each tall and bearded man a rifle swings,
And under each greatcoat a bayonet clings;
The Sheriff on his sturdy cob astride
Talks with the chief, who marches by their side,
And, creeping on behind them, Paudeen Dhu
Pretends his needful duty much to rue.
Six big-boned labourers, clad in common frieze,
Walk in the midst, the Sheriff's staunch allies;
Six crowbar men, from distant county brought,—
Orange, and glorying in their work, 'tis thought,
But wrongly,—churls of Catholics are they,
And merely hired at half a crown a day.

The hamlet clustering on its hill is seen,
A score of petty homesteads, dark and mean;
Poor always, not despairing until now;
Long used, as well as poverty knows how,
With life's oppressive trifles to contend.
This day will bring its history to an end.
Moveless and grim against the cottage walls
Lean a few silent men: but someone calls
Far off; and then a child 'without a stitch'
Runs out of doors, flies back with piercing screech,
And soon from house to house is heard the cry
Of female sorrow, swelling loud and high,
Which makes the men blaspheme between their teeth.
Meanwhile, o'er fence and watery field beneath,
The little army moves through drizzling rain;
A 'Crowbar' leads the Sheriff's nag; the lane
Is enter'd, and their plashing tramp draws near;
One instant, outcry holds its breath to hear;

'Halt!'—at the doors they form in double line,
And ranks of polish'd rifles wetly shine.

The Sheriff's painful duty must be done;
He begs for quiet—and the work's begun.
The strong stand ready; now appear the rest,
Girl, matron, grandsire, baby on the breast,
And Rosy's thin face on a pallet borne;
A motley concourse, feeble and forlorn.
One old man, tears upon his wrinkled cheek,
Stands trembling on a threshold, tries to speak,
But, in defect of any word for this,
Mutely upon the doorpost prints a kiss,
Then passes out for ever. Through the crowd
The children run bewilder'd, wailing loud;
Where needed most, the men combine their aid;
And, last of all, is Oona forth convey'd,
Reclined in her accustom'd strawen chair,
Her aged eyelids closed, her thick white hair
Escaping from her cap; she feels the chill,
Looks round and murmurs, then again is still.

Now bring the remnants of each household fire;
On the wet ground the hissing coals expire;
And Paudeen Dhu, with meekly dismal face,
Receives the full possession of the place . . .

202　　　　　Four ducks on a pond,
　　　　　　A grass bank beyond,
　　　　　　A blue sky of spring,
　　　　　　White birds on the wing:
　　　　　　What a little thing
　　　　　　To remember for years—
　　　　　　To remember with tears!

W. B. YEATS
1865–1939

To Ireland in the Coming Times

Know, that I would accounted be
True brother of a company
That sang, to sweeten Ireland's wrong,
Ballad and story, rann and song;
Nor be I any less of them,
Because the red-rose-bordered hem
Of her, whose history began
Before God made the angelic clan,
Trails all about the written page.
When Time began to rant and rage
The measure of her flying feet
Made Ireland's heart begin to beat;
And Time bade all his candles flare
To light a measure here and there;
And may the thoughts of Ireland brood
Upon a measured quietude.

Nor may I less be counted one
With Davis, Mangan, Ferguson,
Because, to him who ponders well,
My rhymes more than their rhyming tell
Of things discovered in the deep,
Where only body's laid asleep.
For the elemental creatures go
About my table to and fro,
That hurry from unmeasured mind
To rant and rage in flood and wind;
Yet he who treads in measured ways
May surely barter gaze for gaze.
Man ever journeys on with them
After the red-rose-bordered hem.
Ah, faeries, dancing under the moon,
A Druid land, a Druid tune!

While still I may, I write for you
The love I lived, the dream I knew.
From our birthday, until we die,
Is but the winking of an eye;

And we, our singing and our love,
What measurer Time has lit above,
And all benighted things that go
About my table to and fro,
Are passing on to where may be,
In truth's consuming ecstasy,
No place for love and dream at all;
For God goes by with white footfall.
I cast my heart into my rhymes,
That you, in the dim coming times,
May know how my heart went with them
After the red-rose-bordered hem.

204   *Red Hanrahan's Song About Ireland*

The old brown thorn-trees break in two high over Cummen Strand,
Under a bitter black wind that blows from the left hand;
Our courage breaks like an old tree in a black wind and dies,
But we have hidden in our hearts the flame out of the eyes
Of Cathleen, the daughter of Houlihan.

The wind has bundled up the clouds high over Knocknarea,
And thrown the thunder on the stones for all that Maeve can say.
Angers that are like noisy clouds have set our hearts abeat;
But we have all bent low and low and kissed the quiet feet
Of Cathleen, the daughter of Houlihan.

The yellow pool has overflowed high up on Clooth-na-Bare,
For the wet winds are blowing out of the clinging air;
Like heavy flooded waters our bodies and our blood;
But purer than a tall candle before the Holy Rood
Is Cathleen, the daughter of Houlihan.

205   *On Those that Hated 'The Playboy*
of the Western World', 1907

Once, when midnight smote the air,
Eunuchs ran through Hell and met
On every crowded street to stare
Upon great Juan riding by:
Even like these to rail and sweat
Staring upon his sinewy thigh.

Easter 1916

I have met them at close of day
Coming with vivid faces
From counter or desk among grey
Eighteenth-century houses.
I have passed with a nod of the head
Or polite meaningless words,
Or have lingered awhile and said
Polite meaningless words,
And thought before I had done
Of a mocking tale or a gibe
To please a companion
Around the fire at the club,
Being certain that they and I
But lived where motley is worn:
All changed, changed utterly:
A terrible beauty is born.

That woman's days were spent
In ignorant good-will,
Her nights in argument
Until her voice grew shrill.
What voice more sweet than hers
When, young and beautiful,
She rode to harriers?
This man had kept a school
And rode our wingèd horse;
This other his helper and friend
Was coming into his force;
He might have won fame in the end,
So sensitive his nature seemed,
So daring and sweet his thought.
This other man I had dreamed
A drunken, vainglorious lout.
He had done most bitter wrong
To some who are near my heart,
Yet I number him in the song;
He, too, has resigned his part
In the casual comedy;
He, too, has been changed in his turn,
Transformed utterly:
A terrible beauty is born.

Hearts with one purpose alone
Through summer and winter seem
Enchanted to a stone
To trouble the living stream.
The horse that comes from the road,
The rider, the birds that range
From cloud to tumbling cloud,
Minute by minute they change;
A shadow of cloud on the stream
Changes minute by minute;
A horse-hoof slides on the brim,
And a horse plashes within it;
The long-legged moor-hens dive,
And hens to moor-cocks call;
Minute by minute they live:
The stone's in the midst of all.

Too long a sacrifice
Can make a stone of the heart.
O when may it suffice?
That is Heaven's part, our part
To murmur name upon name,
As a mother names her child
When sleep at last has come
On limbs that had run wild.
What is it but nightfall.
No, no, not night but death;
Was it needless death after all?
For England may keep faith
For all that is done and said.
We know their dream; enough
To know they dreamed and are dead;
And what if excess of love
Bewildered them till they died?
I write it out in a verse—
MacDonagh and MacBride
And Connolly and Pearse
Now and in time to be,
Wherever green is worn,
Are changed, changed utterly:
A terrible beauty is born.

September 25, 1916

207 *The Seven Sages*

The First. My great-grandfather spoke to Edmund Burke
  In Grattan's house.
The Second.   My great-grandfather shared
  A pot-house bench with Oliver Goldsmith once.
The Third. My great-grandfather's father talked of music,
  Drank tar-water with the Bishop of Cloyne.
The Fourth. But mine saw Stella once.
The Fifth.   Whence came our thought?
The Sixth. From four great minds that hated Whiggery.
The Fifth. Burke was a Whig.
The Sixth.   Whether they knew or not,
  Goldsmith and Burke, Swift and the Bishop of Cloyne
  All hated Whiggery; but what is Whiggery?
  A levelling, rancorous, rational sort of mind
  That never looked out of the eye of a saint
  Or out of drunkard's eye.
The Seventh.   All's Whiggery now,
  But we old men are massed against the world.
The First. American colonies, Ireland, France and India
  Harried, and Burke's great melody against it.
The Second. Oliver Goldsmith sang what he had seen,
  Roads full of beggars, cattle in the fields,
  But never saw the trefoil stained with blood,
  The avenging leaf those fields raised up against it.
The Fourth. The tomb of Swift wears it away.
The Third.   A voice
  Soft as the rustle of a reed from Cloyne
  That gathers volume; now a thunder-clap.
The Sixth. What schooling had these four?
The Seventh.   They walked the roads
  Mimicking what they heard, as children mimic;
  They understood that wisdom comes of beggary.

208 *Coole Park and Ballylee, 1931*

  Under my window-ledge the waters race,
    Otters below and moor-hens on the top,
  Run for a mile undimmed in Heaven's face
    Then darkening through 'dark' Raftery's 'cellar' drop,

Run underground, rise in a rocky place
In Coole demesne, and there to finish up
Spread to a lake and drop into a hole.
What's water but the generated soul?

Upon the border of that lake's a wood
Now all dry sticks under a wintry sun,
And in a copse of beeches there I stood,
For Nature's pulled her tragic buskin on
And all the rant's a mirror of my mood:
At sudden thunder of the mounting swan
I turned about and looked where branches break
The glittering reaches of the flooded lake.

Another emblem there! That stormy white
But seems a concentration of the sky;
And, like the soul, it sails into the sight
And in the morning's gone, no man knows why;
And is so lovely that it sets to right
What knowledge or its lack had set awry,
So arrogantly pure, a child might think
It can be murdered with a spot of ink.

Sound of a stick upon the floor, a sound
From somebody that toils from chair to chair;
Beloved books that famous hands have bound,
Old marble heads, old pictures everywhere;
Great rooms where travelled men and children found
Content or joy; a last inheritor
Where none has reigned that lacked a name and fame
Or out of folly into folly came.

A spot whereon the founders lived and died
Seemed once more dear than life; ancestral trees,
Or gardens rich in memory glorified
Marriages, alliances and families,
And every bride's ambition satisfied.
Where fashion or mere fantasy decrees
We shift about—all that great glory spent—
Like some poor Arab tribesman and his tent.

We were the last romantics—chose for theme
Traditional sanctity and loveliness;
Whatever's written in what poets name
The book of the people; whatever most can bless
The mind of man or elevate a rhyme;
But all is changed, that high horse riderless,
Though mounted in that saddle Homer rode
Where the swan drifts upon a darkening flood.

209   *The Circus Animals' Desertion*

I

I sought a theme and sought for it in vain,
I sought it daily for six weeks or so.
Maybe at last, being but a broken man,
I must be satisfied with my heart, although
Winter and summer till old age began
My circus animals were all on show,
Those stilted boys, that burnished chariot,
Lion and woman and the Lord knows what.

II

What can I but enumerate old themes?
First that sea-rider Oisin led by the nose
Through three enchanted islands, allegorical dreams,
Vain gaiety, vain battle, vain repose,
Themes of the embittered heart, or so it seems,
That might adorn old songs or courtly shows;
But what cared I that set him on to ride,
I, starved for the bosom of his faery bride?

And then a counter-truth filled out its play,
The Countess Cathleen was the name I gave it;
She, pity-crazed, had given her soul away,
But masterful Heaven had intervened to save it.
I thought my dear must her own soul destroy,
So did fanaticism and hate enslave it,
And this brought forth a dream and soon enough
This dream itself had all my thought and love.

And when the Fool and Blind Man stole the bread
Cuchulain fought the ungovernable sea;
Heart-mysteries there, and yet when all is said
It was the dream itself enchanted me:
Character isolated by a deed
To engross the present and dominate memory.
Players and painted stage took all my love,
And not those things that they were emblems of.

III

Those masterful images because complete
Grew in pure mind, but out of what began?
A mound of refuse or the sweepings of a street,
Old kettles, old bottles, and a broken can,
Old iron, old bones, old rags, that raving slut
Who keeps the till. Now that my ladder's gone,
I must lie down where all the ladders start,
In the foul rag-and-bone shop of the heart.

PÁDRAIG Ó HÉIGEARTAIGH

1871–1936

(Translated from the Irish)

210

My sorrow, Donncha, my thousand-cherished
      under this sod stretched,
this mean sod lying on your little body
      —my utter fright . . .
If this sleep were on you in Cill na Dromad
      or some grave in the West
it would ease my sorrow, though great the affliction
      and I'd not complain.

Spent and withered are the flowers scattered
      on your narrow bed.
They were fair a while but their brightness faded,
      they've no gloss or life.

And my brightest flower that in soil grew ever
        or will ever grow
rots in the ground, and will come no more
        to lift my heart.

Alas beloved, is it not great pity
        how the water rocked you,
your pulses powerless and no one near you
        to bring relief?
No news was brought me of my child in peril
        or his cruel hardship
—O I'd go, and eager, to Hell's deep flag-stones
        if I could save you.

The moon is dark and I cannot sleep.
        All ease has left me.
The candid Gaelic seems harsh and gloomy
        —an evil omen.
I hate the time that I pass with friends,
        their wit torments me.
Since the day I saw you on the sands so lifeless
        no sun has shone.

Alas my sorrow, what can I do now?
        The world grinds me
—your slight white hand, like a tree-breeze, gone from
        my frowning brows,
and your little honeymouth, like angels' music
        sweet in my ears
saying to me softly: 'Dear heart, poor father,
        do not be troubled.'

And O, my dear one! I little thought
        in my time of hope
this child would never be a brave swift hero
        in the midst of glory
with deeds of daring and lively thoughts
        for the sake of Fódla
—but the One who framed us of clay on earth
        not so has ordered.

J. M. SYNGE
1871–1909

211   *On an Anniversary*

After reading the dates in a book of lyrics

With Fifteen-ninety or Sixteen-sixteen
We end Cervantes, Marot, Nashe or Green;
Then Sixteen-thirteen till twoscore and nine
Is Crashaw's niche, that honey-lipped divine.
And so when all my little work is done
They'll say I came in Eighteen-seventy-one,
And died in Dublin . . . What year will they write
For my poor passage to the stall of night?

212   *To the Oaks of Glencree*

My arms are round you, and I lean
Against you, while the lark
Sings over us, and golden lights, and green
Shadows are on your bark.

There'll come a season when you'll stretch
Black boards to cover me:
Then in Mount Jerome I will lie, poor wretch,
With worms eternally.

213   *A Question*

I asked if I got sick and died, would you
With my black funeral go walking too,
If you'd stand close to hear them talk or pray
While I'm let down in that steep bank of clay.

And, No, you said, for if you saw a crew
Of living idiots pressing round that new
Oak coffin—they alive, I dead beneath
That board—you'd rave and rend them with your teeth.

214

Winter

With little money in a great city

There's snow in every street
Where I go up and down,
And there's no woman, man, or dog
That knows me in the town.

I know each shop, and all
These Jews, and Russian Poles,
For I go walking night and noon
To spare my sack of coals.

215

The Curse

*To a sister of an enemy of the author's
who disapproved of 'The Playboy'*

Lord, confound this surly sister,
Blight her brow with blotch and blister,
Cramp her larynx, lung, and liver,
In her guts a galling give her.

Let her live to earn her dinners
In Mountjoy with seedy sinners:
Lord, this judgment quickly bring,
And I'm Your servant, J. M. Synge.

P. H. PEARSE
1879–1916

(Translated from the Irish)

216

Renunciation

Naked I saw thee,
O beauty of beauty,
And I blinded my eyes
For fear I should fail.

I heard thy music,
O melody of melody,
And I closed my ears
For fear I should falter.

I tasted thy mouth,
O sweetness of sweetness,
And I hardened my heart
For fear of my slaying.

I blinded my eyes,
And I closed my ears,
I hardened my heart
And I smothered my desire.

I turned my back
On the vision I had shaped,
And to this road before me
I turned my face.

I have turned my face
To this road before me,
To the deed that I see
And the death I shall die.

(Translated by the author)

PADRAIC COLUM
1881–1972

217   *A Poor Scholar of the Forties*

My eyelids red and heavy are,
With bending o'er the smold'ring peat.
I know the Aeneid now by heart,
My Virgil read in cold and heat,
In loneliness and hunger smart.
   And I know Homer, too, I ween,
   As Munster poets know Ossian.

And I must walk this road that winds
'Twixt bog and bog, while east there lies
A city with its men and books,
With treasures open to the wise,
Heart-words from equals, comrade-looks;
　　Down here they have but tale and song,
　　They talk Repeal the whole night long.

'You teach Greek verbs and Latin nouns',
The dreamer of Young Ireland said.
'You do not hear the muffled call,
The sword being forged, the far-off tread
Of hosts to meet as Gael and Gall—
　　What good to us your wisdom store,
　　Your Latin verse, your Grecian lore?'

And what to me is Gael or Gall?
Less than the Latin or the Greek.—
I teach these by the dim rush-light,
In smoky cabins night and week.
But what avail my teaching slight?
　　Years hence, in rustic speech, a phrase,
　　As in wild earth a Grecian vase!

218　　　　　*An Old Woman of the Roads*

O, to have a little house!
To own the hearth and stool and all!
The heaped up sods against the fire,
The pile of turf against the wall!

To have a clock with weights and chains
And pendulum swinging up and down!
A dresser filled with shining delph,
Speckled and white and blue and brown!

I could be busy all the day
Clearing and sweeping hearth and floor,
And fixing on their shelf again
My white and blue and speckled store!

I could be quiet there at night
Beside the fire and by myself,
Sure of a bed and loth to leave
The ticking clock and the shining delph!

Och! but I'm weary of mist and dark,
And roads where there's never a house nor bush,
And tired I am of bog and road,
And the crying wind and the lonesome hush!

And I am praying to God on high,
And I am praying Him night and day,
For a little house—a house of my own—
Out of the wind's and the rain's way.

219   *She Moved Through the Fair*

My young love said to me, 'My brothers won't mind,
And my parents won't slight you for your lack of kind.'
Then she stepped away from me, and this she did say,
'It will not be long, love, till our wedding day.'

She stepped away from me and she moved through the fair,
And fondly I watched her go here and go there,
Then she went her way homeward with one star awake,
As the swan in the evening moves over the lake.

The people were saying no two were e'er wed
But one had a sorrow that never was said,
And I smiled as she passed with her goods and her gear,
And that was the last that I saw of my dear.

I dreamt it last night that my young love came in,
So softly she entered, her feet made no din;
She came close beside me, and this she did say,
'It will not be long, love, till our wedding day.'

220 *June*

Broom out the floor now, lay the fender by,
And plant this bee-sucked bough of woodbine there,
And let the window down. The butterfly
Floats in upon the sunbeam, and the fair
Tanned face of June, the nomad gipsy, laughs
Above her widespread wares, the while she tells
The farmers' fortunes in the fields, and quaffs
The water from the spider-peopled wells.

The hedges are all drowned in green grass seas,
And bobbing poppies flare like Elmo's light,
While siren-like the pollen-stainèd bees
Drone in the clover depths. And up the height
The cuckoo's voice is hoarse and broke with joy.
And on the lowland crops the crows make raid,
Nor fear the clappers of the farmer's boy,
Who sleeps, like drunken Noah, in the shade.

And loop this red rose in that hazel ring
That snares your little ear, for June is short
And we must joy in it and dance and sing,
And from her bounty draw her rosy worth.
Ay! soon the swallows will be flying south,
The wind wheel north to gather in the snow,
Even the roses spilt on youth's red mouth
Will soon blow down the road all roses go.

221 *A Fear*

I roamed the woods today and seemed to hear,
As Dante heard, the voice of suffering trees.
The twisted roots seemed bare contorted knees,
The bark was full of faces strange with fear.

I hurried home still wrapt in that dark spell,
And all the night upon the world's great lie
I pondered, and a voice seemed whisp'ring nigh,
'You died long since, and all this thing is hell!'

222   *Thomas MacDonagh*

He shall not hear the bittern cry
In the wild sky, where he is lain,
Nor voices of the sweeter birds
Above the wailing of the rain.

Nor shall he know when loud March blows
Thro' slanting snows her fanfare shrill,
Blowing to flame the golden cup
Of many an upset daffodil.

But when the Dark Cow leaves the moor,
And pastures poor with greedy weeds,
Perhaps he'll hear her low at morn
Lifting her horn in pleasant meads.

AUSTIN CLARKE
1896–1974

223   *Tenebrae*

This is the hour that we must mourn
With tallows on the black triangle,
Night has a napkin deep in fold
To keep the cup; yet who dare pray
If all in reason should be lost,
The agony of man betrayed
At every station of the cross?

223 Tenebrae] a Holy Week office, commemorating the death and resurrection
of Christ   tallows on the black triangle] after each Psalm one of the fifteen candles is
extinguished from the triangular candlestick on the altar, to signify the Apostles' desertion
of Christ. The last candle is placed behind the altar until the end of the service, depicting
Christ's burial, in its disappearance, and resurrection, in its reappearance   a napkin
deep in fold / To keep the cup] the chalice is kept covered by the humeral veil

O when the forehead is too young,
Those centuries of mortal anguish,
Dabbed by a consecrated thumb
That crumbles into dust, will bring
Despair with all that we can know;
And there is nothing left to sing,
Remembering our innocence.

I hammer on that common door,
Too frantic in my superstition,
Transfix with nails that I have broken,
The angry notice of the mind.
Close as the thought that suffers him,
The habit every man in time
Must wear beneath his ironed shirt.

An open mind disturbs the soul,
And in disdain I turn my back
Upon the sun that makes a show
Of half the world, yet still deny
The pain that lives within the past,
The flame sinking upon the spike,
Darkness that man must dread at last.

224   from *Civil War*

They are the spit of virtue now,
Prating of law and honour,
But we remember how they shot
Rory O'Connor.

225   *The Straying Student*

On a holy day when sails were blowing southward,
A bishop sang the Mass at Inishmore,
Men took one side, their wives were on the other
But I heard the woman coming from the shore:
And wild in despair my parents cried aloud
For they saw the vision draw me to the doorway.

223 Dabbed by a consecrated thumb] in the ritual of Ash Wednesday

Long had she lived in Rome when Popes were bad,
The wealth of every age she makes her own,
Yet smiled on me in eager admiration,
And for a summer taught me all I know,
Banishing shame with her great laugh that rang
As if a pillar caught it back alone.

I learned the prouder counsel of her throat,
My mind was growing bold as light in Greece;
And when in sleep her stirring limbs were shown,
I blessed the noonday rock that knew no tree:
And for an hour the mountain was her throne,
Although her eyes were bright with mockery.

They say I was sent back from Salamanca
And failed in logic, but I wrote her praise
Nine times upon a college wall in France.
She laid her hand at darkfall on my page
That I might read the heavens in a glance
And I knew every star the Moors have named.

Awake or in my sleep, I have no peace now,
Before the ball is struck, my breath has gone,
And yet I tremble lest she may deceive me
And leave me in this land, where every woman's son
Must carry his own coffin and believe,
In dread, all that the clergy teach the young.

226   *Penal Law*

Burn Ovid with the rest. Lovers will find
A hedge-school for themselves and learn by heart
All that the clergy banish from the mind,
When hands are joined and head bows in the dark.

326

227   *Her Voice Could Not Be Softer*

Suddenly in the dark wood
She turned from my arms and cried
As if her soul were lost,
And O too late I knew,
Although the blame was mine,
Her voice could not be softer
When she told it in confession.

228   *Martha Blake at Fifty-One*

Early, each morning, Martha Blake
    Walked, angeling the road,
To Mass in the Church of the Three Patrons.
    Sanctuary lamp glowed
And the clerk halo'ed the candles
    On the High Altar. She knelt
Illumined. In gold-hemmed alb,
    The priest intoned. Wax melted.

Waiting for daily Communion, bowed head
    At rail, she hears a murmur.
Latin is near. In a sweet cloud
    That cherub'd, all occurred.
The voice went by. To her pure thought,
    Body was a distress
And soul, a sigh. Behind her denture,
    Love lay, a helplessness.

Then, slowly walking after Mass
    Down Rathgar Road, she took out
Her Yale key, put a match to gas-ring,
    Half filled a saucepan, cooked
A fresh egg lightly, with tea, brown bread,
    Soon, taking off her blouse
And skirt, she rested, pressing the Crown
    Of Thorns until she drowsed.

In her black hat, stockings, she passed
   Nylons to a nearby shop
And purchased, daily, with downcast eyes,
   Fillet of steak or a chop.
She simmered it on a low jet,
   Having a poor appetite,
Yet never for an hour felt better
   From dilatation, tightness.

She suffered from dropped stomach, heartburn
   Scalding, water-brash
And when she brought her wind up, turning
   Red with the weight of mashed
Potato, mint could not relieve her.
   In vain her many belches,
For all below was swelling, heaving
   Wamble, gurgle, squealch.

She lay on the sofa with legs up,
   A decade on her lip,
At four o'clock, taking a cup
   Of lukewarm water, sip
By sip, but still her daily food
   Repeated and the bile
Tormented her. In a blue hood,
   The Virgin sadly smiled.

When she looked up, the Saviour showed
   His Heart, daggered with flame
And, from the mantel-shelf, St Joseph
   Bent, disapproving. Vainly
She prayed for in the whatnot corner
   The new Pope was frowning. Night
And day, dull pain, as in her corns,
   Recounted every bite.

She thought of St Teresa, floating
   On motes of a sunbeam,
Carmelite with scatterful robes,
   Surrounded by demons,
Small black boys in their skin. She gaped
   At Hell: a muddy passage
That led to nothing, queer in shape,
   A cupboard closely fastened.

Sometimes, the walls of the parlour
   Would fade away. No plod
Of feet, rattle of van, in Garville
   Road. Soul now gone abroad
Where saints, like medieval serfs,
   Had laboured. Great sun-flower shone.
Our Lady's Chapel was borne by seraphs,
   Three leagues beyond Ancona.

High towns of Italy, the plain
   Of France, were known to Martha
As she read in a holy book. The sky-blaze
   Nooned at Padua,
Marble grotto of Bernadette.
   Rose-scatterers. New saints
In tropical Africa where the tsetse
   Fly probes, the forest taints.

Teresa had heard the Lutherans
   Howling on red-hot spit,
And grill, men who had searched for truth
   Alone in Holy Writ.
So Martha, fearful of flame lashing
   Those heretics, each instant,
Never dealt in the haberdashery
   Shop, owned by two Protestants.

In ambush of night, an angel wounded
   The Spaniard to the heart
With iron tip on fire. Swooning
   With pain and bliss as a dart
Moved up and down within her bowels
   Quicker, quicker, each cell
Sweating as if rubbed up with towels,
   Her spirit rose and fell.

St John of the Cross, her friend, in prison
   Awaits the bridal night,
Paler than lilies, his wizened skin
   Flowers. In fifths of flight,
Senses beyond seraphic thought,
   In that divinest clasp,
Enfolding of kisses that cauterize,
   Yield to the soul-spasm.

Cunning in body had come to hate
    All this and stirred by mischief
Haled Martha from heaven. Heart palpitates
    And terror in her stiffens.
Heart misses one beat, two . . . flutters . . . stops.
    Her ears are full of sound.
Half fainting, she stares at the grandfather clock
    As if it were overwound.

The fit had come. Ill-natured flesh
    Despised her soul. No bending
Could ease rib. Around her heart, pressure
    Of wind grew worse. Again,
Again, armchaired without relief,
    She eructated, phlegm
In mouth, forgot the woe, the grief,
    Foretold at Bethlehem.

Tired of the same faces, side-altars,
    She went to the Carmelite Church
At Johnson's Court, confessed her faults,
    There, once a week, purchased
Tea, butter in Chatham St. The pond
    In St Stephen's Green was grand.
She watched the seagulls, ducks, black swan,
    Went home by the 15 tram.

Her beads in hand, Martha became
    A member of the Third Order,
Saved from long purgatorial pain,
    Brown habit and white cord
Her own when cerges had been lit
    Around her coffin. She got
Ninety-five pounds on loan for her bit
    Of clay in the common plot.

Often she thought of a quiet sick-ward,
    Nuns, with delicious ways,
Consoling the miserable: quick
    Tea, toast on trays. Wishing
To rid themselves of her, kind neighbours
    Sent for the ambulance,
Before her brother and sister could hurry
    To help her. Big gate clanged.

No medical examination
  For the new patient. Doctor
Had gone to Cork on holidays.
  Telephone sprang. Hall-clock
Proclaimed the quarters. Clatter of heels
  On tiles. Corridor, ward,
A-whirr with the electric cleaner,
  The creak of window cord.

She could not sleep at night. Feeble
  And old, two women raved
And cried to God. She held her beads.
  O how could she be saved?
The hospital had this and that rule.
  Day-chill unshuttered. Nun, with
Thermometer in reticule,
  Went by. The women mumbled.

Mother Superior believed
  That she was obstinate, self-willed.
Sisters ignored her, hands-in-sleeves,
  Beside a pantry shelf
Or counting pillow-case, soiled sheet.
  They gave her purgatives.
Soul-less, she tottered to the toilet.
  Only her body lived.

Wasted by colitis, refused
  The daily sacrament
By regulation, forbidden use
  Of bed-pan, when meals were sent up,
Behind a screen, she lay, shivering,
  Unable to eat. The soup
Was greasy, mutton, beef or liver,
  Cold. Kitchen has no scruples.

The Nuns had let the field in front
  As an Amusement Park,
Merry-go-round, a noisy month, all
  Heltering-skeltering at darkfall,
Mechanical music, dipper, hold-tights,
  Rifle-crack, crash of dodgems.
The ward, godless with shadow, lights,
  How could she pray to God?

Unpitied, wasting with diarrhoea
  And the constant strain,
Poor Child of Mary with one idea,
  She ruptured a small vein,
Bled inwardly to jazz. No priest
  Came. She had been anointed
Two days before, yet knew no peace:
  Her last breath, disappointed.

229   *Japanese Print*

        Both skyed
        In south-west wind beyond
        Poplar and fir-tree, swallow,
        Heron, almost collide,
        Swerve
        With a rapid
        Dip of wing, flap,
        Each in an opposite curve,
        Fork-tail, long neck outstretched
        And feet. All happened
        Above my head. The pair
        Was disappearing. Say I
        Had seen, half hint, a sketch on
        Rice-coloured air,
        Sharako, Hokusai!

230   *Anacreontic*

        They say that Byron, though lame
        In the wrong foot, danced the Sir Roger
        To the old-fashioned tune of De Coverly
        With Lady Caroline Lamb.
        But others had done the same.
        The middle-aged banker, Sam Rogers,
        Twice shared a covering letter
        With her. But O when she'd seen the
        Translator of Anacreon,
        Young Thomas Moore in the wax-light,
        Step to her bed without shame,
        A naked Cupid, all rosy,

All roundy, no epicene
Lisping in anapaestics,
Softly she blew out the flame-tip,
Glimmered in white, as the moon rose,
And unpetalled the rose-bud from Paestum.

PATRICK KAVANAGH
1904–1967

231   *Sanctity*

To be a poet and not know the trade,
To be a lover and repel all women;
Twin ironies by which great saints are made,
The agonising pincer-jaws of Heaven.

232   *On Looking into E. V. Rieu's Homer*

Like Achilles you had a goddess for mother,
For only the half-god can see
The immortal in things mortal;
The far-frightened surprise in a crow's flight
Or the moonlight
That stays for ever in a tree.

In stubble fields the ghosts of corn are
The important spirits that imagination heeds.
Nothing dies; there are no empty
Spaces in the cleanest-reaped fields.

It was no human weakness when you flung
Your body prostrate on a cabbage drill—
Heart-broken with Priam for Hector ravaged;
You did not know why you cried,
This was the night he died—
Most wonderful-horrible
October evening among those cabbages.

The intensity that radiated from
The Far Field Rock—you afterwards denied—
Was the half-god seeing his half-brothers
Joking on the fabulous mountain-side.

233 *Kerr's Ass*

We borrowed the loan of Kerr's big ass
To go to Dundalk with butter,
Brought him home the evening before the market
An exile that night in Mucker.

We heeled up the cart before the door,
We took the harness inside—
The straw-stuffed straddle, the broken breeching
With bits of bull-wire tied;

The winkers that had no choke-band,
The collar and the reins . . .
In Ealing Broadway, London Town
I name their several names

Until a world comes to life—
Morning, the silent bog,
And the God of imagination waking
In a Mucker fog.

234 *Epic*

I have lived in important places, times
When great events were decided, who owned
That half a rood of rock, a no-man's land
Surrounded by our pitchfork-armed claims.
I heard the Duffys shouting 'Damn your soul'
And old McCabe stripped to the waist, seen
Step the plot defying blue cast-steel—
'Here is the march along these iron stones'.
That was the year of the Munich bother. Which
Was more important? I inclined

To lose my faith in Ballyrush and Gortin
Till Homer's ghost came whispering to my mind.
He said: I made the Iliad from such
A local row. Gods make their own importance.

235 *Canal Bank Walk*

Leafy-with-love banks and the green waters of the canal
Pouring redemption for me, that I do
The will of God, wallow in the habitual, the banal,
Grow with nature again as before I grew.
The bright stick trapped, the breeze adding a third
Party to the couple kissing on an old seat,
And a bird gathering materials for the nest for the Word
Eloquently new and abandoned to its delirious beat.
O unworn world enrapture me, encapture me in a web
Of fabulous grass and eternal voices by a beech,
Feed the gaping need of my senses, give me ad lib
To pray unselfconsciously with overflowing speech
For this soul needs to be honoured with a new dress woven
From green and blue things and arguments that cannot be proven.

236 *Lines Written on a Seat on the Grand Canal, Dublin, 'Erected to the Memory of Mrs Dermot O'Brien'*

O commemorate me where there is water,
Canal water preferably, so stilly
Greeny at the heart of summer. Brother
Commemorate me thus beautifully
Where by a lock Niagarously roars
The falls for those who sit in the tremendous silence
Of mid-July. No one will speak in prose
Who finds his way to these Parnassian islands.
A swan goes by head low with many apologies,
Fantastic light looks through the eyes of bridges—
And look! a barge comes bringing from Athy
And other far-flung towns mythologies.
O commemorate me with no hero-courageous
Tomb—just a canal-bank seat for the passer-by.

SAMUEL BECKETT

1906–

Two Poems

I

Cascando

1

why not merely the despaired of
occasion of
wordshed

is it not better abort than be barren

the hours after you are gone are so leaden
they will always start dragging too soon
the grapples clawing blindly the bed of want
bringing up the bones the old loves
sockets filled once with eyes like yours
all always is it better too soon than never
the black want splashing their faces
saying again nine days never floated the loved
nor nine months
nor nine lives

2

saying again
if you do not teach me I shall not learn
saying again there is a last
even of last times
last times of begging
last times of loving
of knowing not knowing pretending
a last even of last times of saying
if you do not love me I shall not be loved
if I do not love you I shall not love

the churn of stale words in the heart again
love love love thud of the old plunger
pestling the unalterable

whey of words
terrified again
of not loving
of loving and not you
of being loved and not by you
of knowing not knowing pretending
pretending

I and all the others that will love you
if they love you

3
unless they love you

1936

2

Saint-Lô

Vire will wind in other shadows
unborn through the bright ways tremble
and the old mind ghost-forsaken
sink into its havoc

1946

238   *Four Poems*

I

Dieppe

again the last ebb
the dead shingle
the turning then the steps
towards the lighted town

1937

2

my way is in the sand flowing
between the shingle and the dune
the summer rain rains on my life
on me my life harrying fleeing
to its beginning to its end

337

my peace is there in the receding mist
when I may cease from treading these long shifting thresholds
and live the space of a door
that opens and shuts

1948

3

what would I do without this world faceless incurious
where to be lasts but an instant where every instant
spills in the void the ignorance of having been
without this wave where in the end
body and shadow together are engulfed
what would I do without this silence where the murmurs die
the pantings the frenzies towards succour towards love
without this sky that soars
above its ballast dust

what would I do what I did yesterday and the day before
peering out of my deadlight looking for another
wandering like me eddying far from all the living
in a convulsive space
among the voices voiceless
that throng my hiddenness

1948

4

I would like my love to die
and the rain to be falling on the graveyard
and on me walking the streets
mourning the first and last to love me

1948

(Translated from the French by the author)

PADRAIC FALLON

1906–1974

Kiltartan Legend

Penelope pulls home
Rogue-lord, artist, world wanderer,
Simply by sitting in a house,
Its sturdy genius;
Of all sirens the most dangerous.

She'll sit them out,
The curious wonders, the ventriloquial voices,
Spacious landfalls, the women, beds in the blue;
Her oceanography
The garden pond, her compass a knitting needle.

The arc-lamped earth, she knows,
Will burn away and she
Still potter among her flowers waiting for him;
Apollo runs before
Touching the blossoms, her unborn sons.

Knitting, unknitting at the half heard
Music of her tapestry, afraid
Of the sunburned body, the organs, the red beard
Of the unshipped mighty male
Home from the fairy tale;

Providing for him
All that's left of her she ties and knots
Threads everywhere; the luminous house
Must hold and will
Her trying warlord home.

Will she know him?
Dignity begs the question that must follow.
She bends to the web where her lord's face
Glitters but has no fellow,
And humbly, or most royally, adds her own.

Lakshmi

A sheet of paper, placed
Over this dangerous bronze figure,
Covers up the East
And the dancer's narrow waist,

India gone, sunken
The archaic shining knot; white paper
Is the churned-up ocean
That cast her upwards, buttocks in motion,

Helmeted hair, enormous
Ear-rings and all, the necklace
In sacred circles; there was
Dancing here that folded into a lotus.

The bare breasts still now, the nubs
At rest, but the twisted rhombs
Of the hips still echo
Temple gongs.

The belly is so young
And the undented navel. Instruments
Should sound like this,
Keeping distance

Like the long arm that falls to the gathering fingers,
Hand sinister, that knows space
Is precious and must not spill.
The two legs are tough with grace—

And since they are the bearers, yield nothing
To immodest silks, who must tower
Up from their native earth
To carry a little flower

Where, coppered above
The heartbeat, on its fine meridian floats
A face flawed with neither age or youth;
Here Ganges pours

But merely rounds the bud
She contemplates, that must not dwindle;
On her right hand it rides, and earth
Turns quietly on the spindle.

Assumption

Some Syrian rainmaker
Invoking a minor image of power found her
Intrude, O enormous magic, and his hands
Dissolve in showers over many lands;
Earth turned woman, or woman into earth, he
Left this wild image to Syrian sorcery.
But O how they tamed her, the Greeks, the civilising
Mythologising Alexandrian schoolmen
And the soft Italians with the Christian eyes
Who ferried her over the tideless Mediterranean;
The muted breasts, the quiet, and on the top
A face bright as a waterdrop.

Assumed into heaven, she,
A statue among statuary,
Consumes in her single fire the line
Of barbarous virgins who dwelt between
Trinities in their season.
Heaven and earth are in division;
The gross fertilities, the ram, the bull,
Left out-of-doors while in her shuttered parlour
When she bares the nipple
No rye rises, no wheaten flower;
Only her dreams stir
The peacock presences of air.

This mild lady
Calms the gross ambitions with a steady
Country look. No drums, no dances,
No midnight fires, no sacrifice of princes;
She takes her pail among the cows
And bolts her fowl in the fowl house;

Evoe, if the sun-headed god is gone, there's still
The house to be done, white linen hung
Upon the hedge. The serene axle
Goes round and round in a crucifixion,
But earth is a pot of flowers. Foreign tongues
Commune above her in a drift of wings.

242   *Painting of my Father*

I

I saw him to the last, the grey
Casting of the face,
The crabbed hands like this
Yielding to the cluster of the Rosary;

I who barbered you occasionally
And filled your pipe
Dropping into your deafness the odd item
Of family news that never
Exactly reached you,

For you were away already.

So your true going was a sort
Of mutual release. 'Lord', you whispered hanging
That day in my arms naked
As Jesus down from the cross,
'Take me away'.

Now for me this vague distress
And a guilt that grows;
What is it that one owes a father?

And cannot pay,

Liaison lost with the broad
Dialect of the child where words
Were the throbs of a countryside
Big like a sheepshearing or small
As the lark pinned high above
The water meadows where we drank our tea,
The trout waiting in the fishing river;

Eternal precincts
Of a huge present tense, as if
You were not due to be left
Abandoned like an old
Settlement;
The young being
Unscrupulous in their growing up.

So you wanted little of me towards the end,
Barbering, a light
For the old pipe,
And an ear, my ear, any ear, when you spilled over
The intolerable burden
Of being a very old man.

II

An image that wounds;
Better even
The figure of power, the
All father,
Jahwah, Helios or another; not
That I'd like you in big translations
Who were rich enough
As your own man

For you were daylight's own fellow and over
The moonsuck of the mother
All male and master under heaven;
And that's how you come into mind,
In taut middleage when you were quite
The masher,
Velvet collar, tan velour
Overcoat, plush hat and handmade boot,
In those streets round the cattlemarket where
Our evenings were a summer saunter;

Hanlon's Corner, Stoneybatter,
The Broadstone, MGWR,
Where trains run no more,

And I half expect round any corner
The hastening dandy, country
Things still clinging;
Blue the gaze;
Delicate the gait, the dancer,
Angler, Fowler, Hurler, football player;

Tomorrow
Formally as a bullfighter he'll pace
The horned pens and the cattle slobber,
Face the loss or net the profit
Stonily
As befits the gambler;

And at noon lean
Recomposed on the railed wall
By the City Arms, yarning, true Ulyssean,
Over a shoe shine.

III

And now here
Above the walnut desk, the only familiar in
This strange hallucinatory land I found
Late, you stare out; again
All age, all pain, at the very end
Of your long span: not you indeed
But every man;
Just waiting.

Land's End some few miles away; the tide
Is white round the Mount; a bird
Stands on the sundial on the lawn; Spring
Is hovering;
And in the tulip tree—hallucination—some
Medieval person reads a tome

(To disappear battered
By a rainshower with his
Monkshood, creature of air;
The bird stays on, real enough;
A woodpecker)

A country ironed out
Into saints and menhirs where
You never put a foot,

Where the weather camps for an hour before
It stamps the soft shires, taking over
The whole south of England at a blow.

LOUIS MacNEICE

1907–1963

243   *Carrickfergus*

I was born in Belfast between the mountain and the gantries
   To the hooting of lost sirens and the clang of trams:
Thence to Smoky Carrick in County Antrim
   Where the bottle-neck harbour collects the mud which jams

The little boats beneath the Norman castle,
   The pier shining with lumps of crystal salt;
The Scotch Quarter was a line of residential houses
   But the Irish Quarter was a slum for the blind and halt.

The brook ran yellow from the factory stinking of chlorine,
   The yarn-mill called its funeral cry at noon;
Our lights looked over the lough to the lights of Bangor
   Under the peacock aura of a drowning moon.

The Norman walled this town against the country
   To stop his ears to the yelping of his slave
And built a church in the form of a cross but denoting
   The list of Christ on the cross in the angle of the nave.

I was the rector's son, born to the anglican order,
   Banned for ever from the candles of the Irish poor;
The Chichesters knelt in marble at the end of a transept
   With ruffs about their necks, their portion sure.

The war came and a huge camp of soldiers
  Grew from the ground in sight of our house with long
Dummies hanging from gibbets for bayonet practice
  And the sentry's challenge echoing all day long;

A Yorkshire terrier ran in and out by the gate-lodge
  Barred to civilians, yapping as if taking affront:
Marching at ease and singing 'Who Killed Cock Robin?'
  The troops went out by the lodge and off to the Front.

The steamer was camouflaged that took me to England—
  Sweat and khaki in the Carlisle train;
I thought that the war would last for ever and sugar
  Be always rationed and that never again

Would the weekly papers not have photos of sandbags
  And my governess not make bandages from moss
And people not have maps above the fireplace
  With flags on pins moving across and across—

Across the hawthorn hedge the noise of bugles,
  Flares across the night,
Somewhere on the lough was a prison ship for Germans,
  A cage across their sight.

I went to school in Dorset, the world of parents
  Contracted into a puppet world of sons
Far from the mill girls, the smell of porter, the salt-mines
  And the soldiers with their guns.

244   *The Sunlight on the Garden*

      The sunlight on the garden
      Hardens and grows cold,
      We cannot cage the minute
      Within its nets of gold,
      When all is told
      We cannot beg for pardon.

Our freedom as free lances
Advances towards its end;
The earth compels, upon it
Sonnets and birds descend;
And soon, my friend,
We shall have no time for dances.

The sky was good for flying
Defying the church bells
And every evil iron
Siren and what it tells:
The earth compels,
We are dying, Egypt, dying

And not expecting pardon,
Hardened in heart anew,
But glad to have sat under
Thunder and rain with you,
And grateful too
For sunlight on the garden.

245   *Autobiography*

In my childhood trees were green
And there was plenty to be seen.

Come back early or never come.

My father made the walls resound,
He wore his collar the wrong way round.

Come back early or never come.

My mother wore a yellow dress;
Gentle, gently, gentleness.

Come back early or never come.

When I was five the black dreams came;
Nothing after was quite the same.

Come back early or never come.

The dark was talking to the dead;
The lamp was dark beside my bed.

Come back early or never come.

When I woke they did not care;
Nobody, nobody was there.

Come back early or never come.

When my silent terror cried,
Nobody, nobody replied.

Come back early or never come.

I got up; the chilly sun
Saw me walk away alone.

Come back early or never come.

246   *House on a Cliff*

Indoors the tang of a tiny oil lamp. Outdoors
The winking signal on the waste of sea.
Indoors the sound of the wind. Outdoors the wind.
Indoors the locked heart and the lost key.

Outdoors the chill, the void, the siren. Indoors
The strong man pained to find his red blood cools,
While the blind clock grows louder, faster. Outdoors
The silent moon, the garrulous tides she rules.

Indoors ancestral curse-cum-blessing. Outdoors
The empty bowl of heaven, the empty deep.
Indoors a purposeful man who talks at cross
Purposes, to himself, in a broken sleep.

247   *Soap Suds*

This brand of soap has the same smell as once in the big
House he visited when he was eight: the walls of the bathroom open
To reveal a lawn where a great yellow ball rolls back through a hoop
To rest at the head of a mallet held in the hands of a child.

And these were the joys of that house: a tower with a telescope;
Two great faded globes, one of the earth, one of the stars;
A stuffed black dog in the hall; a walled garden with bees;
A rabbit warren; a rockery; a vine under glass; the sea.

To which he has now returned. The day of course is fine
And a grown-up voice cries Play! The mallet slowly swings,
Then crack, a great gong booms from the dog-dark hall and the ball
Skims forward through the hoop and then through the next and then

Through hoops where no hoops were and each dissolves in turn
And the grass has grown head-high and an angry voice cries Play!
But the ball is lost and the mallet slipped long since from the hands
Under the running tap that are not the hands of a child.

DENIS DEVLIN

1908–1959

248   from *Memoirs of a Turcoman Diplomat*

OTELI ASIA PALAS, INC.

Evenings ever more willing lapse into my world's evening,
Birds, like Imperial emblems, in their thin, abstract singing,
Announce some lofty Majesty whose embassies are not understood,
Thrushes' and finches' chords, like the yellow and blue skies changing
    place,
I hold my stick, old-world, the waiters know me,
And sip at my European drink, while sunlight falls,
Like thick Italian silks over the square houses into the Bosphorus.
Ladies, I call you women now, from out my emptied tenderness,
All dead in the wars, before and after war,
I toast you my adventures with your beauty!
Where the domes of Sinan shiver like ductile violets in the rain of light.

To the Franks, I suppose it's ugly, this brick and oblong,
When a rare sunlight, rare birdsong,
Compose the absolute kingdom far in the sky
The Franks must ask how it was known, how reached, how governed,
    how let die?
This woman who passes by, sideways, by your side:
There was one you loved for years and years;
Suddenly the jaw is ugly, the shoulders fall,
Provoking but resentment, hardly tears.

THE GOLDEN HORN

We all have a magic kingdom, some have two,
And cry: 'O my city on the Golden Horn, and O my you!'
Discover, in the bee flaunting his black and gold among the foliage in the
    frieze,
You are not what you thought, you are someone like all these,
The most ardent young man turn, at the drop of a black hat,
Into some rabbity sort of clerk, some heart-affairs diplomat,
A John of the Cross into a Curia priest.
It was years ago. It is not now like when the century began—
Though apple and peach lie brilliant on the dark,
And mineral worlds on the dark sky shine,
And the red mouth breathes in; thine is mine,
And the careless Atlantic inhales the Thames, the Tagus and the Seine,
Murmuring back and murmuring forward beasts and sonata scores and
    Ophelian rags—
Where a girl in her balldress was a light on the wave,
Where a dying flare was like a firefly on the wave,
Where all the waves shivered with phosphorous under the moon's
    glacial withdrawal—
'Me voici ignorant': so a poet my father read.
The Empire born again, old pedants will rake up the dead.

My father thought my feeling could take fire by the vibrant Seine
And a tough intellect be constructed in Gottingen,
He thought, the citadels of Anatolia I could justify
Making what's hungry full, what's ragged spry.
Opalescent on the unbloodied green, the Sultan's battle horse,
The hungry cavalry, rearing and screaming in the mist:
We put them down, these Franks, in their sweaty leather and blas-
    phemous curse,
Our salaried Levantine admirals sank their trading ships.

It happened: the Prophet conquered with murder in his hand and
   honour in his crescent lips.

Put it down to a thick heart and a thick pate,
Such puritanic temperament's outgrown:
Now some international Secretary-General throws a lump of bait
And laughs and says my country's not my own.

There was a professor who said: 'The horse must go!'
And certain poets praised him to their shame,
Except in County Cork and Mexico
And where the quick darlings to us from the Cossacks came.
In the Foreign Office, they humorously ask my advice,
My father had money, I was posted from place to place:
What can I tell them? even if I got it right?
There would be protocol about the right time and the right place,
And even not too sentimental about the corps of horse
Dancing between the up-country captains' harsh knees
They could assert that horses than humanity were worse—'

And that our Westernising dictator, though free was no longer free
When at Smyrne he tumbled the chatterbox Greeks into the sea,
Turk lieutenants, waxed moustaches and all, and spiritless mugs of tea.

.   .   .   .

THE WHITE CITY

The Sava and the Danube like two horses folded, mane on mane,
And there were dogs which lapped the water up:
Pale sunlight and pale water, as if some great poet
Said there was peace, like Goethe, and there was peace.

The sunlight pressing on the eyelids, on the waters;
Only ten years ago the invaders came,
The pretty guide talked on and showed our party—
In which were former Nazis, former Fascists—
Photo-posters of men hanging like blotting paper,
Dirty blood on dirty children, dirty mothers
The willowy waters of the Sava bathed;
Only three hundred years ago
Sulymein the Magnificent
Sick and sad outside Belgrade.

Who knows his expectations, free or slave?
Join me, Johannes, down this pretty brace:
One said, or could have sung, Come out with me,
The other, A truce to talk of genocide, and nation and race!

Tuck in your trews, Johannes, my boy, be led by me,
These girls are kind. And we're all the rage now, whisky-flushed men of
    our age,
The callow and the sallow and the fallow wiped off the page!

249   *Ank'hor Vat*

      The antlered forests
      Move down to the sea.
      Here the dung-filled jungle pauses

      Buddha has covered the walls of the great temple
      With the vegetative speed of his imagery

      Let us wait, hand in hand

      No Western god or saint
      Ever smiled with the lissome fury of this god
      Who holds in doubt
      The wooden stare of Apollo
      Our Christian crown of thorns:

      There is no mystery in the luminous lines
      Of that high, animal face
      The smile, sad, humouring and equal
      Blesses without obliging
      Loves without condescension;
      The god, clear as spring-water
      Sees through everything, while everything
      Flows through him

      A fling of flowers here
      Whose names I do not know
      Downy, scarlet gullets
      Green legs yielding and closing

While, at my mental distance from passion,
The prolific divinity of the temple
Is a quiet lettering on vellum.

Let us lie down before him
His look will flow like oil over us.

The Lancet

Brilliant fierce eagles
And goldfishes asleep.

Lips to drink and instruments for singing
Tight hedgerows gripped the fields, now loose and drowsed.
I moved about in the dark, all was quiet
The skies swollen with unshed thunder
Along the clay path my footsteps
Ominously, softly counted time.

Everyside are spread the fruitful plains
Villages live and die
Beneath the million-citied sap, the indifferent fosterage
Of trees; a bloom of night!
As the bloom of black grapes to your nocturnal sky:
So am I near to freedom.

Now and then a shout floats up
In the court
Where the colleagues
Are drinking and musing. None
Will propose an enigma.

Look straight into my eyes when you drink: Yes;
The same enchantment as ever makes me yours!

Your hair dims
I narrow my eyes to slits and I see
Gold copes gliding
The market places foaming with white smocks
Cantilenas of men and women chained and chanting
Each mouth fabulous
With its proper version.

I have been held back
From acts of particular kindness;
I have skulked in the halls of anger
And with meanness have blighted
The blossom of generous givers

But make it that I tremble
In Babylon choirs, in sonorous congregation
The celebration of belled buildings
And turn by turn stare without terror on
The rapt ravelling and unravelling of tidal generations
In which I am born and give birth and die;
And above that sea
Simple and full the sun.

The drinkers topple over
Come, we are still asleep
Avoid the lunar marshes

Darkness slips
From my face, your voice
Clamours in my blood
The same enchantment as ever!
Your drowsy head,
Dishevelled, falls on my shoulder.
The streams in their beds
Never tire of habit
The same enchantment!
Ebony doors open, my love
Is unfulfilled, yield!
The brothers of the sun, the eagles,
Are fixed among the wavering skies, yield!
Bear fruit of me.

251   *Venus of the Salty Shell*

Round a cleft in the cliffs to come upon
The Athenians standing with their friendly gods
Serious on the shore.

The fresh violet of the Middle Sea
Blooms and is gone; and there

The tremble of a difference from the foam
Foam forms a shell which bears
The smiling idol of Love
Brightness shadowy through brightness.

The space of a moment love lightens the body
Only when love comes free as air
Like the goddess on the dove-drawn shell
Riding upon the speckled hawthorn waves
Into the rocky ways of the sea-republic.
Look at that hand gently to the breast!
She smiles as if turning all the orchards of summer
Into one brittle petal to touch.

The old men do not remember
The women of their youth,
The young men bend at point like setters.
There is need; she, the desired-with-cries,
Fanned by the ivory air, on the ache of birth
Advances as though her nakedness
Were the first glad woman's for these men

And nearer and the cries of the men
Stop, they are struck still.
The doves, the hawthorn merge in the wrack and foam.

252   *Wishes for Her*

Against Minoan sunlight
Slight-boned head,
Buildings with the thin climb of larks
Trilling off whetstone brilliants,
Slight head, nor petal nor marble
Night-shell
Two, one and separate.

Love in loving, all
A fledgling, hard-billed April,
Soil's gaudy chemistry in fission and fuse.
And she
Lit out of fire and glass
Lightning
The blue flowers of vacant thunder.

In the riverlands
Stained with old battlefields, old armour
In which their child, rust, sighs,
Strangers lost in the courtyard,
I lie awake.
The ice recedes, on black silk
Rocks the seals sway their heads.

No prophet deaths
In the webbed tensions of memory,
No harm
Night lean with hunters.
I wish you well, wish
Tall angels whose rib-freezing
Beauty attend you.

253   *Little Elegy*

I will walk with a lover of wisdom
A smile for Senator Destiny
But I shall gladly listen.

Her beauty was like silence in a cup of water
Decanting all but the dream matter
The figures of reality
Stood about, Dantesque and pitiful.
Can anyone tell me her name?
I will love her again and again
Girl on skis, arrow and bow in one,
Masked in glass, graceful,
Hard as a word in season.

I saw a round, Bavarian goodman
And a Harvard student with a Mohican's lope
Colliding with huge nosegays
Then laughter burst above their flowers:
Absent of mind, they had their wits about them
I laughed at them both outright
And at simpering, peasant statues
Graces and gods would they be!
It was a heady springtime in Munich
Many I knew confided in me

Popu, the champion cyclist
Sigmund, deriding tyrants
And Carlos, who made love shyly
To a furtive, gentle girl
And came to my door, stammering,
'She loves me, you know.'
'She loves me, you know.'
But geography separated them
And geography keeps them apart
Now they live forgotten in each other's heart.

II

The sun was full on, the bird-breed
Gradually found their wings.
The baroque churches glowed like the Book of Kells.
We two, with butterbrot and sweetmilk
Over the snow beneath blue winds
Went far and wide.
Busy, alone, we all go far and wide
Who once listened to each other's
Fair vows and counsel.
Of those that go out of the cafés and gardens
Some lie in prisons
Some die of unhappiness
Indeed, it is so!

This is all I can remember
Quarrelling, gusts of confidence
The class climbing through faun nights
And her I would meet
As though I were unconscious
In vacant, bright-columned streets
And beings in love's tunic scattered to the four winds
For no reason at all
For no reason that I can tell.

MÁIRTÍN Ó DIREÁIN

1910–1988

(Translated from the Irish)

Homage to John Millington Synge

The thing that brought you among my people
from rich distance to rough rock
was something in the vital clay,
a trace escaping of woe and loss.

It was not from stone you took your stories,
but the wonders in stories by the fire;
not care for the stony cell or flag
—there are no groans out of dead ground.

Deirdre met you there on the road;
Naoise's *currach* turned Ceann Gainnimh.
Deirdre and Naoise took their way
—and Pegeen was nagging at Shauneen.

Always in your fist, that book . . .
You cast your words from it in a spell:
Deirdre, Naoise, Pegeen took shape
and gave a hero-leap from its pages.

My people's way is failing fast,
the wave no longer a guarding wall.
But till Cuan Wood comes to Inis Meán
the words you gathered here will be
alive still in a foreign tongue.

currach] skin boat   Ceann Gainnimh] Sandy Head   Cuan Wood] where
Deirdre lived in Scotland   Inis Meán] the middle Aran Island

SEÁN Ó RÍORDÁIN

1916–1977

(Translated from the Irish)

255   *Death*

    Death was at hand.
    I said I would go
    with no grief or delay.
    I looked at myself
    in wonder
    and said:
    'So that's
    all I was . . .
    Goodbye then
    my friend.'

    I look back now
    upon that time
    when death came up
    in his hurry to take me
    and yield I must—
    and I think I know
    the delight of a maid
    as she waits for her love,
    though I am
    no woman.

256   *Claustrophobia*

    Beside the wine
    is a candle, and terror,
    and the image of my Lord
    with all power gone.
    What remains of the night
    crowds into the yard:
    the night rules
    outside my window.
    Unless I can stop
    the candle going out

night will leap
into my lungs,
mind will founder,
my terror take over,
and the night form from me
—I am living dark.
　　Let the candle last
　　one night, I will be
　　a republic of light
　　till the day comes.

Ice Cold

257

I went out on a frosty morning.
A handkerchief was there on a bush.
I took it, to put it into my pocket,
but it was frozen: it slipped from my hand.
No natural cloth sprang there from my grasp
but a thing that died on a bush last night,
and I went searching under my mind
until I had found its likeness—
　　that day I kissed a woman of my people
　　ice cold, stretched out in her box.

The Moths

258

Delicate sound of a moth; a page turning;
a tiny wing destroyed.
In my bedroom on a night in autumn
a delicate thing hurt.

Another night, I saw in dream
two moth wings
wide as the wings of angels
and delicate as women.

I was to restrain them,
not to have them escape,
to possess them, as I held them,
and bring them to full bliss.

But I spilled the holy powder
spattered on each wing
—and I knew I was without digits,
without the digits of manhood for ever.

And the digits stalked away from my blunder
with a new and firm authority,
and everyone could be heard, talking about them,
everyone, except myself.

Delicate sound of a moth; a page turning;
a moth membrane ruined;
an autumn night; moths flying.
Such fierce attention to their tiny uproar.

VALENTIN IREMONGER

1918–

259 ## *The Toy Horse*

Somebody, when I was young, stole my toy horse,
The charm of my morning romps, my man's delight.
For two days I grieved, holding my sorrow like flowers
Between the bars of my sullen angry mind.

Next day I went out with evil in my heart,
Evil between my eyes and at the tips of my hands,
Looking for my enemy at the armed stations,
Until I found him, playing in his garden

With my toy horse, urgent in the battle
Against the enemies of his Unreason's land:
He was so happy, I gave him also
My vivid coloured crayons and my big glass marble.

260 ## *This Houre Her Vigill*

Elizabeth, frigidly stretched,
On a spring day surprised us
With her starched dignity and the quietness
Of her hands clasping a black cross.

With book and candle and holy water dish
She received us in the room with the blind down.
Her eyes were peculiarly closed and we knelt shyly
Noticing the blot of her hair on the white pillow.

We met that evening by the crumbling wall
In the field behind the house where I lived
And talked it over, but could find no reason
Why she had left us whom she had liked so much.

Death, yes, we understood: something to do
With age and decay, decrepit bodies;
But here was this vigorous one, aloof and prim,
Who would not answer our furtive whispers.

Next morning, hearing the priest call her name,
I fled outside, being full of certainty,
And cried my seven years against the church's stone wall.
For eighteen years I did not speak her name

Until this autumn day when, in a gale,
A sapling fell outside my window, its branches
Rebelliously blotting the lawn's green. Suddenly, I thought
Of Elizabeth, frigidly stretched.

RICHARD MURPHY

1927–

from *The Battle of Aughrim* (261–265)

261   *Rapparees*

Out of the earth, out of the air, out of the water
And slinking nearer the fire, in groups they gather:
Once he looked like a bird, but now a beggar.

This fish rainbows out of a pool: 'Give me bread!'
He fins along the lake-shore with the starved.
Green eyes glow in the night from clumps of weed.

The water is still. A rock or the nose of an otter
Jars the surface. Whistle of rushes or bird?
It steers to the bank, it lands as a pikeman armed.

With flint and bundles of straw a limestone hall
Is gutted, a noble family charred in its sleep,
And they gloat by moonlight on a mound of rubble.

The highway trees are gibbets where seventeen rot
Who were caught last week in a cattle-raid.
The beasts are lowing. 'Listen!' 'Stifle the guard!'

In a pinewood thickness an earthed-over charcoal fire
Forges them guns. They melt lead stripped from a steeple
For ball. At the whirr of a snipe each can disappear

Terrified as a bird in a gorse-bush fire,
To delve like a mole or mingle like a nightjar
Into the earth, into the air, into the water.

262   *Wolfhound*

A wolfhound sits under a wild ash
Licking the wound in a dead ensign's neck.

When guns cool at night with bugles in fog
She points over the young face.

All her life a boy's pet.
Prisoners are sabred and the dead are stripped.

Her ear pricks like a crimson leaf on snow,
The horse-carts creak away.

Vermin by moonlight pick
The tongues and sockets of six thousand skulls.

She pines for his horn to blow
To bay in triumph down the track of wolves.

Her forelegs stand like pillars through a siege,
His Toledo sword corrodes.

363

Nights she lopes to the scrub
And trails back at dawn to guard a skeleton.

Wind shears the berries from the rowan tree,
The wild geese have flown.

She lifts her head to cry
As a woman keens in a famine for her son.

A redcoat, stalking, cocks
His flintlock when he hears the wolfhound growl.

Her fur bristles with fear at the new smell,
Snow has betrayed her lair.

'I'll sell you for a packhorse,
You antiquated bigoted papistical bitch!'

She springs: in self-defence he fires his gun.
People remember this.

By turf embers she gives tongue
When the choirs are silenced in wood and stone.

263   *Green Martyrs*

I dream of a headless man
Sitting on a charger, chiselled stone.

A woman is reading from an old lesson:
'. . . who died in the famine.

Royal bulls on my land,
I starved to feed the absentee with rent.

Aughrim's great disaster
Made him two hundred years my penal master.

Rapparees, whiteboys, volunteers, ribbonmen,
Where have they gone?

Coerced into exile, scattered
Leaving a burnt gable and a field of ragwort.'

July the Twelfth, she takes up tongs
To strike me for a crop of calf-bound wrongs.

Her weekly half-crowns have built
A grey cathedral on the old gaol wall.

She brings me from Knock shrine
John Kennedy's head on a china dish.

264   *Orange March*

In bowler hats and Sunday suits,
Orange sashes, polished boots,
Atavistic trainbands come
To blow the fife and beat the drum.

Apprentices uplift their banner
True blue-dyed with 'No Surrender!'
Claiming Aughrim as if they'd won
Last year, not 1691.

On Belfast silk, Victoria gives
Bibles to kneeling Zulu chiefs.
Read the moral, note the date:
'The secret that made Britain great.'

Derry, oakwood of bright angels,
Londonderry, dingy walls
Chalked at night with 'Fuck the Queen!'
Bygone canon, bygone spleen.

265   *Casement's Funeral*

After the noose, and the black diary deeds
Gossiped, his fame roots in prison lime:
The hanged bones burn, a revolution seeds.
Now Casement's skeleton is flying home.

A gun salutes, the troops slow-march, our new
Nation atones for her shawled motherland
Whose welcome gaoled him when a U-boat threw
This rebel quixote soaked on Banna Strand.

Soldiers in green guard the draped catafalque
With chalk remains of once ambiguous bone
Which fathered nothing till the traitor's dock
Hurt him to tower in legend like Wolfe Tone.

From gaol yard to the Liberator's tomb
Pillared in frost, they carry the freed ash,
Transmuted relic of a death-cell flame
Which purged for martyrdom the diarist's flesh.

On the small screen I watch the packed cortège
Pace from High Mass. Rebels in silk hats now
Exploit the grave with an old comrade's speech:
White hair tossed, a black cape flecked with snow.

266   *High Island*

A shoulder of rock
Sticks high up out of the sea,
A fisherman's mark
For lobster and blue-shark.

Fissile and stark
The crust is flaking off,
Seal-rock, gull-rock,
Cove and cliff.

Dark mounds of mica schist,
A lake, mill and chapel,
Roofless, one gable smashed,
Lie ringed with rubble.

An older calm,
The kiss of rock and grass,
Pink thrift and white sea-campion,
Flowers in the dead place.

Day keeps lit a flare
Round the north pole all night
Like brushing long wavy hair
Petrels quiver in flight.

Quietly as the rustle
Of an arm entering a sleeve,
They slip down to nest
Under altar-stone or grave.

Round the wrecked laura
Needles flicker
Tacking air, quicker and quicker
To rock, sea and star.

THOMAS KINSELLA

1928–

267   *A Hand of Solo*

Lips and tongue
wrestle the delicious
        life out of you.

A last drop.
Wonderful.
        A moment's rest.

In the firelight glow
the flickering
        shadows softly

come and go up on the shelf:
red heart and black spade
        hid in the kitchen dark.

Woman throat song
help my head
        back to you sweet.

                *

Hushed, buried green baize.
Slide and stop. Black spades. Tray. Still.
Red deuce. Two hearts. Blood-clean. Still.

Black flash. Jack Rat grins.
She drops down. Silent. Face disk blank. Queen.

The Boss spat in the kitchen fire.
His head shook.

Angus's fat hand brushed in all the pennies.
His waistcoat pressed the table.

Uncle Matty slithered the cards together
and knocked them. Their edges melted. Soft gold.

Angus picked up a bright penny and put it
in my hand: satiny, dream-new disk of light . . .

'Go on out in the shop and get yourself something.'
'Now, Angus . . .'
                      'Now, now, Jack. He's my luck.'
'Tell your grandmother we're waiting for her.'

She was settling the lamp.
Two yellow tongues rose and brightened.
The shop brightened.

Her eyes glittered.
A tin ghost beamed, Mick McQuaid
nailed across the fireplace.

'Shut the kitchen door, child of grace.
Come here to me.
Come here to your old grandmother.'

Strings of jet beads wreathed her neck
and hissed on the black taffeta
and crept on my hair.

'. . . You'd think I had three heads!'
My eyes were squeezed shut against the key
in the pocket of her apron. Her stale abyss . . .

Old knuckles pressed on the counter,
then were snatched away. She sat down at the till
on her high stool, chewing nothing.

The box of Indian apples
was over in the corner
by the can of oil.

I picked out one of the fruit,
a rose-red hard wax
turning toward gold, light like wood,

and went at it with little bites,
peeling off bits of skin
and tasting the first traces of the blood.

When it was half peeled,
with the glassy pulp exposed like cells,
I sank my teeth in it

loosening the packed mass of dryish beads
from their indigo darkness.
I drove my tongue among them

and took a mouthful, and slowly
bolted them. My throat filled
with a rank, Arab bloodstain.

268   *Ancestor*

I was going up to say something,
and stopped. Her profile against the curtains
was old, and dark like a hunting bird's.

It was the way she perched on the high stool,
staring into herself, with one fist
gripping the side of the barrier around her desk
—or her head held by something, from inside.
And not caring for anything around her
or anyone there by the shelves.
I caught a faint smell, musky and queer.

I may have made some sound—she stopped rocking
and pressed her fist in her lap; then she stood up
and shut down the lid of the desk, and turned the key.
She shoved a small bottle under her aprons
and came toward me, darkening the passageway.

Ancestor . . . among sweet- and fruit-boxes.
Her black heart . . .
                         Was that a sigh?
—brushing by me in the shadows,
with her heaped aprons, through the red hangings
to the scullery, and down to the back room.

269   *Tear*

I was sent in to see her.
A fringe of jet drops
chattered at my ear
as I went in through the hangings.

I was swallowed in chambery dusk.
My heart shrank
at the smell of disused
organs and sour kidney.

The black aprons I used to
bury my face in
were folded at the foot of the bed
in the last watery light from the window

(Go in and say goodbye to her)
and I was carried off
to unfathomable depths.
I turned to look at her.

She stared at the ceiling
and puffed her cheek, distracted,
propped high in the bed
resting for the next attack.

The covers were gathered close
up to her mouth,
that the lines of ill-temper still
marked. Her grey hair

was loosened out like
a young woman's all over
the pillow, mixed with the shadows
criss-crossing her forehead

and at her mouth and eyes,
like a web of strands tying down her head
and tangling down toward the shadow
eating away the floor at my feet.

I couldn't stir at first, nor wished to,
for fear she might turn and tempt me
(my own father's mother)
with open mouth

—with some fierce wheedling whisper—
to hide myself one last time
against her, and bury my
self in her drying mud.

Was I to kiss her? As soon
kiss the damp that crept
in the flowered walls
of this pit.

Yet I had to kiss.
I knelt by the bulk of the death bed
and sank my face in the chill
and smell of her black aprons.

Snuff and musk, the folds against my eyelids,
carried me into a derelict place
smelling of ash: unseen walls and roofs
rustled like breathing.

I found myself disturbing
dead ashes for any trace
of warmth, when far off
in the vaults a single drop

splashed. And I found
what I was looking for
—not heat nor fire,
not any comfort,

but her voice, soft, talking to someone
about my father: 'God help him, he cried
big tears over there by the machine
for the poor little thing.' Bright

drops on the wooden lid for
my infant sister. My own
wail of child-animal grief
was soon done, with any early guess

at sad dullness and tedious pain
and lives bitter with hard bondage.
How I tasted it now—
her heart beating in my mouth!

She drew an uncertain breath
and pushed at the clothes
and shuddered tiredly.
I broke free

and left the room
promising myself
when she was really dead
I would really kiss.

My grandfather half looked up
from the fireplace as I came out,
and shrugged and turned back
with a deaf stare to the heat.

I fidgeted beside him for a minute
and went out to the shop.
It was still bright there
and I felt better able to breathe.

Old age can digest
anything: the commotion
at Heaven's gate—the struggle
in store for you all your life.

How long and hard it is
before you get to Heaven,
unless like little Agnes
you vanish with early tears.

Wyncote, Pennsylvania: A Gloss

A mocking-bird on a branch
outside the window, where I write,
gulps down a wet crimson berry,
shakes off a few bright drops
from his wing, and is gone
into a thundery sky.

Another storm coming.
Under that copper light
my papers seem luminous.
And over them I will take
ever more painstaking care.

JOHN MONTAGUE

1929–

Above the Pool

We were nearly
pressed against each other
on the stairs
(you, one step above
with your mother:
I, one step below
with my aunt)

of the white mosque
of a cinema
in Bundoran, high above
the small hotels, ice-cream
parlours, the Atlantic
working against
roguey rocks.

And my eyes
were asking yours,
and yours were asking mine
for something more

than a glance on a stair;
the seawrack odour
of Donegal air.

We crossed
on the wooden stairs
above the bathing pool
next day, and you halted
with your sun-warmed hair
expectant eyes, wedge-heeled
wartime shoes

waiting for me
to speak, while hit tunes
from the Majestic ballroom
sobbed in my brain:
I'll close my eyes,
Shine on, Victory Moon,

And I walked on
balancing all my hunger for
that mysterious other
against my need to be alone,
to hug rocks, search blue pools
for starfish, in this
my last summer of loneliness.

272   *All Legendary Obstacles*

All legendary obstacles lay between
Us, the long imaginary plain,
The monstrous ruck of mountains
And, swinging across the night,
Flooding the Sacramento, San Joaquin,
The hissing drift of winter rain.

All day I waited, shifting
Nervously from station to bar
As I saw another train sail
By, the San Francisco Chief or
Golden Gate, water dripping
From great flanged wheels.

At midnight you came, pale
Above the negro porter's lamp.
I was too blind with rain
And doubt to speak, but
Reached from the platform
Until our chilled hands met.

You had been travelling for days
With an old lady, who marked
A neat circle on the glass
With her glove, to watch us
Move into the wet darkness
Kissing, still unable to speak.

273   *Hero's Portion*

*When dining they all sit not on chairs, but on the ground, strewing beneath them wolf- or
dog-skins. . . . Beside them are the hearths blazing with fire, with cauldrons and spits
with great pieces of meat; brave warriors are honoured by the finest portions.*

(Diodorus Siculus)

I

A steaming hunk of meat
landed before him—

it was red & running
with blood & his stomach

rose & fell to see it
his juices churned to meet it
his jaws opened to chew it

cracking & splitting down
to the marrow stuffed bone
which he licked & sucked

as clean as a whistle

before he sighed 'Enough!'
and raised his gold ringed arms

to summon one
of the waiting women
to squat across his lap

375

while the musician pulled
his long curved nails
through the golden hair
of his harp.

II

What song to sing?
the blind man said:

*sing the hero
who lost his head*

*sing the hero
who lopped it off*

*sing the torso
still propped aloft*

*sing the nobles
who judged that fall*

*sing the sword
so fierce & tall*

*sing the ladies
whose bowels crave*

*its double edge
of birth & grave.*

III

Timbers creak
in the banquet hall;
the harper's fingers
are ringed with blood
& the ornate battle sword
sheathed in its scabbard.
The king has fallen asleep
under the weight of his crown
while in the corner a hound
& bitch are quarrelling
over the hero's bone.

Mother Cat

The mother cat
opens her claws
like petals

bends her spine
to expose her
battery of tits

where her young
toothless snouts
screwed eyes

on which light
cuffs mild
paternal blows

jostle & cry
for position
except one

so boneless
& frail it
pulls down

air, not milk.
Wan little scut
you are already

set for death
never getting
a say against

the warm circle
of your mother's
breast, as she

arches voluptuously
in the pleasure
of giving life

JOHN MONTAGUE

to those who
claim it, bit-
ten navel cords

barely dried,
already fierce
at the trough.

SEAMUS HEANEY

1939–

275   *Docker*

There, in the corner, staring at his drink.
The cap juts like a gantry's crossbeam,
Cowling plated forehead and sledgehead jaw.
Speech is clamped in the lips' vice.

That fist would drop a hammer on a Catholic—
Oh yes, that kind of thing could start again;
The only Roman collar he tolerates
Smiles all round his sleek pint of porter.

Mosaic imperatives bang home like rivets;
God is a foreman with certain definite views
Who orders life in shifts of work and leisure.
A factory horn will blare the Resurrection.

He sits, strong and blunt as a Celtic cross,
Clearly used to silence and an armchair:
Tonight the wife and children will be quiet
At slammed door and smoker's cough in the hall.

276   *Bogland*

for T. P. Flanagan

We have no prairies
To slice a big sun at evening—
Everywhere the eye concedes to
Encroaching horizon,

378

Is wooed into the cyclops' eye
Of a tarn. Our unfenced country
Is bog that keeps crusting
Between the sights of the sun.

They've taken the skeleton
Of the Great Irish Elk
Out of the peat, set it up
An astounding crate full of air.

Butter sunk under
More than a hundred years
Was recovered salty and white.
The ground itself is kind, black butter

Melting and opening underfoot,
Missing its last definition
By millions of years.
They'll never dig coal here,

Only the waterlogged trunks
Of great firs, soft as pulp.
Our pioneers keep striking
Inwards and downwards,

Every layer they strip
Seems camped on before.
The bogholes might be Atlantic seepage.
The wet centre is bottomless.

277   *Sunlight*

There was a sunlit absence.
The helmeted pump in the yard
heated its iron,
water honeyed

in the slung bucket
and the sun stood
like a griddle cooling
against the wall

of each long afternoon.
So, her hands scuffled
over the bakeboard,
the reddening stove

sent its plaquc of heat
against her where she stood
in a floury apron
by the window.

Now she dusts the board
with a goose's wing,
now sits, broad-lapped,
with whitened nails

and measling shins:
here is a space
again, the scone rising
to the tick of two clocks.

And here is love
like a tinsmith's scoop
sunk past its gleam
in the meal-bin.

278 *A Constable Calls*

His bicycle stood at the window-sill,
The rubber cowl of a mud-splasher
Skirting the front mudguard,
Its fat black handlegrips

Heating in sunlight, the 'spud'
Of the dynamo gleaming and cocked back,
The pedal treads hanging relieved
Of the boot of the law.

His cap was upside down
On the floor, next his chair.
The line of its pressure ran like a bevel
In his slightly sweating hair.

He had unstrapped
The heavy ledger, and my father
Was making tillage returns
In acres, roods, and perches.

Arithmetic and fear.
I sat staring at the polished holster
With its buttoned flap, the braid cord
Looped into the revolver butt.

'Any other root crops?
Mangolds? Marrowstems? Anything like that?'
'No.' But was there not a line
Of turnips where the seed ran out

In the potato field? I assumed
Small guilts and sat
Imagining the black hole in the barracks.
He stood up, shifted the baton-case

Further round on his belt,
Closed the domesday book,
Fitted his cap back with two hands,
And looked at me as he said goodbye.

A shadow bobbed in the window.
He was snapping the carrier spring
Over the ledger. His boot pushed off
And the bicycle ticked, ticked, ticked.

279   *The Guttural Muse*

Late summer, and at midnight
I smelt the heat of the day:
At my window over the hotel car park
I breathed the muddied night airs off the lake
And watched a young crowd leave the discotheque.

Their voices rose up thick and comforting
As oily bubbles the feeding tench sent up
That evening at dusk—the slimy tench
Once called the 'doctor fish' because his slime
Was said to heal the wounds of fish that touched it.

A girl in a white dress
Was being courted out among the cars:
As her voice swarmed and puddled into laughs
I felt like some old pike all badged with sores
Wanting to swim in touch with soft-mouthed life.

DEREK MAHON

1941–

280   *A Disused Shed in Co. Wexford*

Let them not forget us, the weak souls among the asphodels.
                    (Seferis, *Mythistorema*)

for J. G. Farrell

Even now there are places where a thought might grow—
Peruvian mines, worked out and abandoned
To a slow clock of condensation,
An echo trapped for ever, and a flutter
Of wildflowers in the lift-shaft,
Indian compounds where the wind dances
And a door bangs with diminished confidence,
Lime crevices behind rippling rainbarrels,
Dog corners for bone burials;
And in a disused shed in Co. Wexford,

Deep in the grounds of a burnt-out hotel,
Among the bathtubs and the washbasins
A thousand mushrooms crowd to a keyhole.
This is the one star in their firmament
Or frames a star within a star.
What should they do there but desire?
So many days beyond the rhododendrons
With the world waltzing in its bowl of cloud,
They have learnt patience and silence
Listening to the rooks querulous in the high wood.

They have been waiting for us in a foetor
Of vegetable sweat since civil war days,
Since the gravel-crunching, interminable departure
Of the expropriated mycologist.
He never came back, and light since then
Is a keyhole rusting gently after rain.
Spiders have spun, flies dusted to mildew
And once a day, perhaps, they have heard something—
A trickle of masonry, a shout from the blue
Or a lorry changing gear at the end of the lane.

There have been deaths, the pale flesh flaking
Into the earth that nourished it;
And nightmares, born of these and the grim
Dominion of stale air and rank moisture.
Those nearest the door grow strong—
'Elbow room! Elbow room!'
The rest, dim in a twilight of crumbling
Utensils and broken flower-pots, groaning
For their deliverance, have been so long
Expectant that there is left only the posture.

A half century, without visitors, in the dark—
Poor preparation for the cracking lock
And creak of hinges. Magi, moonmen,
Powdery prisoners of the old regime,
Web-throated, stalked like triffids, racked by drought
And insomnia, only the ghost of a scream
At the flash-bulb firing squad we wake them with
Shows there is life yet in their feverish forms.
Grown beyond nature now, soft food for worms,
They lift frail heads in gravity and good faith.

They are begging us, you see, in their wordless way,
To do something, to speak on their behalf
Or at least not to close the door again.
Lost people of Treblinka and Pompeii!
'Save us, save us,' they seem to say,
'Let the god not abandon us
Who have come so far in darkness and in pain.
We too had our lives to live.
You with your light meter and relaxed itinerary,
Let not our naive labours have been in vain!'

281 *Derry Morning*

The mist clears and the cavities
Glow black in the rubbled city's
Broken mouth. An early crone,
Muse of a fitful revolution
Wasted by the fray, she sees
Her *aisling* falter in the breeze,
Her oak-grove vision hesitate
By empty wharf and city gate.

Here it began, and here at least
It fades into the finite past
Or seems to: clattering shadows whop
Mechanically over pub and shop.
A strangely pastoral silence rules
The shining roofs and murmuring schools;
For this is how the centuries work—
Two steps forward, one step back.

Hard to believe this tranquil place,
Its desolation almost peace,
Was recently a boom-town wild
With expectation, each unscheduled
Incident a measurable
Tremor on the Richter Scale
Of world events, each vibrant scene
Translated to the drizzling screen.

What of the change envisioned here,
The quantum leap from fear to fire?
Smoke from a thousand chimneys strains
One way beneath the returning rains
That shroud the bomb-sites, while the fog
Of time receives the ideologue.
A Russian freighter bound for home
Mourns to the city in its gloom.

aisling] vision of promise. See note to poems 136 and 138

The Woods

Two years we spent
down there, in a quaint
outbuilding bright with recent paint.

A green retreat,
secluded and sedate,
part of a once great estate,

it watched our old
bone-shaker as it growled
with guests and groceries through heat and cold,

and heard you tocsin
meal-times with a spoon
while I sat working in the sun.

Above the yard
an old clock had expired
the night Lenin arrived in Petrograd.

Bourbons and Romanovs
had removed their gloves
in the drawing-rooms and alcoves

of the manor house;
but these illustrious
ghosts never imposed on us.

Enough that the pond
steamed, the apples ripened,
the conkers on the gravel opened.

Ragwort and hemlock,
cinquefoil and ladysmock
throve in the shadows at the back;

beneath the trees
foxgloves and wood-anemones
looked up with tearful metamorphic eyes.

We woke the rooks
on narrow, winding walks
familiar from the story books,

or visited
a disused garden shed
where gas-masks from the war decayed;

and we knew peace
splintering the thin ice
on the bath-tub drinking-trough for cows.

But how could we
survive indefinitely
so far from the city and the sea?

Finding, at last,
too creamy for our taste
the fat profusion of that feast,

we travelled on
to doubt and speculation,
our birthright and our proper portion.

Another light
than ours convenes the mute
attention of those woods tonight—

while we, released
from that pale paradise,
ponder the darkness in another place.

SEAMUS DEANE

1941–

283

Scholar I

I splashed water on my face
And one glabrous drop
Ran down my neck and back
In a zig-zag chill.

As I climbed into bed,
Dazed with reading,
I felt the naked sheet
Sigh for the fool.

Sleep on the glazed eye,
Acrid paste on the tooth—
Is there a book that I
Would not burn for the truth?

284   *Scholar II*

I remember at times
How irresponsible I have
Become. No ruling passion
Obsesses me, although passions
Are what I play among.
I'll know the library in a city
Before I know there is a slum.
I could wish the weight of
Learning would bring me down
To where things are done.

I remember the thief who fell
Half way down the wall
Of the Houghton Library because
His rope broke under the extra
Weight of the Gutenberg Bible.
Perhaps he came from a slum,
Hired to rifle the mint of published
Knowledge too. I could have told him
The difference a book would have made.

Saved him perhaps his broken leg.
Told him the new Faust stories
Of a thousand men who made
The same error and now lie
Under the weight of that beautiful,
Intransitive print. He had to fail.
And now he lies, perhaps for years,

With other slum-children in a jail,
The university of the third degree,
While in other circles move the frail
Inquirers, trailing printed liberty.

MICHAEL HARTNETT

1941–

285   *All That is Left . . .*

All that is left and definite
is the skull:
the dull fibres and flesh are gone.
the long femur survives perhaps,
or the wreck of ribs,
but nothing plasmic.
no alien could figure how it loved,
longed to avoid death.
he could perhaps by reconstruction
see it stood,
see, if the tarsals were intact,
it fled, it grasped.
but how could sight be guessed at,
the eyeballs gone?
how could he envision blood,
arteries and heart
flaked down and dusted?
or hair, wave-long and starred,
that sparked out under fingers,
under amber?
all that is left and definite
is the skull full of cockroaches,
and hollow fragile strands in twos
rayed like tendrils
out about a root.

286   *I Have Heard Them Knock*

I have heard them knock
on my dimension
like chimes of glass on glass
or one water-drop
falling a long unlit way
into a deep well,
    but I have never known
    the eternal word for 'enter'.

And they have loosed
melodic pulses in my ears
like cut-glass pendants
struck by fine steel needles,
    but I have never known
    the eternal word for 'yes'.

And moods from their tangent world
have urged me in,
talked me my mind a tapestry
with one flaw,
that flaw the way I can come in
and live their chiming world.
    but I have never known
    the eternal word for 'open'.

287   *The possibility that has been overlooked is the future*

I look along the valley of my gun.
An otter examines the air,
silver in the sun.
I have hunted him for many days.
I will not kill him where he stands:
double death in the breeches
demands he be given a chance.
I take stock, warm metal in my hands.
Will he swim upstream,
water from his nose a bright arrowhead?
Will he swim downstream
coiling in bubbles to the riverbed?

Will he swim upstream,
where an ashtree's roots are naked?
There is a chance he will swim towards me.
Will he take it?

288   from *A Farewell to English*

.   .   .   .   .

II

Half afraid to break a promise
made to Dinny Halpin Friday night
I sat down from my walk to Camas
Sunday evening, Doody's Cross,
and took off my burning boots
on a gentle bench of grass.
The cows had crushed the evening
green with mint
springwater from the roots
of a hawkfaced firtree on my right
swamped pismires bringing home
their sweet supplies
and strawberries looked out
with ferret's eyes.
These old men walked on the summer road
sugán belts and long black coats
with big ashplants and half-sacks
of rags and bacon on their backs.
They stopped before me with a knowing look
hungry, snotnosed, half-drunk.
I said grand evening
and they looked at me awhile
then took their roads
to Croom, Meentogues and Cahirmoyle.
They looked back once,

Croom] the area of Co. Limerick associated with the poet Aindrias Mac Craith
(d. 1795); seat of the last 'courts' of Irish poetry; Hartnett's birthplace   Meentogues]
birthplace of Aogán Ó Rathaille   Cahirmoyle] site of the house of John Bourke,
patron of Dáibhí Ó Bruadair

black moons of misery
sickling their eye-sockets,
a thousand years of history
in their pockets.

III

Chef Yeats, that master of the use of herbs
could raise mere stew to a glorious height,
pinch of saga, soupçon of philosophy
carefully stirred in to get the flavour right,
and cook a poem around the basic verbs.
Our commis-chefs attend and learn the trade,
bemoan the scraps of Gaelic that they know:
add to a simple Anglo-Saxon stock
Cuchulainn's marrow-bones to marinate,
a dash of Ó Rathaille simmered slow,
a glass of University hic-haec-hoc:
sniff and stand back and proudly offer you
the celebrated Anglo-Irish stew.

EXPLANATORY AND
BIOGRAPHICAL NOTES

1. A *rath* is a circular fortification and dwelling-place. This one is the fort of Rathangan, Co. Kildare.

2. Tailtiu, with Tara, was a royal settlement with sloping outer embankments. The poem is attributed to the widow of King Aed Mac Ainmirech who was killed in 598—but it could possibly date to the eighth century.

3. A pagan view of the arrival of the Christians. The early Irish tonsure was cut straight across through the hair, striking the poet as being cut out by an adze.

4. This is *Amra Choluim Chille*, the earliest datable poem in the Irish tradition. It is firmly associated with the death-date of the saint in 597. Colum Cille, 'the sanctuary dove', was the earliest of the saintly exiles and became the subject of a later folk literature (see poems 54–8 and notes). The *Amra* was copied through the generations as an act of devotion and became obscure in places in the process.

5. Saint Columbanus was a contemporary of Saint Colum Cille. He went into exile in the final decade of the sixth century, first in Gaul, then in Italy, where he established the monastery of Bobbio. The poem has been given a completely figurative interpretation, as a pious exhortation, but the opening seems drawn from actual experience.

EIGHTH CENTURY

7. This poem is known also as 'The Deer's Cry'. It is said to have been composed by Saint Patrick to deceive his pursuers into believing that he and his followers were a herd of deer.

8. Cú Chuimne was an eighth-century monk; a Latin hymn of his to the Virgin Mary has survived.

9. These are the final stanzas of a very long devotional poem mostly in praise of Christ's attributes. The poet lived in the mid eighth century in the area of the present counties Louth and Monaghan.

EIGHTH/NINTH CENTURY

10. Derdriu's lament, and her death, come at the end of *The Exile of the Sons of Uisliu*, an eighth- or ninth-century pre-tale of the prose epic *Táin Bó Cuailnge*, 'The Great Cattle-Raid'.

11. The description of the two bulls is taken from passages of *retoiric*, or obscure verse, in another pre-tale, the ninth-century *Quarrel of the Two Pig-Keepers*.

12, 13. The Morrígan, or 'Great Queen', is a goddess of war usually appearing in the shape of a scald-crow. These prophetic utterances are taken from the main body of *The Táin* in its earlier, eighth-century, version; they are made by the gloating bird as the opposing armies draw closer for the last battle. The *Badb* (poem 12) is another manifestation of the war goddess, also in bird shape.

NINTH CENTURY

15. This poem is sometimes attributed to Suibne Geilt, 'Mad Sweeney' (see no. 60). But the main body of Suibne poetry is later by several centuries, and there seems no reason not to take this as an early example of hermitage or monastic poetry. The title 'An Ivied Tree-Top' is suggested by the ninth-century scribe.

16. This poem, one of the most famous in the literature, survives in numerous manuscripts and versions. The speaker is referred to in later folklore and poetry as the voice of Ireland and the goddess of sovereignty. In the original poem she has retired from the world and is living out her life in penance. The version given here is selected from a number of available versions, chosen for general cohesion and omitting some difficulties.

17. Dínertech was killed at the battle of Carn Conaill in 649. He had come to help Créide's father, Guaire—king of Aidne in south Co. Galway, and of the whole of Connacht—who was defeated by Diarmait the king of Ireland.

18–25. A series of anonymous lyrics and glosses by early Christian 'saints'. Poems of the kind are very numerous, and were preserved in later manuscripts—in some cases merely for their technical interest. They range from expressions of simple devotion through a keen appreciation of the natural detail surrounding the remote early hermitages, and the domestic peace there, to an allegorical—sometimes even imagistic—use of these elements.

24. Guaire was king of Connacht in the mid seventh century (and father of Créide, whose lament for Dínertech is given at no. 17 above). Marbán was his half-brother.

There is some doubt as to the location of Marbán's hermitage, subject of this rhapsody which gathers up so many of the motifs of early Irish nature poetry. Druim Rolach is unidentified; there is a Roigne (line 19) in Co. Kilkenny, but this seems an unlikely site in the circumstances. A more likely possibility is suggested in line 20: Mucruime is the plain between Athenry and Galway, and Moenmag the plain around Loughrea, east of Guaire's kingdom of Aidne in south Co. Galway.

25. The Calendar, or 'festology', of Oengus was compiled at the beginning of the ninth century in the monastery at Tallaght (now a suburb of Dublin). The compiler is said to have been a 'spouse of God', Oengus Céile Dé, but more than one 'culdee', or anchorite, was so named (see poem 45). The Christian invasion foreseen in poem 3 is complete, as the poet sets the *cahirs*—the great ecclesiastical establishments such as Clonmacnoise, Ferns, and Glendalough, with their potent saints—against the deserted *dúns* and *raths*, the pagan fortresses of Cruachan, Tara, and Emain Macha with their vanished kings.

26. This poem, a masterpiece of metrical technique in the original Irish, occurs in the prose tale *The Boyhood Deeds of Finn Mac Cumhaill*. It is composed by Finn to prove his poetic skill, after he has undergone the three ritual requirements of prophetic marrow-chewing, divination, and incantation. This translation is based on the version tentatively established from a fifteenth-century text by Gerard Murphy.

27. Mael Mhuru died in 887.

28. The form of this epigram is cited in an eleventh-century metrical tract as an example of the syllabic form *baise fri tóin*, lit. 'a slap on the buttocks'.

30–4. Saint and scholar . . . Donatus was an Irish cleric, bishop of Fiesole in the middle of the ninth century. His major work is a life of Saint Brigit in Latin hexameters. Sedulius was a scholar who settled as 'scholasticus' of the Cathedral school in Liège in 848 and helped establish a colony of Irish scholars there under the patronage of Bishop Hartgar. Besides such scholarly activities as the production of an edition of the Greek text of Saint Paul's Epistles and commentaries on the Psalms and on Saint Jerome, Sedulius wrote many poems, and has been suggested as the ancestor of goliardic poetry. He is possibly the author of the Irish epigram following (no. 35).

35. This Irish epigram occurs among the marginalia in a manuscript produced by the circle of Sedulius Scottus. See above.

36. An early reference to the Vikings.

38. This farewell to summer, as with the welcome in poem 26, is attributed to Finn Mac Cumhaill. It was preserved only by way of commentary on a single word in a text of the *Amra Choluim Chille* (poem 4).

40. This poem occurs in a prose tale in which Líadan agrees to marry Cuirithir, but instead becomes a nun. Cuirithir then becomes a monk. Líadan, after a time, seeks out Cuirithir in his solitary cell, but he leaves her, and she stays there until her death.

41. Three incantations attributed to the poet Amergin Glúngel, the 'Bright-kneed', in *Lebor Gabála*, the 'Book of Invasions'. This is a work of pseudo-history which purports to describe the first settlement of Ireland.

Amergin's first invocation calms the ocean when the voyagers are driven westward by a storm until they are lost and weary; the second is uttered as Amergin sets his right foot for the first time on the soil of Ireland; the third is to ensure the fertility of the land and seas of Ireland.

The invocations are given an ancient tone, but were probably composed as late as the tenth century.

TENTH CENTURY

43. A poem discovered and published by Professor James Carney, who draws attention to the still-current element of the sneeze as a bad omen, and to the idea of the three sods of earth allotted in a human life: the sod of birth, the sod of death, and the sod of burial.

44. Saint Manchán died in 665. His hermitage was at Liath, in Co. Offaly; the place is still called Lemanaghan.

45. The poet, a 'spouse of God', like the compiler of *Félire Oenghusso* (poem 25), prefixed this prayer for forgiveness to *Saltair na Rann*, a verse psalter completed in 987 and consisting of 150 poems on the Bible story and the Redemption.

ELEVENTH CENTURY

48–50. The poet was a member of the religious community at Armagh and noted for his wisdom, piety, and poetry. He died, recorded as 'the chief sage of Ireland', in 1086. In poem 48 he addresses the virgin by name, *Crínóc*, lit. 'ancient-young', but with a pun on 'young' and 'virgin'. She is addressed as a loved and respected teacher, and it used to be thought that the subject was a *virgo subintroducta*, a spiritual wife who would live with a priest or hermit. It was Professor James Carney who made the convincing suggestion that the poet, in old age, has come once more on the psalm-book he used in his school-days and is moved to address it as a lost love (and in terms which one might use with a female warrior who instructs the young, as Scáthach instructed Cúchulainn in the story of his training in arms). A student would have made his first acquaintance with the Psalms at the age of seven.

53. Bishop Patrick ruled the small Hiberno-Norse city of Dublin from 1074 to 1084. The *Prologue* is prefixed to a prose treatise, *De tribus habitaculis animae*, on Heaven and Hell. A gloss identifies the 'pleasant patron' as a Bishop Wulfstan, and names Aldwin as the 'comrade' at the close. Bishop Patrick kept up a regular connection with religious settlements in England and, returning from one of these visits, was drowned.

ELEVENTH/TWELFTH CENTURY

54–8. Apart from the poem associated with the historical figure of the saint himself (no. 4) there is a later literature connected with Colum Cille as a devotional or folk figure. This literature ranges from individual quatrains to a full-length biography by Adamnán. Texts of the poems are not in all cases 'fixed' and the selection used here takes Gerard Murphy's version for no. 54 and Tomás F. Ó Rathile's version for no. 56.

The following is some of the basic information which the poems take for granted: that Colum Cille was a kinsman of the Clan Chonaill, one of the two great peoples of the North (the other being the Clan Eogain—both descendants of Niall); his people defeated the High King of Ireland, partly owing to Colum Cille's prayers, at the battle of Cúl Dreimne in 561; these events led finally to the saint's lifelong exile on the island of Iona in the kingdom of Alba, or Scotland.

56. The poem in this form was pieced together by Professor Tomás F. Ó Rathile in his *Measgra Dánta*. The second stanza, and the fourth last, are usually given as separate poems.

59. A poem from the metrical *Dindsenchas*, or lore of place-names, where it is attributed to Finn Mac Cumhaill—who would here be exercising an important function of the poet in preserving and communicating information about notable places, their names and characteristics.

TWELFTH CENTURY

60. The tradition of Suibne Geilt, a name usually translated 'Mad Sweeney', places him in the seventh century. He went mad during the battle of Mag Rath and lived the rest of his life as a wild man. The stanzas given here are chosen from a large body of nature poetry associated with Suibne. In the final stanza of the selection Suibne prophesies his own death. This took place at 'Mo Ling's House', St Mo Ling's Monastery—now known as St Mullins—in Co. Carlow. In the version referred to, Suibne is killed by the peak of a deer's horn placed so as to go through him when he bends to drink.

61–6. These poems are taken from *Acallam na Senórach*, 'The Conversation of the Elders'. This is a long and popular compilation of stories about Finn Mac Cumhaill and his warriors, the Fianna. The stories are told to Saint Patrick by Oisín, son of Finn, and Caílte, Finn's old enemy. These warriors managed, in their own notable stories, to survive three hundred years into Christian times.

62. Caílte has already told Saint Patrick how Cael fought in the battle of Fionn Trágha (Anglicized 'Ventry') and was drowned on the last day of the battle. He now finishes the tale. The place-names refer to various physical features in the area—ridges, a headland, a lake, etc. Only some of these can be identified.

63. This poem records the end of a family feud, when Finn Mac Cumhaill has hunted Goll Mac Morna to his death. Cumhall, son of Tréanmór, was a warrior in the service of Conn. Cumhall stole the girl Muirne, the druid's daughter, and Conn sent to ask for her return. Cumhall refused and Conn sent an army after her, led by Goll Mac Morna, who killed Cumhall at the battle of Cnucha. Muirne was then returned to her father but he refused her because she was pregnant. She later gave birth to Finn.

THIRTEENTH CENTURY

68–71. The second of these poems was composed in 1213, after an angry incident involving the poet's killing of an insulting servant sent to him at his home in Lissadell, Co. Sligo, by the Domhnall of the poem. The episode led to the poet's exile finally in Scotland (hence the epithet 'Albanach'). The tale is told in the Annals of the Four Masters. The poem is addressed as an appeal for support to the Norman prince Richard FitzWilliam de Burgo. The structure which Muireadhach gives the poem is worth noting: establishing the primacy first of FitzWilliam, then of the poet in his own sphere—equals against an insignificant world, with poets flocking to FitzWilliam's house because of Muireadhach's fame.

The third poem is an elegy for the poet's wife Maol Mheadha.

In the fourth poem, the word 'knife' in Irish is feminine. The poem turns in the final stanza to address the carver at the feast.

72. An extreme example of the outlook of the professional poet. The references cited as precedents for giving due honour to the poet include Saints Patrick and Colum Cille, ancient kings of Ireland, and figures from saga and mythological literature—and not least Jesus Christ, who is expected to reward the poet with Heaven for his 'lovely craft'. The Domhnall addressed in the second-last stanza is probably Domhnall Óg Ó Domhnaill, chief of the O'Donnells. Giolla Brighde composed his inaugural ode.

The text used is that selected from the full text and edited by Eleanor Knott in *Irish Syllabic Poetry* (Cork, 1934).

73. New Ross in Co. Wexford was one of the earliest towns settled by the Normans and remained an important port, rivalling Dublin for a time.

This poem was written either by a professional Anglo-Norman trouvère, or by a visiting French monk or friar, to celebrate the entrenchment of the town in 1265. It is of interest for the lively view it gives of an early stage in the settlement of the 'stranger'.

The translation from which the selection is taken was made in 1831 by Mrs George Maclean and published in T. Crofton Croker's *Popular Songs of Ireland*. The four lines on Friday's work, indistinct in the original, were left untranslated; these have been supplied.

FOURTEENTH CENTURY

74. The poet Gofraidh Fionn Ó Dálaigh was a native of Duhallow, Co. Cork, and was regarded by later poets as a great stylist. The parable of the child in prison was taken from the *Gesta Romanorum* and was often given without the five introductory stanzas. It remained possibly the single most popular religious poem in Irish for centuries.

75. Gearóid Iarla, 'Gerald the Earl' Fitzgerald, fourth Earl of Desmond so called, is mentioned in the Annals of the Four Masters as excelling 'all the English and many of the Irish in knowledge of the Irish language, poetry, and history'. He was Lord Chief Justice of Ireland in 1367 and 'disappeared' into Lough Gur, and into folklore, in 1398.

76-7. Much of the early English poetry produced in Ireland has been lost, but various scraps survive indicating poetic activity of various kinds. These two fragments are dated approximately 1300/1350. The actual Irish origin of the first song has been disputed. The second fragment is the only surviving fragment of a *cantilena* or ballad sung at the time in the town of Kilkenny.

78-9. The first considerable body of verse in English appears in a manuscript made in the Franciscan Grey Friars abbey in Kildare in the first half of the fourteenth century. The contents include English, French, and Latin prose and verse. Many items are merely copies, but some appear to have been composed by the 'Frere Michel' who claims authorship in the last stanza of *Swet Jesus*.

FOURTEENTH/FIFTEENTH CENTURY

80. Tadhg Óg Ó hUigínn has been described as 'chief Preceptor of the poets of Ireland and Scotland'; he composed ceremonial and religious poetry, including an inauguration ode for the O'Neill in 1397.

In this poem he laments the death of his teacher and elder brother who died in 1391, and gives an insight into the procedures and values of the great formal schools of poetry. These schools broke up each year toward the end of March. Methods of teaching made use entirely of memory and required recitation by teacher and student together in darkness; the image in the eighteenth stanza is from falconry, where training in darkness is also involved.

FIFTEENTH CENTURY

81–2. Two poems from an anonymous sequence attributed to the traditional figure of a tenth-century queen Gormlaith, daughter of the high king Flann Sinna and widow of the king Niall Glúndubh, 'Black-Knee', who fell in battle against the Vikings.

83. *The Mayor of Waterford's Letter* (1487): five stanzas out of a total of forty-four. The Earl of Kildare and other Anglo-Irish lords, in a short-lived rebellion, proclaimed Lambert Simnel, the son of a Dublin organ-maker, King of England and Lord of Ireland. Waterford refused to recognize the 'counterfeit king'.

From the 'Hanmer Papers', items collected by the English clergyman Meredith Hanmer, who lived in Ireland from 1591 to his death in 1604. The collection is printed in the Addenda to the *State Papers Relating to Ireland, 1601–1603*.

FIFTEENTH/SIXTEENTH CENTURY: ANONYMOUS LOVE POETRY

84–94. These anonymous love lyrics represent the 'domestication' of Western European *amour courtois*—French and Provençal and, later, English—which came to Ireland in the wake of the Norman invasion. The process was not, of course, confined to these two centuries: Robin Flower has commented on the way in which poems written 300 or 400 years apart can strike upon the ear as contemporary (see nos. 75, 96–8, and 118). As to an earlier influence in the other direction see note to nos. 30–4.

95. From the 'Hanmer Papers': see note to no. 83. Possibly the earliest translation into English of an Irish song. The original is not known.

SIXTEENTH CENTURY

96–8. The poet was king of Tír Conaill, the present Donegal.

99. This poem was composed in the mid sixteenth century by Lochlann Óg Ó Dálaigh, a bardic poet from Co. Clare, in praise of three young kinsmen of the ruling O'Briens: Tadhg, Conchubar, and a younger Tadhg.

Among the many formal usages (references to the 'host of Cas'—the Dál gCais, ruling family of the O'Briens; 'the half of Conn', or Northern half of Ireland; the long-established use of the goddess-name Banba for the country as a whole) the immediacies of the time can be felt, not least the reminder to the nobles of their responsibilities toward the poets.

100. Tadhg Dall—'the blind'—Ó hUigínn (an ancestor was Tadhg Óg Ó hUigínn: poem 80) lived at the point of highest development of the bardic system, an 'Augustan' period of technical mastery and apparent social stability. In the words of Eleanor Knott, editor of his poems, 'it was the poet's trade to flatter . . . and for his livelihood he depended on the rewards for his efforts . . .'. He would be feared also (and run some risk—see the following poem) for his satire.

The praise poem, a glowing record of a visit to the Norman castle in Enniskillen in the time of a prince of the Maguires, is of interest for the picture it gives (however formalized) of life in a noble Gaelic settlement of the period. It has been suggested that the smoke in the first stanza on p. 146 may be from the heat of valorous effort.

102–3. Laoiseach Mac an Bháird was a Monaghan poet of the late sixteenth century. In his work there is the first occurrence of the great theme of the coming of the final 'stranger' and the ruin of the old order.

The tree of the first poem was removed by the new authorities very likely because it was associated with an ancient inauguration site. This particular tree has not been identified. The 'schools' are the schools of poetry.

In the second poem criticism is aimed at one of two brothers who has apparently chosen Tudor ways, while the other has taken to the hills in revolt— an indication of the shape of much future history.

104. Possibly a continuation of the theme of the ruin of the old order. The poet, under the new conditions of threat, grows conscious of the value of his manuscripts, poem-book, harp, 'chess'-board, and emblematic weapons. The 'orphan' of the final stanza is the 'little book' of the first stanza.

105. *The Praise of Waterford* (1545); the city of Waterford, having remained loyal during the rebellion of Lambert Simnel in the fifteenth century (see poem 83), proved loyal again in the sixteenth during the rebellion of Perkin Warbeck. Wherefore 'the citie's armes are deckt with this golden word Intacta manet'.

From the 'Hanmer Papers': see note to no. 83. These stanzas are selected from a total of twenty-four.

106. From the 'Hanmer Papers': see note to no. 83.

SEVENTEENTH CENTURY

107–9. The early seventeenth century is the last period when any sense of stability was possible for the old Gaelic order. These few anonymous poems are from that time.

110–11. Ó hEoghusa was poet to the Maguires of Fermanagh. He records the final phase of the unsuccessful struggle for survival of the Gaelic aristocracy in the few years preceding the 'Flight of the Earls' in 1607. Poem 110 deals sourly with the associated general drop in poetic standards; in the sixth stanza the reference is to an Irish parable in which forty wise men took shelter in a cave while the rest of the world stayed out in the rain and called them fools. Poem 111 is the original of Mangan's celebrated 'version'—see poem 185.

112–13. Ó Gnímh was a member of a hereditary poetic family attached to the O'Neills. His poetry, with its close-down of all positive feeling, dates—like Ó hEoghusa's, and Ó Hifearnáin's following—to the time of confiscations and plantations in the early seventeenth century.

113. Here, after a rehearsal of the calamities that have befallen the poets, a possibility of survival is seen at the hands of the generous-hearted Art Mac

Aonghusa, a Northern prince whose heroic ancestry is made a feature of the poem.

114. The final bardic voice ... Ó Hifearnáin anticipates the extreme predicament of Ó Rathaille in the following century (poem 140). His poetic skill is seen to be pointless, with the disappearance of everything of supportive significance in the legendary past, of the last patron in the present, and of every illusion of survival. Ó Hifearnáin, in another bitter poem, warns against the craft of verse.

115 ff. For the 'new' poets, Céitinn and others, see the Introduction, p. xxv.

115–16. Céitinn—usually Anglicized Geoffrey Keating, a priest and a scholar—is noted primarily for a major history of Ireland, the first true history as distinct from the legendary pseudo-histories of the past.

The first of these poems was composed after the 'Flight of the Earls' in 1607 and laments the downfall of the great families of Ireland. There are references to the dynasties of Munster, the O'Neills, the Fitzgeralds, etc.

There is some doubt as to the authorship of the second lyric.

117. Born near Cashel in Co. Tipperary, Haicéad became a Dominican priest on the Continent. On his return he took an active interest in worldly affairs and wrote many ill-tempered occasional poems.

118. Feiritéar was a chieftain of Norman descent who ruled in the Dingle Peninsula, Co. Kerry, where he is still something of a folk hero. In 1641 he joined in the rebellion against the Elizabethan colonists. When this failed he went into hiding. He was captured and publicly hanged in Killarney.

In the final stanza of this poem the acrostic in the original Irish seems to give the name 'Husae' (Hussey).

119–22. Ó Bruadair managed to spend the early part of his career as a professional poet, attached to various Gaelic families, notably the Fitzgeralds. For the last twenty years of his life, from about 1678, he was reduced to manual labour. He died in misery.

123. This poem is attributed to Tomás Láidir, 'Thomas the Strong', a celebrated hero of the Costello family who had lost their lands in the Cromwellian dispossessions in Connaught. He and Úna Nic Dhiarmada—Anglicized 'MacDermot'—were in love, but he was not made welcome by her family. He made a number of proposals but was repeatedly refused. He made one last formal proposal and left, swearing that if he crossed Áth na Donóige—a ford in the Donogue river—on the journey home, without an answer, he would never marry Úna. He rode slowly, and waited a long time in the ford itself, but finally, on the mocking advice of his own servant, he crossed to the opposite bank. A messenger came soon after with news that he had been accepted, but he refused to go back on his oath. Úna died shortly afterward. Tomás killed the servant who gave him the evil counsel, and composed the famous song *Úna Bhán*.

The song survives in numerous versions; there is no established text.

124–5. Luke Wadding, a Franciscan priest and scholar, was Catholic bishop of Ferns, Co. Wexford, during the troubled post-Cromwellian period. He went into exile, probably after the confiscation of the family land, and spent much of his life on the Continent. His carols appeared in *A Smale Garland*, first published in Ghent. Some of the songs became very popular and helped establish a special tradition of carol-singing in Co. Wexford.

126. A song written in mockery of the arrival of General Richard Talbot, newly created Earl of Tyrconnell by the Catholic King James II in Dublin in 1688. The refrain is a parody of the Irish language. The song was an extraordinary success and became a marching song of the victorious Williamite armies. It is sometimes attributed to Lord Wharton, who claimed to have 'sung a deluded prince out of three kingdoms'.

127. The Williamites' final victory was at the Battle of the Boyne, celebrated still with music and public ritual in the North of Ireland. The Orange victory song exists in a number of versions; the one given here appears to be the oldest. A version by a Colonel Blacker is almost as famous; it begins:

> July the first, in Oldbridge town,
>   There was a grievous battle,
> Where many a man lay on the ground
>   By the cannons that did rattle.
> King James he pitched his tents between
>   The lines for to retire,
> But King Billy threw his bomb balls in
>   And set them all on fire . . .

EIGHTEENTH CENTURY

128. Séamas Dall, 'the Blind', Mac Cuarta was a travelling poet from Co. Louth. He depended on local patronage in his native county and in the Boyne valley.

129–35. Jonathan Swift was born in Dublin of English parents. He was a posthumous child, adopted by an uncle and educated at Kilkenny School and Trinity College, Dublin. He went to England as a 'client' of Sir William Temple and, on Temple's estate at Moor Park, met 'Stella'—Esther Johnson, daughter of Temple's steward—while she was still a child, forming with her the most devoted and lasting relationship of his life.

He was ordained priest in the Anglican Church in 1695 and given the parish of Laracor in Ireland, and finally (after manifesting his gifts as a satirist) made Dean of St Patrick's Cathedral in Dublin, a position which he regarded as permanent exile. After Temple's death, Swift arranged that Stella settle in Ireland, until her death in 1728.

Swift was declared of unsound mind in 1742 and died in 1745.

The original of poem 130 is the Irish poem *Pléaráca na Ruarcach* by Aodh Mac Gabhráin, a little-known poet from Cavan who lived in the first half of the eighteenth century. The *Pléaráca* became famous when set to music by the blind musician Carolan (who seems to have been known to Swift).

136–40. Ó Rathaille's is one of the major Irish poetic careers, his work responding to all the significant circumstances of his time and place. He was born in Kerry, near Killarney, and suffered in the wake of the Williamite wars.

Poems 136 and 138 are two of a genre of *aisling*, or vision poems, developed by Ó Rathaille as a medium expressing hope in a Jacobite return. The places named in poem 138 are in Co. Limerick.

137. This poem is set in the bleak westernmost region, by the Atlantic seaboard, where Ó Rathaille took refuge on the dispossession of his patron family, the McCarthys, after the Battle of the Boyne.

139. It was the Brownes, a Catholic family of Elizabethan planter stock, who supplanted the McCarthys (poem 137); they proved understanding, on the whole, of Irish traditional ways, including the place of the poet. Sir Valentine, however, who succeeded to the estates in 1720, was an exception. He refused Ó Rathaille some important request and earned this bitter poem.

140. In this poem the lords of Munster are dispossessed and the great rivers of Ireland are muffled and reddened with blood. It was composed by Ó Rathaille in his last illness, with all hope of political restoration gone and, consequently, of any improvement in his personal fortunes under any of the great patron families.

141. Mac Giolla Ghunna was born in Co. Fermanagh and studied for a time for the priesthood, but left and became a rake-poet. Only a few of his poems survive.

142–9. Oliver Goldsmith was born in Pallas, Co. Longford, the son of a Protestant clergyman. The family soon moved to Lissoy, a village in Co. Westmeath.

Goldsmith was unsettled from an early age. He attended various schools before entering Trinity College, Dublin, in 1744. There he had a mixed academic career, including gambling, flute-playing, and an abortive attempt, 'in a fit of despair', to migrate to America. After taking a poor BA degree he tried divinity and law before settling as a physician in Edinburgh.

In 1755 he made a tour of Europe on foot, and wrote the first draft of *The Traveller*. In 1757 he finally began to establish himself as a writer in London, becoming friendly with Samuel Johnson.

The Traveller was finally published in 1764 and was an immediate success. *The Vicar of Wakefield* was published in 1766, and *The Deserted Village* in 1770. Macaulay has analysed *The Deserted Village* as follows:

> The village in its happy days is a true English village. The village in its decay is an Irish village . . . [Goldsmith] had never seen in his native island such a rural paradise, such a seat of plenty, content, and tranquillity, as his 'Auburn'. He had assuredly never seen in England all the inhabitants of such a paradise turned out of their homes in one day and forced to emigrate in a body to America . . .

The poem 'Retaliation' arose from a contest at a meeting of a 'company of gentlemen' when Garrick and Goldsmith proposed to write each other's epitaphs. Garrick spoke extempore:

> Here lies Nolly Goldsmith, for shortness called Noll,
> Who wrote like an angel, but talk'd like poor Poll.

Goldsmith took some weeks to produce his 'Retaliation'.

150–1. Eoghan Rua—'the Red-haired'—is possibly the specimen-case of the Irish poet in the evil days. He was born in the same part of Kerry as Ó Rathaille and, after a while in the British army or navy, became a travelling schoolteacher and labourer, and a famous folk-figure and wit. He composed many poems in the *aisling* form, all of great colour and virtuosity, embodying the remote hope of a return of the Stuarts and the consequent righting of all wrongs.

153. Eibhlín Dhubh, 'the Dark One', was a member of the O'Connell family of Co. Kerry; she was an aunt of Daniel O'Connell. In 1767 she married Art Ó Laoghaire, who had been in the Hungarian Hussars, and they lived near Macroom in Co. Cork. In 1773 Ó Laoghaire, after a quarrel with Abraham Morris, the High Sheriff, was killed by Morris's bodyguard.

The lament is a traditional 'keen', a *caoineadh* uttered by Eibhlín Dhubh at different stages during her husband's obsequies: over the dead body; at its dressing for the coffin; at a first temporary burial; and at the final burial in the grounds of the monastery of Kilcrea, Co. Cork. It is not a poem, in the sense of a prepared or formal response, but a unique extempore fusion of traditional device and individual genius.

154. Brian Merriman was born the illegitimate son of a country gentleman in Co. Clare. He worked as farmer and schoolteacher: *The Midnight Court* is his only known poem of any significance.

It is full of social, literary, and historical reference, and opens with a parody of the standard *aisling* (see poems 138 and 151). The messenger from the *sí*, or the other world, who accosts the poet is herself a parody of womanly characteristics, and the vision of the poem—far from offering Ireland political hope of any kind in her troubles—traces all problems to the country's bachelors.

The date toward the end of the poem—of the Court's decree, and presumably of the poem itself—works out at 1780.

155–6. Richard Brinsley Sheridan was born in Dublin, but the family moved to England when he was young. He was educated at Harrow. He was involved in a romantic courtship, surviving a violent duel. On account of his talent and wit, and of Mrs Sheridan's accomplishments as a singer, the couple were received into 'the best society'.

With *The Rivals* in 1775 and *The School for Scandal* in 1777 he began a brilliant theatrical career. Later this declined, through a combination of extravagance and bad management, and Sheridan died in poverty.

SEVENTEENTH TO NINETEENTH CENTURIES: FOLK POETRY

One of the great riches of the Irish tradition is its store of songs, of every kind and arising from every occasion: love-songs and laments, political party-songs and satires, religious incantations, maledictions, comic narratives. These songs exist in great profusion in both languages. In Irish, in addition to folk-song as ordinarily understood, there are many prayers and charms, and many great art songs sung in the *sean nós*, or 'old style'. In the songs in English there is often a distinctive element due to a translation or borrowing effect from the Irish.

162. A political love-poem . . . The black rose is an emblem of Ireland.

163. Kilcash was a great house of the Butler family near Clonmel, Co. Tipperary.

168–73. A Jacobite lament and a group of songs from the French invasion of 1796 and the rebellion of 1798.

169. *Shan Van Vocht*, lit. 'poor old woman': Ireland in her guise of hag or *cailleach*.

170. Napper Tandy was involved with Wolfe Tone in the United Irishmen.

171. 'Croppies' was a derogatory term for the rebels in Wexford in 1798; it derived from the practice of cropping the hair short in the French Revolutionary manner.

172–3. Two songs from the victorious side. The imagery here is still functional in North of Ireland politics.

174. A ballad in Dublin slang.

NINETEENTH AND TWENTIETH CENTURIES

175. 'Blind Raftery' was born in Mayo. He was blind from childhood and travelled around the west of Ireland singing his songs and playing the fiddle. He is the blind poet of Yeats's 'The Tower' and the poem 'Coole Park and Ballylee, 1931'.

176–82. Thomas Moore was born in Dublin. He studied law in Trinity College, Dublin, and London, but turned early toward a literary career and managed to combine lyrical and social—and financial—success to an extraordinary degree. His *Irish Melodies* were published in instalments between 1807 and 1834, with musical settings by Sir John Stevenson; many of them established themselves as standard 'Irish lyrics', and have so remained.

Moore remained detached from the political activities of his time, but his songs sometimes contain the ingredients of a crude nationalism, and are largely responsible for the Harp and Shamrock imagery usually associated with it.

Early in his career Moore made the acquaintance of Robert Emmet. The first song in the selection speaks in the voice of Sarah Curran, Emmet's beloved, as she mourns him after the abortive Rising in Dublin, and his execution, in 1803.

'The Petition of the Orangemen of Ireland' is one of many satirical poems written by Moore on contemporary issues. He published a selection in *Odes upon Cash, Corn, Catholics and other matters*, London, 1828.

See Introduction, pp. xxvi–xxvii.

183–93. James Clarence Mangan was born in Dublin into a very poor family, and led a life of misery and deprivation, with alcohol contributing to an early death.

He began work as a young boy in a scrivener's office, and continued as an occasional journalist. His works include, besides some personal poems of great bleakness, a body of important translations from the Irish. Mangan knew no Irish himself; the 'versions' were made from texts produced by others, including the scholars Eugene O'Curry and John O'Donovan.

Yeats regarded Mangan, with Davis and Ferguson, as in some sense his colleague in an Irish poetic tradition (poem 203); he thought 'The Nameless One' 'quite wonderful'.

It was Mangan whom Joyce selected as the subject for his paper before the University Literary and Historical Society in 1902. He drew attention to Mangan's work repeatedly throughout his career.

Poem 183 is a version of no. 162, and no. 185 is a version of no. 111.

194–8. Sir Samuel Ferguson was born in Belfast. He was a lawyer and antiquarian, keeper of public records, and President of the Royal Irish Academy. His publications include *Lays of the Western Gael*, from which 'The Burial of King Cormac' and 'Aideen's Grave' are taken (Ferguson's introductory notes are given below); *Lays of the Red Branch*, a set of verse retellings of sagas from the Ulster cycle, from which 'Deirdre's Lament' is taken; and *Congal*, an epic in five books.

194. 'Cormac, son of Art, son of Con Cead-Catha (*i.e.*, Hundred-Battle), enjoyed the sovereignty of Ireland through the prolonged period of forty years, commencing from AD 213. During the latter part of his reign, he resided at Sletty on the Boyne, being, it is said, disqualified for the occupation of Tara by the personal blemish he had sustained in the loss of an eye, by the hand of Angus "Dread-Spear", chief of the Desi, a tribe whose original seats were in the barony of Deece, in the county of Meath. It was in the time of Cormac and his son Carbre, if we are to credit the Irish annals, that Finn, son of Comhal, and the Fenian heroes, celebrated by Ossian, flourished. Cormac has obtained the reputation of wisdom and learning, and appears justly entitled to the honour of having provoked the enmity of the Pagan priesthood, by declaring his faith in a God not made by hands of men.'

195. 'Aideen, daughter of Angus of Ben-Edar (now the Hill of Howth), died of grief for the loss of her husband, Oscar, son of Ossian, who was slain at the battle of Gavra (*Gowra*, near Tara in Meath), AD 284. Oscar was entombed in the rath or earthen fortress that occupied part of the field of battle, the rest of the slain being cast in a pit outside. Aideen is said to have been buried on Howth, near the mansion of her father, and poetical tradition represents the Fenian heroes as present at her obsequies. The Cromlech in Howth Park has been supposed to be her sepulchre. It stands under the summits from which the poet Atharne is said to have launched his invectives against the people of Leinster, until, by the blighting effect of his satires, they were compelled to make him atonement for the death of his son.'

197. This poem appeared not among Ferguson's collected poetry but in Lady Ferguson's *Life*. The occasion of the poem was the 'Phoenix Park murders' of Burke and Cavendish by the 'Invincibles'. In Lady Ferguson's words:

Carey, who gave the signal, while waiting for the appearance of the unsuspecting victims, was an onlooker at a game of polo then being played in the Park. His supposed meditations are analysed by Ferguson in a poem written partly to show how readily Browning's mannerisms might be imitated.

198. The 'Lament for Thomas Davis' was, likewise, 'uncollected'. Sir Charles Gavan Duffy records that:

Ferguson, who lay on a bed of sickness when Davis died, impatient that for the moment he could not declare it in public, asked me to come to him, that he might ease his heart by expressing in private his sense of what he had lost. He read me fragments of a poem written under these circumstances the most Celtic in structure and spirit of all the elegies laid on the tomb of Davis. The last verse sounded like a prophecy; it was, at any rate, a powerful incentive to take up our task anew.

199–200. Thomas Davis was born in Mallow, Co. Cork. He studied law at

Trinity College, Dublin. He joined Daniel O'Connell's Repeal Association, but agitated against O'Connell's time-consuming constitutional procedures.

In 1842 Davis established the *Nation* newspaper. Many of the poems he wrote for the paper have become classic utterances of impassioned nationalism.

201–2. William Allingham was born in Ballyshannon, Co. Donegal. He settled in London and became friendly with Tennyson, Carlyle, and Rossetti, and edited *Fraser's Magazine*. He wrote a great many poems and songs and a long serious narrative in iambic pentameter, *Laurence Bloomfield in Ireland*, on landlordism and associated matters (1864). The short 'gloss' 'Four ducks on a pond' is untypical in its directness and simplicity and usually proves unforgettable.

203–9. On W. B. Yeats, see Introduction, pp. xxvi–xxvii.

210. Pádraig Ó hÉigeartaigh emigrated from Co. Kerry to Springfield, Massachusetts, as a child. He sent this lament on his son's death to Patrick Pearse's paper *An Claidheamh Soluis* ('The Sword of Light') at the turn of the century; a number of phrases out of Pearse's translation are included.

211–15. J. M. Synge studied Irish and music and spent a while on the Aran Islands, and wrote a book about his experiences there (see poem 254). The life and literature of the Irish-speaking people proved a rich source of material for his plays for the Abbey Theatre.

216. Patrick Pearse was born in Dublin. He studied law, lectured on Irish language and literature in the National University, edited the official newspaper of the Gaelic League, *An Claidheamh Soluis*, and established a bilingual school. His ideal of an Ireland free of English rule, expressed in this poem (which is sometimes entitled 'Ideal') led him into open rebellion and death.

217–19. Padraic Colum was born in Longford. He wrote a number of plays for the Irish Theatre and later taught in the United States. He wrote and edited many books, including collections of folklore, but it is in a few early 'folk' lyrics, risking bathos in their dramatic simplicity, that his poetic achievement lies.

220–2. Francis Ledwidge was born in Slane, Co. Meath. He was a farm labourer and, later, secretary of the local farm labourers' union. Lord Dunsany encouraged him in his early writing and also, it would seem, into joining Dunsany's own regiment in the First World War; Ledwidge was killed in Belgium. The lament for Thomas MacDonagh, one of the 1916 leaders—see poem 222—recalls certain early Irish poetry in its use of internal rhyme.

223–30. Austin Clarke was born in Dublin and spent a long career in relative obscurity as poet, verse dramatist, novelist, and journalist. His is probably the most vital talent in Irish poetry after Yeats, with a career full of change and continuous renewal until his death in 1974. After an early stage of involvement with the old sagas, the poetry turned to matters of faith, conscience, and apostasy, with the poet in 'Tenebrae' an agonized Luther. The atmosphere of life as lived under the Catholic Church in Ireland until the 1950s can be felt in poems 226–8. The poetry of Clarke's old age represents an escape into serene, sensual paganism, with the visual punning of poem 226, on prayer and 'sin'—not to mention the title—freed of all guilt in poem 230.

228. Clarke worked throughout his life at the form of the long poem, and finally achieved an idiosyncratic diction which enabled him to sustain a high intensity throughout long narratives. Some of these are harshly satirical, some darkly inward-looking; this one is unique in its humane understanding and restraint.

231–6. Patrick Kavanagh was born in Iniskeen, Co. Monaghan, and lived as a small farmer until 1939 when he migrated to Dublin and undertook a career as poet, literary journalist, and novelist. His best early poems look hard and direct at his surroundings—the universal emerging from the familiar particulars. He spent his middle life attempting to educate the unworthy in matters of Art and Life, and suffered greatly in the process. During a final illness he wrote a number of sonnets embodying a newly discovered wisdom in resignation (poems 235 and 236).

237–8. Samuel Beckett was born in Dublin but has spent most of his life in France (where he was Joyce's secretary for a while), writing in French and translating his own work into English, mainly plays and novels. Nobel Prize 1969.

239–42. Padraic Fallon was born in Athenry, Co. Galway, and worked in the Irish Civil Service, initially in Dublin (where he met AE and the last of the 'Renaissance'), then as a customs official in Wexford. He was reticent in the book publication of his poetry; his collected *Poems*, published in the year of his death, gave the first adequate view of his career.

243–7. Louis MacNeice's father was rector in Carrickfergus in Northern Ireland. MacNeice was born in Belfast, educated in England, and settled in London, where he was part of the great poetic group of the thirties with W. H. Auden.

248–53. Denis Devlin was born in Scotland. He made a career in the Irish diplomatic service. A range of reference based on this, and on modern Continental and American literature, made his work untypical of Irish poetry as hitherto familiar. Such translations as he made were from the French, including poems of St John Persse; his friends included Allen Tate and Robert Penn Warren, who co-edited his *Selected Poems* in an American edition. His reputation remains largely hidden, despite such clear and open poetry as 'Little Elegy'—or the long poem *Memoirs of a Turcoman Diplomat* where the voice (obviously speaking close to Devlin's own) gives access to a restless and sensual intellect.

254. Máirtín Ó Direáin was born in the Aran Islands, where Irish is still the spoken language of the people.

255–8. Seán Ó Ríordáin was born in Cork. His early work was influenced for a time by W. H. Auden, but rapidly discovered its own voice. It was a very hard voice, alert and introspective. It is the last voice in Irish in the anthology.

259–60. Valentin Iremonger was born in Dublin and has worked in the Irish diplomatic service.

261 ff. For general discussion of more recent choices see Introduction, pp. xxviii–xxx.

261–6. Richard Murphy was born in Mayo and educated in Britain. He has taught poetry in American universities.

'Rapparees' and 'Wolfhound' were published originally as separate poems. They found their places later in the historical sequence *The Battle of Aughrim* (1968), along with other poems dealing with contemporary manifestations of the same, and related, historical events.

267–70. Thomas Kinsella was born in Dublin. He worked in the Irish Department of Finance until 1955, and is currently Professor of English in Temple University, Philadelphia, directing a study programme in Dublin in the Irish tradition. He has translated *The Táin* and *An Duanaire: Poems of the Dispossessed 1600–1900*.

271–4. John Montague was born in the United States and brought up in Northern Ireland; he lived a while in Paris. He has taught poetry in American universities and is currently at University College, Cork. Editor, *Faber Book of Irish Verse*.

275–9. Seamus Heaney was born in Derry. He has taught in Queen's University, Belfast, and in a teachers' training college in Dublin; he is currently Boylston Professor of Rhetoric and Oratory at Harvard University.

280–2. Derek Mahon was born in Belfast. He is an English teacher and lecturer in Northern Ireland and Dublin.

283–4. Seamus Deane was born in Derry. He lectures in English at University College, Dublin.

285–8. Michael Hartnett was born in Limerick.

SOURCES AND ACKNOWLEDGEMENTS

1. Gerard Murphy, *Early Irish Lyrics* (Oxford, 1956).
2–3. James Carney, *Medieval Irish Lyrics* (Dublin, 1967).
4. R. I. Best and Osborn Bergin (eds.), *Lebor na hUidre* (Dublin, 1929). Ending supplied from *Leabhar Breac*: RIA facsimile (Dublin, 1876).
5. Carney, op. cit.
6–7. David Greene and Frank O'Connor (eds.), *A Golden Treasury of Irish Poetry* (London, 1967).
8–9. Carney, op. cit.
10–13. Thomas Kinsella (trans.), *The Táin* (Dublin/Oxford, 1969).
14. Kuno Meyer, *Bruchstücke der Älteren Lyrik Irlands* (Berlin, 1919).
15–18. Murphy, op. cit.
19. Ibid.; with Kuno Meyer, *Zeitschrift für Celtische Philologie* (Halle A. S., 1897), vol. VIII.
20. Murphy, op. cit.
21. Greene and O'Connor, op. cit.
22–4. Murphy, op. cit.
25. Whitley Stokes (ed.), *Félire Oenghusso* (Dublin, 1880).
26. Murphy, op. cit.
27. Meyer, op. cit.
28. Murphy, op. cit.
29. Kuno Meyer, *A Primer of Irish Metrics* (Dublin, 1909).
30. Stephen Gaselee (ed.), *The Oxford Book of Medieval Latin Verse*, (Oxford, 1928).
31–6. Carney, op. cit.
37. Kuno Meyer (ed.), *Revue Celtique* (London, 1903), vol. xi.
38. Murphy, op. cit.
39. Carney, op. cit.
40. Murphy, op. cit.
41. R. A. S. Macalister and John MacNeill (eds.), *Lebor Gabála* (*Of the Conquests of Ireland*) (Dublin, 1916).
42. Murphy, op. cit.
43. Carney, op. cit.
44–5. Murphy, op. cit.
46. Kuno Meyer, *Bruchstücke der Älteren Lyrik Irlands* (Berlin, 1919).
47. Murphy, op. cit.
48–9. Carney, op. cit.
50. Greene and O'Connor, op. cit.
51. Kuno Meyer, *The Gaelic Journal* (Dublin, February 1892), vol. iv.
52. Greene and O'Connor, op. cit.
53. Aubrey Gwynn (ed.), *The Writings of Bishop Patrick, 1074–1084* (Dublin, 1955).
54–5. Murphy, op. cit.

56. Thomas F. O'Rahilly (ed.), *Measgra Dánta: Miscellaneous Irish Poems* (Cork, 1927).

57–8. Murphy, op. cit.

59. Edward Gwynn (ed.), *Metrical Dindsenchas* (Dublin, 1924), Part IV.

60–2. Murphy, op. cit.

63. Eoin MacNeill (ed.), *Duanaire Finn* (London, 1908).

64–6. Murphy, op. cit.

67. Eleanor Knott (ed.), *Irish Syllabic Poetry* (Cork, 1934).

68–71. Osborn Bergin (ed.), *Irish Bardic Poetry* (Dublin, 1970).

72. Knott, op. cit.

73. T. Crofton Croker (ed.), *The Popular Songs of Ireland* (London, 1839).

74. Knott, op. cit.; with five introductory stanzas from text ed. Revd L. McKenna in *Timthire an Chroidhe Neamhtha (Messenger of the Sacred Heart)* (Dublin, 1918), vol. VIII (ii).

75. Thomas F. O'Rahilly (ed.), *Dánta Grá: An Anthology of Irish Love Poetry* (Cork, 1925).

76–7. Russell K. Alspach, *Irish Poetry from the English Invasion to 1798* (Pennsylvania University Press, 1960).

78–9. W. Heuser (ed.), *Die Kildare Gedichte* (Bonn, 1904).

80–2. Bergin, op. cit.

83. T. Crofton Croker, op. cit.

84–9. Seán Ó Tuama (ed.), *An Duanaire: Poems of the Dispossessed 1600–1900*, trans. Thomas Kinsella (Dublin, 1981).

90–4. T. F. O'Rahilly, op. cit.

95. Alspach, op. cit.

96–8. T. F. O'Rahilly, op. cit.

99. Bergin, op. cit.

100–1. Eleanor Knott (ed.), *The Bardic Poems of Tadhg Dall Ó hUigínn* (London, 1922).

102–4. Bergin, op. cit.

105. T. Crofton Croker, op. cit.

106. Alspach, op. cit.

107–9. Ó Tuama and Kinsella, op. cit.

110–14. Bergin, op. cit.

115–22. Ó Tuama and Kinsella, op. cit.

123. Douglas Hyde (ed.), *Love Songs of Connacht* (London and Dublin, 1893).

124–5. Luke Wadding, *A Smale Garland of Pious and Goodly Songs*, in *The Wexford Carols*, ed. Diarmaid Ó Muirithe, (Dolmen Press, 1982).

126. T. Crofton Croker, *The Historical Songs of Ireland* (London, 1841).

127. Stopford A. Brooke and T. W. Rolleston (eds.), *A Treasury of Irish Poetry* (London, 1903).

128. Ó Tuama and Kinsella, op. cit.

129–35. Harold Williams (ed.), *The Poems of Jonathan Swift* (Oxford, 1937).

136–41. Ó Tuama and Kinsella, op. cit.

142–9. Austin Dobson (ed.), *The Complete Poetical Works of Oliver Goldsmith* (Oxford, 1906).

150–3. Ó Tuama and Kinsella, op. cit.

154. Ibid.; text completed from *Cúirt an Mheon-Oíche*, ed. Liam P. Ó Murchú (Dublin, 1982).

155. Richard Brinsley Sheridan, *The School for Scandal* (1777).

156. Richard Brinsley Sheridan, *The Duenna* (1775).

157–67. Ó Tuama and Kinsella, op. cit.

168–74. Oral tradition; no settled versions. Versions are included here from: *The Ballad Poetry of Ireland*, ed. Sir Charles Gavan Duffy (Dublin, 1869); and *The Golden Treasury of Irish Songs and Lyrics*, ed. Charles Welsh (New York, 1907).

175. Ó Tuama and Kinsella, op. cit.

176–81. *The Poetical Works of Thomas Moore* (London, 1862).

182. Thomas Moore, *Odes Upon Cash, Corn, Catholics and other matters* (London, 1828).

183–93. James Clarence Mangan, *Poems*, Centenary Edition, ed. D. J. O'Donoghue (Dublin London, 1903).

194–6. Sir Samuel Ferguson, *Lays of the Western Gael and other Poems* (London/Dublin, 1897).

197. Lady Ferguson, *Sir Samuel Ferguson in the Ireland of his Day* (London, 1896).

198. Brooke and Rolleston, op. cit.

199–200. Thomas Davis, *National Ballads, Songs and Poems*, ed. Wallis (Dublin London, 1876).

201. William Allingham, *Laurence Bloomfield in Ireland* (London, 1864).

202. William Allingham, *Poems*, selected and arranged by Lady Allingham (London, 1912).

203–9. W. B. Yeats, 'On Those that Hated "The Playboy of the Western World"', copyright 1912 by Macmillan Publ. Co., renewed 1940 by Bertha Georgie Yeats. 'Easter 1916', copyright 1924 by Macmillan Publ. Co., renewed 1952 by Bertha Georgie Yeats. 'The Seven Sages' and 'Coole Park and Ballylee, 1931', copyright 1933 by Macmillan Publ. Co., renewed 1961 by Bertha Georgie Yeats. 'The Circus Animals' Desertion', copyright 1940 by Georgie Yeats, renewed 1968 by Bertha Georgie Yeats, Michael Butler Yeats and Anne Yeats. 'To Ireland in the Coming Times' and 'Red Hanrahan's Song about Ireland': all reprinted from *Collected Poems* (London: Macmillan, 2/e, 1950; New York: Macmillan Publ. Co., 1956). By permission of A. P. Watt Ltd., on behalf of Michael B. Yeats and Macmillan London, Ltd, and Macmillan Publishing Company.

210. Ó Tuama and Kinsella, op. cit.

211–15. John M. Synge, *Plays, Poems and Prose* (London, 1941).

216. Padraic H. Pearse, *Collected Works* (Dublin/London, 1917).

217–19. Padraic Colum, *The Poet's Circuits* (Dolmen Press, 1981).

220–2. Francis Ledwidge, *The Collected Poems* (London, 1919).

223–30. Austin Clarke, *Collected Poems* (Dolmen Press, 1974). By permission of R. Dardis Clarke.

231–6. Patrick Kavanagh, *Collected Poems* (2/e, 1972). Reprinted by permission of Mrs Katherine Kavanagh and Martin, Brian & O'Keeffe Ltd.

237–8. Samuel Beckett, *Collected Poems 1930–1978* (John Calder Ltd., 1984).

Published in the USA in *Collected Poems in English and French* (Grove Press, Inc., 1977), © 1977 by Samuel Beckett. Reprinted by permission of John Calder (Publishers) Ltd., and Grove Press Inc.

239–42. Padraic Fallon, *Poems* (Dolmen Press, 1974). Reprinted by permission of Brian Fallon.

243–7. Louis MacNeice, *Selected Poems* (Faber). Reprinted by permission of David Higham Associates Ltd.

248–53. Denis Devlin, *Collected Poems* (Dolmen Press, 1964).

254. Máirtín Ó Direáin, 'Homage to John Millington Synge', from *Ó Morna agus Dánta Eile* (Dublin, 1957), trans. Thomas Kinsella.

255–8. Seán Ó Ríordáin, 'Death', from *Eireaball Spideoige* (Dublin, 1952); 'Claustrophobia', 'Ice Cold', and 'The Moths', from *Brosna* (Dublin, 1964), all trans. Thomas Kinsella.

259–60. Valentin Iremonger, 'The Troy Horse', 'This House Her Virgill' from *Horan's Field and Other Reservations* (The Dolmen Press, 1972). © 1972 Valentin Iremonger. By permission of the author.

261–5. Richard Murphy, *The Battle of Aughrim* (1963). Reprinted by permission of Faber & Faber Ltd., and the author.

266. Richard Murphy, *High Island*. Reprinted by permission of Faber & Faber Ltd., and the author.

267–70. Thomas Kinsella, *Poems 1956–1973* (Dolmen Press, 1980).

271–4. John Montague, 'Above the Pool', from *Poisoned Lands* (Dolmen Press, 1977); 'All Legendary Obstacles' from *A Chosen Light* (Dolmen Press, 1967); 'Hero's Portion' and 'Mother Cat' both from *A Slow Dance* (Dolmen Press, 1975). By permission of the author.

275–9. Seamus Heaney, 'Docker' from *Death of a Naturalist* (1966), reprinted by permission of Faber & Faber Ltd. 'Bogland' from *Door into the Dark* (Faber), published in the USA in *Poems 1965–1975* (FS&G). Copyright © 1969, 1975, 1980 by Seamus Heaney. Reprinted by permission of Farrar, Straus, & Giroux, Inc. 'Sunlight' from *North*, reprinted by permission of Faber & Faber Ltd. 'A Constable Calls' from *North* (Faber), published in the USA in *Poems 1965–1975* (FS&G). Copyright © 1969, 1975, 1980 by Seamus Heaney. Reprinted by permission of Faber & Faber Ltd., and Farrar, Straus, & Giroux, Inc. 'The Guttural Muse' from *Field Work*. Copyright © 1976, 1979, by Seamus Heaney. Reprinted by permission of Faber & Faber Ltd., and Farrar, Straus, & Giroux, Inc.

280–2. Derek Mahon, 'A Disused Shed in Co. Wexford', *Poems 1962–1978* © Derek Mahon 1979. Reprinted by permission of Oxford University Press. 'Derry Morning' and 'The Woods' from *The Hunt by Night* © Derek Mahon 1982. Reprinted by permission of Oxford University Press.

283–4. Seamus Deane, *Rumours* (Dolmen Press, 1977). By permission of the author.

285–8. Michael Hartnett, 'All That is Left' and 'I Have Heard Them Knock' from *Poems in English* (Dolmen Press, 1977). By permission of the author. 'The possibility that has been overlooked is the future' and 'A Farewell to English' from *A Farewell to English*, enlarged edition, The Gallery Press (Dublin, 1978). By permission of the publisher.

INDEX OF FIRST LINES

The references are to the numbers of the poems

415

INDEX OF AUTHORS

The references are to the numbers of the poems

OXFORD

MORE OXFORD PAPERBACKS

Details of a selection of other books follow. A complete list of Oxford Paperbacks, including The World's Classics, Twentieth-Century Classics, OPUS, Past Masters, Oxford Authors, Oxford Shakespeare, and Oxford Paperback Reference, is available in the UK from the General Publicity Department, Oxford University Press (JN), Walton Street, Oxford OX2 6DP.

In the USA, complete lists are available from the Paperbacks Marketing Manager, Oxford University Press, 200 Madison Avenue, New York, NY 10016.

Oxford Paperbacks are available from all good bookshops. In case of difficulty, customers in the UK can order direct from Oxford University Press Bookshop, 116 High Street, Oxford, Freepost, OX1 4BR, enclosing full payment. Please add 10 per cent of published price for postage and packing.

THE TAIN

Translated by Thomas Kinsella

The Tain is a translation from the *Tàin Bó Cuailnge*, centre-piece of the eighth-century Ulster cycle of heroic tales, and Ireland's nearest approach to a great epic. It tells the story of a giant cattle-raid, the invasion of Ulster by the armies of Medb and Ailill, queen and king of Connacht, and their allies, seeking to carry off the great Brown Bull of Cuailnge.

'This magnificent version of the early epic . . . deserves to be as widely read for its literary significance as it is already widely coveted for its beauty as a book.' *Listener*

'Kinsella has given us something both old and new . . . a most distinguished book.' *Irish Times*

THE OXFORD BOOK OF BALLADS

Selected and Edited by James Kinsley

This anthology of the traditional ballads of England and Scotland was first published a little over a decade ago to replace Sir Arthur Quiller-Couch's *Oxford Book* published in 1910. It is proving to be an equally enduring collection. Nearly all the texts are based on single versions as close as possible to oral traditions, and more than eighty tunes are included.

THE NEW OXFORD BOOK OF LIGHT VERSE

Chosen by Kingsley Amis

'extremely funny and absorbing . . . a reflection, of course, of the sureness of Amis's taste' *Times Literary Supplement*

'very comprehensive and enjoyable' *Observer*

'Full of good stuff.' *New Statesman*

THE OXFORD BOOK OF CONTEMPORARY VERSE, 1945–1980

Compiled by D. J. Enright

This anthology offers substantial selections from the work of forty British, American, and Commonwealth poets who have emerged and confirmed their talents since 1945.

'There is more pithy and Johnsonian good sense in his short introduction than in all the many books that have been written about modern poetry . . . one of the best personal anthologies I have come across.' John Bayley in the *Listener*

THE OXFORD BOOK OF SATIRICAL VERSE

Chosen by Geoffrey Grigson

'one of the best anthologies by the best modern anthologist.'
New York Review of Books

'an immense treasury of wit, exuberance, controlled malice and uncontrolled rage.' *Times Literary Supplement.*

THE OXFORD BOOK OF SHORT POEMS

Chosen and Edited by P. J. Kavanagh and James Michie

P. J. Kavanagh and James Michie have chosen the best poems in English of less than 13 lines in length for this unique and exciting anthology.

'One of the best of Oxford anthologies and a wonderful literal demonstration of Pound's remark about poetry being a matter of gists and piths.' *Guardian*

'delightful and unexpected' *Sunday Times*

'an excellent anthology' *British Book News*

ADVENTURES WITH MY HORSE

Penelope Shuttle

Penelope Shuttle, in her fourth collection, continues her inspired exploration of areas in our lives that are habitually blurred and betrayed by our over-visual, de-natured culture. The horse of the poems is both a real horse and the animal force of imagination. The adventures are those of the sensuous life. She writes about the relationship between woman and child, between woman and unborn child; about the everyday rhythms of the living house; and about the quality of uncompromised work.

Oxford Poets

ON BALLYCASTLE BEACH

Mebdh McGuckian

This is a mature and complex collection, the third book from Mebdh McGuckian, one of the leading Ulster poets of her generation, whose mysterious and unsettling poems continue to perturb and fascinate the reader.

'one of the richest and most provocative collections of poetry to have appeared in recent years' *The Times* (of Mebdh McGuckian's first full length book, *The Flower Master*)

Oxford Poets

THE OXFORD BOOK OF WAR POETRY

Chosen and edited by Jon Stallworthy

'full of good things . . . many old favourites . . . and quite a few genuine surprises' Vernon Scannell, *Guardian*

There can be no area of human experience that has generated a wider range of feeling than war: hope and fear; exhilaration and humiliation; hatred and love. Man's early war-songs were generally exhortations to action, or celebrations of action. More recently, war poetry has been implicitly, if not explicitly, anti-war as poets more and more have responded to 'man's inhumanity to man'—and to women and children.

This great shift in social awareness is revealed in the 250 poems included in this anthology. The selection is arranged chronologically by conflict, to produce a history of warfare as seen by the most eloquent observers and chroniclers. After an unsparing scrutiny of two World Wars and Vietnam, violence in Northern Ireland and El Salvador, the anthology ends with chilling visions of the 'Next War'.

SHIBBOLETH

Michael Donaghy

This is Michael Donaghy's first full-length collection. His work has a wit and grace reminiscent of the metaphysical poets, and his subjects range widely, responding in unexpected ways to his curiosity and inventiveness. Among the varied pieces collected here are a number of love poems remarkable for their blend of tenderness and irony; a terse 'news item'; playful 'translations' of a mythical Welsh poet; and an interview with Marcel Duchamp.

The title poem 'Shibboleth' won second prize in the National Poetry Competition of 1987.

Oxford Poets

THE AIR SHOW

Peter Scupham

Peter Scupham's seventh collection is a sequence of poems interlinked by his childhood memories of the Second World War.

The intense rumours, sights and sounds of war accompany his move from Derby to a Cambridgeshire village, and are ever-present during his holidays with grandparents in Lincolnshire. Old toys, period postcards, and revisiting places of the past all help him in his attempt to crack the 'Enigma', the coded complex signals transmitted by the child he once was. Scupham's undisputed skills as an eloquent craftsman-poet are brought to bear on this haunting and moving theme.

'Scupham ranks among the most arresting of newer English poets.' *Spectator*

Oxford Poets

BROKEN MOON

Carole Satyamurti

In this first collection of her poems, Carole Satyamurti speaks in a distinctive voice—accurate, compassionate, intelligent, and with a finely judged sense of the ludicrous. Many of the poems bear witness to the strategies, and the small, important victories of people attempting to deal with loss and deficiency in their lives: a man with a speech impediment speaks in words of his own invention; a disabled child wrestles with a difficult piece on the piano; women from several cultures, and of different ages, negotiate a sort of balance for, and between, themselves.

Oxford Poets

METRO

George Szirtes

A new volume from the highly praised Hungarian-born poet.

'One of the very best of our poets under forty. You might encapsulate his manner of writing by describing it as a contest between picturable reality and the over-world of the imagination.' Peter Porter, *Observer*

Oxford Poets

I'M DEADLY SERIOUS

Chris Wallace-Crabbe

This is Chris Wallace-Crabbe's second book of poems to appear in Britain. His style ranges from playful ballads to mystic pieces, embracing European, American, and Australian influences.

'He is a resourceful and romantic-spirited poet.' Peter Porter

Oxford Poets

COLLECTED POEMS 1988

David Gascoyne

David Gascoyne's first collection of poems was published in 1932, when he was only sixteen. Now, after fifty years later, still writing and translating, he has attracted a readership of several generations to his extraordinary work and career.

Collected Poems 1988 includes much previously uncollected work, revises the contents of the previous edition, and adds a substantial section of Gascoyne's more recent poems. It asserts the continuing importance of Gascoyne as a major poet of the twentieth century.

Oxford Poets

ONE AND OTHER POEMS

Thomas Kinsella

This book contains, in one volume, the second series of Pepper-canister publications: '*One*' (1974), '*A Technical* Supplement' (1976), and a group of poems published in 1978 as '*Song of the Night and Other Poems*'.

THE AUTOMATIC ORACLE

Peter Porter

In this new collection—the second since his *Collected Poems* (1983)—Peter Porter's tone is instantly recognizable, but his preoccupations seem to belong even more to the times we live in, and those times are political and dangerous.

The 'oracle' of the title is the English language itself; the poet a 'priest' who is bound to carry messages to the world outside, and to be a guardian of words and their responsibilities. Familiar themes, of childhood, dreams, paintings, also recur, in a complex and mature volume which deploys a great variety of skilful verse forms.

Winner of the Poetry Whitbread Prize 1988.